Poetry: Its Power and Wisdom

AN INTRODUCTORY STUDY

Ann Dorothea Ferguson

POETRY

Its Power and Wisdom

⁂

An Introductory Study

BY FRANCIS X. CONNOLLY
FORDHAM UNIVERSITY

CHARLES SCRIBNER'S SONS
New York

B-9.61[H]

PRINTED IN THE UNITED STATES OF AMERICA

Library of Congress Catalog Card Number 60-9296

ACKNOWLEDGMENTS

Pages v-vi constitute an extension of the copyright page.

"Lark" by Josephine Miles from *Lines at Intersection.* Reprinted by permission of The Macmillan Company.

"The Man He Killed" and "The Darkling Thrush" by Thomas Hardy from *Collected Poems.* Reprinted by permission of The Macmillan Company and Macmillan & Company Ltd.

"From the Spanish Cloister" and "To A Modern Poet" by Gilbert Keith Chesterton. Reprinted by permission of Dodd, Mead & Company, Inc. from *The Collected Poems of G. K. Chesterton.* Copyright 1911, 1932 by Dodd, Mead & Company, Inc. By permission of Methuen & Co. Ltd. and Miss Collins.

"Winter," "The Dunce," "The Listeners" and "An Epitaph" by Walter de la Mare. Reprinted by permission of the Literary Trustees of Walter de la Mare and the Society of Authors as their representative.

"Cargoes" by John Masefield from *Collected Poems.* Reprinted by permission of The Macmillan Company.

"Ambition" by W. H. Davies from *Collected Poems of W. H. Davies.* Reprinted by permission of Mrs. H. M. Davies and Jonathan Cape Ltd.

"Eight O'Clock," "Into My Heart An Air that Kills," "Is My Team Plowing," and "With Rue My Heart is Laden" by A. E. Housman from *Complete Poems* by A. E. Housman. Copyright 1940, by Henry Holt and Company, Inc. Copyright © 1959, by Henry Holt and Company, Inc. By permission of the publishers. Reprinted by permission of the Society of Authors as the literary representative of the Trustees of the Estate of the late A. E Housman, and Messrs. Jonathan Cape Ltd., publishers of A. E. Housman's *Collected Poems.*

"Richard Cory" by Edwin Arlington Robinson from *The Children of the Night* (Charles Scribner's Sons).

"Ars Poetica" by Archibald MacLeish from *The Collected Poems of Archi-*

bald MacLeish 1917-1952. Reprinted by permission of Houghton Mifflin Company.

"The Lake Isle of Innisfree," "The Scholars," "When You are Old," and "Byzantium" by William Butler Yeats from *Collected Poems.* Copyright 1933, 1951. Reprinted by permission of The Macmillan Company, The Macmillan Company of Canada and Mrs. Yeats.

"Siasconset Song" from *Letter From a Distant Land* by Philip Booth. Copyright 1951 by Philip Booth. Originally printed in *The New Yorker.* Reprinted by permission of The Viking Press, Inc.

"Fern Hill" by Dylan Thomas from *The Collected Poems of Dylan Thomas.* Copyright 1939, 1942, 1946 by New Directions. Copyright 1952, 1953 by Dylan Thomas. Reprinted by permission of New Directions, J. M. Dent & Sons Ltd., and the Trustees of the Dylan Thomas Estate.

"The Bee" by John Fandel. Reprinted by permission of the author and *The Commonweal.*

"Tarantella" by Hilaire Belloc. Reprinted by permission of A. D. Peters.

"The Silken Tent" and "Stopping by Woods on a Snowy Evening" by Robert Frost from *Complete Poems of Robert Frost.* Copyright, 1930, 1949, by Henry Holt and Company, Inc. By permission of the publishers.

"Snow" by Louis MacNeice from *Poems 1925-1940.* Copyright 1937 by Louis MacNeice. Reprinted by permission of Random House, Inc. and Faber and Faber Ltd.

"All Lovely Things" by Conrad Aiken from *Collected Poems* by Conrad Aiken. Copyright, 1953 by Conrad Aiken. Reprinted by permission of Oxford University Press, Inc.

"Preludes," "Journey of the Magi," "The Hollow Men" and selections from "Burnt Norton" by T. S. Eliot. From *Collected Poems 1909-1935* by T. S. Eliot, copyright, 1936, by Harcourt, Brace and Company, Inc. Reprinted by permission of Harcourt, Brace and Company, Inc. and Faber and Faber Ltd.

"Anecdote of the Jar" by Wallace Stevens. Reprinted from *The Collected Poems of Wallace Stevens* by Wallace Stevens, by permission of Alfred A. Knopf, Inc. Copyright 1923, 1931, 1954 by Wallace Stevens.

"The Albatross" by Charles Baudelaire. Translated by Warren Carrier. From *Reading Modern Poetry.* Copyright 1955 by Scott, Foresman and Company, Chicago, and reprinted with their permission.

"The Panther" by Rainer Maria Rilke. Translated by Paul Engle. From *Reading Modern Poetry.* Copyright 1955 by Scott, Foresman and Company, Chicago, and reprinted with their permission.

"In Schrafft's" by W. H. Auden from *Nones* by W. H. Auden. Copyright 1949 by W. H. Auden. Dedicatory epistle from *Nones* by W. H. Auden. Copyright 1951 by W. H Auden. Reprinted by permission of Random House, Inc. "Musée des Beaux Arts" by W. H. Auden from *The Collected Poetry of*

W. H. Auden. Copyright 1940 by W. H. Auden. Reprinted by permission of Random House, Inc. and Faber and Faber Ltd.

"In Waste Places" by James Stephens. Reprinted by permission of The Macmillan Company and Cynthia Stephens.

"When First We Met" by Robert Bridges. From *The Shorter Poems of Robert Bridges* by permission of the Clarendon Press, Oxford.

"Spring," "Pied Beauty," "The Windhover," "Felix Randal," "The Leaden Echo and The Golden Echo," "Thou Art Indeed Just, Lord" and four lines from "The Wreck of the Deutschland" by Gerard Manley Hopkins from *Poems of Gerard Manley Hopkins.* Third edition edited by W. H. Gardner. Copyright 1948 by Oxford University Press, Inc. Reprinted by permission.

"Here Lies a Lady" by John Crowe Ransom. Reprinted from *Selected Poems* by John Crowe Ransom, by permission of Alfred A. Knopf, Inc. Copyright 1924, 1945 by Alfred A. Knopf, Inc.

"Envoi" by Ezra Pound from *Personae.* Copyright 1926 by Ezra Pound. Reprinted by permission of New Directions.

"The Recurrence" by Edwin Muir from *Collected Poems* by Edwin Muir. Reprinted by permission of Faber and Faber Ltd.

"Poetry" by Marianne Moore from *Selected Poems.* Reprinted by permission of The Macmillan Company and Faber and Faber Ltd.

"The Show" by Wilfred Owen from *The Poems of Wilfred Owen.* All rights reserved. Reprinted by permission of New Directions and Chatto and Windus Ltd.

"The Groundhog" and lines from "If I Could Only Live at the Pitch That Is Near Madness" by Richard Eberhart from *Selected Poems* by Richard Eberhart. Copyright 1951. Reprinted by permission of Oxford University Press, Inc. and Chatto and Windus Ltd.

"Buick" by Karl Shapiro from *Poems 1940-1953* by Karl Shapiro. Copyright 1941 by Karl Jay Shapiro. Reprinted by permission of Random House, Inc.

"Colloquy in Black Rock" by Robert Lowell from *Lord Weary's Castle,* copyright, 1944, 1946 by Robert Lowell. Reprinted by permission of Harcourt, Brace and Company, Inc. and Faber and Faber Ltd.

"Still, Citizen Sparrow" by Richard Wilbur from *Ceremony and Other Poems,* copyright, 1948, 1949, 1950 by Richard Wilbur. Reprinted by permission of Harcourt, Brace and Company, Inc.

Selection from the book *Achievement in American Poetry 1900-1950,* by Louise Bogan. Copyright 1951 by The Henry Regnery Company.

Selection from *English Poetry* by Douglas Bush. Copyright 1952 by Oxford University Press, Inc.

Selection from *Poetry and the Age* by Randall Jarrell. Copyright 1953 by Alfred A. Knopf, Inc.

Selection from *Phases of English Poetry* by Herbert Read. Copyright 1951. Reprinted by permission of New Directions.

PREFACE

Purpose

The principal aim of this book is to provide the reader, particularly the college student beginning a serious study of poetry, with the means of understanding what poetry is, what it does, and how it does it. Hence, it is concerned both with the nature of the poetic experience and with the technique of poetic expression, with the "poetic" knowledge that involves emotion and imagination as well as reason, and with the "thinking out" of that knowledge into language.

Plan

The plan of the book is set forth in the first chapter. There the essential reasons why we read poetry are offered in outline form, together with relatively simple analyses of brief poems. Subsequent chapters develop each separate element with reference either to poetry of all types, as in Chapters II to X and Chapter XIII, or with reference to special types of poetry, as in Chapters XI, XII. The discussion on "The Language of Poetry" has been placed near the end of the book because, it is suggested, the formal discussion of diction, meter, rhyme, and other technical matters should be deferred until the reader has experienced the effects of these elements in a wide variety of poems. It should be noted, too, that these elements are continually pointed out, and in many cases explained, in earlier chapters. However, if one prefers, one may begin with the discussion of the language of poetry, or take it up immediately after the subject is first mentioned in Chapter I.

Glossary

In a book of this kind it is unwise, and often impossible, to avoid mentioning certain key terms before those terms are fully explained. Hence, while every effort has been made to avoid forward references, some will be found, especially in the first chapter, where the overall perspective of the book is explained. For this reason a glossary has been provided. For fuller explanation of important terms, however, the reader should consult the Index.

Bibliography

The brief bibliography includes (1) significant books that have been mentioned in the text; (2) books to which the author is indebted for certain basic assumptions; and (3) books that represent a point of view differing from his own.

Texts

The texts of the poems reproduced are taken, wherever possible, from definitive editions. In general, the versions of early poetry have been normalized. In a few instances, the text of the original edition has been preserved to provide the reader with an opportunity to compare ancient and modern spelling, capitalization, and punctuation.

For Favors Received

The author's chief debt is to the tradition of poetry and to those who introduced him to it, particularly to the late A. M. Fremgen, Robert I. Gannon, Frank P. Grady, and James H. McCabe. During twenty-five years he gained many insights from fellow editors and poets who have been associated with *Spirit,* a Magazine of Poetry, and from his colleagues in the English department of Fordham University. For helpful suggestions on particular points in the present book he is grateful to Mr. J. G. Hopkins, Professors Charles Donahue and Grover Cronin of Fordham, and Professor Barry Ulanov of Barnard College. He thanks Professor James E. Tobin of Queens College and Mr. John Fandel of Manhattan College for rigorous and constructive readings of the entire manuscript on behalf of the publisher. Finally, he acknowledges the endless generosity of Mary T. Connolly.

Dedication

In gratitude for being allowed to share in the common service of poetry during the twenty-five years of Spirit, I wish to dedicate this book to J. G. B., J. G. E. H., C. J. L., A. M. S., and J. E. T., and to all others who serve poetry and the spirit from which it springs.

19 March 1960 F. X. C.

CONTENTS

Poetry: Its Power and Wisdom

AN INTRODUCTORY STUDY

CHAPTER I

Why Do We Read Poetry?

WHY DO WE read poetry? There are as many answers as there are readers. We read it because it stirs us deeply, because it startles our imagination, because it stimulates our thinking, because it lifts up our hearts and because it amuses and entertains us. There are a hundred other reasons why we read poetry. All of them center on poetry itself; on what it is and what it does. Poetry *is* something supremely important. It is the re-creation in language of those experiences, great and small, that men treasure for their own sake. Because it is what it is, poetry *does* something for the human spirit. It has the power to make man intensely aware of himself and his world, to broaden his horizons, to provoke him to observe, to wonder, to aspire, in short, to realize more completely what it is to be a man.

Hence, to answer the question, Why do we read poetry, we must discover what poetry is and what it does. In this chapter we shall begin by describing, in a general way, what are the essential elements of poetry and how each of these elements is related to each other. In later chapters we shall consider each element separately.

The first characteristic that most readers encounter in poetry is its power to compel attention. We need not read a complete poem to feel this power. Even a fragment conveys it, as the lines below reveal.

1.

With rue my heart is laden
For golden friends I had,

For many a rose-lipt maiden
And many a lightfoot lad.

A. E. HOUSMAN

2.

The angels keep their ancient places;—
Turn but a stone, and start a wing!
'Tis ye, 'tis your estrangéd faces,
That miss the many-splendor'd thing.

FRANCIS THOMPSON

3.

Oh what can ail thee, knight-at-arms,
Alone and palely loitering?
The sedge is wither'd from the lake,
And no birds sing.

JOHN KEATS

POETRY IS A VITAL EXPERIENCE

What arrests our attention in reading these verses? Perhaps the tone of voice, more intense than usual, makes us aware that the poet is speaking of an experience that has affected him genuinely and deeply. "This I mean"—A. E. Housman seems to insist—"With *rue* my heart is laden/For *golden* friends I had." "I have discovered an important truth and I cannot be silent," Francis Thompson proclaims, warning his readers that men miss the splendor of God because they have turned away from Him. No less genuine and intense seems the anxious melancholy of Keats's question, "What can ail thee, knight-at-arms. . . ?" Joy and sorrow, love and awe, these and other emotions in the poems above are the expressions of genuine and intense experience.

But it is not the experience alone, however genuine and intense, that compels us to listen. Housman was not the first man to mourn the passing of friends. In one sense human experiences are the commonplaces of daily conversation. We often hear it said, "All my old friends are dead . . . My girl is beautiful . . ." How often we express genuine and intense feelings in such ordinary expressions or in the wording of popular song.

But poets present these perennial human experiences in a new way. Theirs is a fresh view, like that of the child to whom all experience is original. Unlike the child, however, the poet refines his experience. He takes note of its meaning. Josephine Miles's "Lark" makes this evident in a simple, almost matter-of-fact contrast between the inattention characteristic of ordinary experience and the intense attention of the poet's experience.

LARK

Lark hit us in the face with his rising sound.
We were unstruck by wind before and raced
Train, and saw all signs with one eye only,
And were shelled against sky
And all that we went by. 5

Now lark said something in the field and we heard it,
And it mounted and rode upon our ears as we sped.
And we heard windshield rattle and canvas creak thereafter,
And pondered every line
Of hill and sign. 10

JOSEPHINE MILES

Now, lark (representing poetic experience) says something, and we hear it; moreover, we grasp its meaning. Ordinary experience becomes again vital and fresh, every part of it is worth pondering, every part yields a new meaning.

Thus, while poetry is born of vital experience, life itself, it is not ordinary experience. It is an experience that is known, contemplated, enjoyed. As Emerson remarked, "The finest poetry was first experience; but the thought has suffered a transformation since it was first experience."

POETRY TRANSFORMS EXPERIENCE

In what does that transformation consist? Here we face the mystery of poetry and all creative art—a mystery that many have attempted to explain without complete success. Innumerable books, like J. L. Lowes's *The Road to Xanadu,* a study of the creative process in Coleridge, have shown how the poet's day-to-day existence, his physical condition, his emotional states, his readings, his occupations, together with the whole body of his previous personal experience, make up the materials of his poetry.

Other books have traced the transforming power of poetry to the poet's power to feel and to express in the idiom of his age the ideas, attitudes, tones, indeed the unanalyzable quality of his time and place.

Yet neither the poet's experience, however varied and interesting, nor the poet's awareness of the forms and pressures of his own time, account for the most important element in the transformation. They do not explain how the poem becomes a work of art. They do not answer the questions, What does the poet *do* with his actual experience in the poem? How does he manifest his sensibility in language?

To examine the implications of these questions, let us summarize the history of one poem, John Keats's "On First Looking into Chapman's Homer."

In October, 1816, Keats read Chapman's translation of Homer with his friend Charles Cowden Clarke. Exalted by this encounter with Homer's imaginary world, the poet meditated on the experience of that evening during his walk home. His imagination associated his experience of reading Homer with similar experiences; the vision of Balboa discovering the Pacific that he had first read about in William Robertson's *History of America;* the impression of an exceptionally vivid portrait of Cortez by Velásquez; the dramatic illusion of a strange netherworld in Dante's *Inferno* and *Purgatorio* that he had been studying; the great living dream of Coleridge's fantastic "The Rime of the Ancient Mariner." All these imaginative worlds represented his previous travels in the realm of gold—of poetry.

At home he turned to his desk. Within a few hours he had done something about his experiences. He had written this poem:

ON FIRST LOOKING INTO CHAPMAN'S HOMER

Much have I travell'd in the realms of gold,
And many goodly states and kingdoms seen;
Round many western islands have I been
Which bards in fealty to Apollo hold.
Oft of one wide expanse had I been told 5
That deep-brow'd Homer ruled as his demesne:

Yet did I never breathe its pure serene
Till I heard Chapman speak out loud and bold:
Then felt I like some watcher of the skies
When a new planet swims into his ken; 10
Or like stout Cortez, when with eagle eyes
He star'd at the Pacific—and all his men
Look'd at each other with a wild surmise—
Silent, upon a peak in Darien.

JOHN KEATS

Note how the first eight lines translate the *actual* experience of reading in terms of a magical voyage. For Keats, to read a great poem is to travel imaginatively in realms of gold—for poems are "goodly states and kingdoms," ruled by bards who owe allegiance to Apollo, the god of poetry. The speaker has visited many of these realms (Dante's, Coleridge's and others'), but not Homer's, until he heard Chapman speak out loud and bold.

In the last six lines the speaker again translates an actual experience, his response to the imaginative discovery of Homer's demesne, to the comparable experience of a discoverer of the Pacific. Like Cortez,* the appreciative reader of a great poem is not only an adventurer but a conquistador. His is a spiritual conquest; he has come to know the world of the imagination—a world of beauty and grandeur.

From this summary we understand better just how a poet's actual experience became "a spiritual and imaginative world, impalpable and immaterial." True, he built his realm of gold upon the actual world of observation and experience. But he *refined* the ore of experience into the gold of poetry.

The power that transforms actual experience into poetry is poetic genius. That genius cannot be defined save in terms of what the poet does in the poem and what the poem does to the reader. Coleridge described what the poet does in these words: "The poet brings the whole soul of man into activity with the subordination of its faculties to each other according to their

* Keat's reference to Cortez as the discoverer of the Pacific, instead of to Balboa, the actual discoverer, has occasioned much comment. But it should be noted that Cortez more clearly typifies a bold, imaginative adventurer than the less well-known Balboa. Truth of fact in poetry is discussed on p. 106.

relative worth and dignity. . . . He diffuses a tone and spirit of unity, that blends and (as it were) fuses, each into each."

Ideally, the reader responds to the poem with *his* whole soul—by feeling, thinking, imagining intensely.

In responding to the poem, the reader experiences a kind of delight, or pleasure. This delight is not an end in itself but the accompaniment of the reader's total active response to the poem, and a result of his possession of the values embodied in the poem. For man's greatest delight is not in mere sensual gratifications, not even in admiration of artistic skill, but in his coming to know the truths of human experience and in his joyous possession of the fruits of that knowledge, which is wisdom.

We read poetry, then, because it presents *a total experience* in a way that brings the whole soul of man into activity, and this activity results in the active possession of various truths, a possession accompanied by and followed by delight.

A POEM PRESENTS A TOTAL EXPERIENCE

We sense this totality of poetic experience even in so-called simple poems, like Robert Burns's "A Red, Red Rose."

O my Luve's like a red, red rose
  That's newly sprung in June:
O my Luve's like the melodie
  That's sweetly play'd in tune!

As fair art thou, my bonnie lass,
  So deep in luve am I:
And I will luve thee still, my dear,
  Till a' the seas gang dry:

Till a' the seas gang dry, my dear,
  And the rocks melt wi' the sun;
I will luve thee still, my dear,
  While the sands o' life shall run.

And fare thee weel, my only Luve
  And fare thee weel awhile!
And I will come again, my Luve,
  Tho' it were ten thousand mile.

Readers of many generations have read, have sung, and have enjoyed this simple lyric. Why? True, "A Red, Red Rose" does contain a message. Here the speaker bids a girl good-bye. This situation helps make the poem easy to understand. It provides a framework for the comparisons—of love to "a red, red rose," and to a "melodie . . . sweetly played in tune"—and the hyperboles—the poet's promise to love until rocks melt in the sun and the seas run dry.

The message, however, is by no means responsible for the total effect of this poem. Its tender sentiment, its plaintive repetitions, its blend of sadness and gaiety—each element contributes to a total effect much more intense than the mere message, or any other individual element. Burns has organized all these elements into a harmonious whole. The poem can no more be reduced to an element of that whole than a musical composition can be reduced to an isolated bar or phrase.

To take another example, Wordsworth's sonnet, "Evening on Calais Beach," unites emotion, thought, and imagination—the basic elements of all poetic experience. Let us study it in more detail.

> It is a beauteous evening, calm and free,
> The holy time is quiet as a Nun
> Breathless with adoration; the broad sun
> Is sinking down in its tranquillity;
> The gentleness of heaven broods o'er the sea: 5
> Listen! the mighty Being is awake,
> And doth with his eternal motion make
> A sound like thunder—everlastingly.
> Dear Child! dear Girl! that walkest with me here,
> If thou appear untouch'd by solemn thought, 10
> Thy nature is not therefore less divine:
> Thou liest in Abraham's bosom all the year;
> And worshipp'st at the Temple's inner shrine,
> God being with thee when we know it not.

THE EMOTIONAL EXPERIENCE

The reader is at once aware that this poem expresses the emotion, or mood, of awe and reverence. In the first eight lines the speaker describes the evening, not in a factual manner, but in terms of his own feelings. The evening is calm and free, tranquil and gentle. In this stillness the speaker listens to the actual thunder of the sea. Then, with the ear of his soul, he hears the eternal motion of God that sustains everlastingly the ordered tranquillity of the universe. In the last six lines the poet takes note of his daughter who is walking beside him. Unlike himself, his daughter seems unaware of the reality that lies beneath the appearances of this beautiful evening. Speaking to himself, but meaning to be overheard, he protests that she, too, proclaims God's presence for God dwells within her, as she, in her innocence, dwells in the bosom of God.

EMOTION ASSOCIATED WITH THOUGHT

But, while the predominant impression of the poem is the speaker's own feeling or *emotion* of awe and reverence, this impression is rooted in thought. The emotion of awe is a natural response to the poet's contemplation of the evening and his daughter. Indeed, not to respond as he does would be to contradict the implicit aim of his meditation. For in recognizing the holiness of the evening, and the presence of some divine power in his child, the poet discovers the motives or reasons for awe and reverence. Hence, emotion and mood exist within the context of the poet's thought or contemplation.

THOUGHT AND EMOTION REPRESENTED IMAGINATIVELY

The poem, then, is emotional, but its emotion of awe inheres in thought. Moreover, both emotion and thought inhere in the concrete, *imagined* situation. The poet does not merely say: I stand in reverent awe (emotion). Neither does he say: I stand in awe because I am in the presence of God (emotion and thought). Rather he presents a scene that *imaginatively* represents his thoughts and feelings. That scene is not a mere stage setting, but a dramatic situation that calls for some appropriate response in thought and feeling.

Note, for example, how Wordsworth first builds up an image of the evening. He emphasizes its quietness by comparing it to the tranquil poise of a nun breathless in adoration. The sun is sinking tranquilly, and the sea is calm. Thus in the first five lines the imagery rinses our mind of tumultuous noises of daytime. (Here silence and peace are active qualities that soothe our senses the better to stimulate them.) Then the exclamation "Listen!" directs our attention to the distant thunder of the sea, the one mighty sound that reverberates through all the stillness. The sound, too, as we have seen above, suggests the mighty being whose eternal motion sustains the universe.

We have now an image in which a thoughtful poet walks by the sea with his carefree daughter. Moreover, this image reveals the mind and soul of the speaker. Thus, the poem makes us see, think, and feel as the poet does—not in isolated acts of emotion, thought, and imagination, but in a single action in which image fuses into thought and both image and thought are transfused with feeling.

ARTISTIC DESIGN: STRUCTURE

A successful poem presents a total experience in an effective way, that is, in a design, pattern, or structure that shapes all the elements of the poem into a unified and coherent whole.

Note how, in Keats's poem, the design may be outlined thus:

The poet has travelled much in the "realms of gold"—(lines 1-4).

He has heard of Homer but has only now, in Chapman, encountered him—(lines 5-8).

The experience of this encounter is like the silent wonder that affects a "watcher of the skies," or a Cortez—(lines 9-14).

Keats's poem has a clear design; that is, the several parts unite, or coalesce, to create a meaningful whole.

Similarly in "A Red, Red Rose" (p. 6), a design or structure gives form to the emotion, thought, and imagery of the poem. In Stanza 1 the speaker asserts the beauty of his beloved, comparing her to a rose and a melody. In stanzas 2 and 3 he says that his love is as deep as his beloved is fair, and that it will last forever. In stanza 4 he bids farewell to his love and promises to return. As in Keats's sonnet, this lyric clearly displays a meaningful sequence of ideas and impressions. We have just seen how in Wordsworth's sonnet the ideas exhibit a definite pattern, proceeding from an emotional and imaginative description of evening to a dramatic meditation on the divine spirit that sustains the universe.

Other poems are even more formal in their structure. John Milton's sonnet, "On His Blindness," for instance, is designed in two parts: the first states a problem in the form of a question; the second presents an answer to that question.

In the first seven and one-half lines Milton meditates on the biblical injunction that each man must employ his talents fruitfully. (See Matthew 25:14-30.) But how can the poet be expected to employ his talent for poetry and scholarship, since both require sight? These thoughts lead him to question, in self-excusing fashion, the pertinence of the parable of the talents to his own case. Note, too, the irony implied by the language: his *light* is spent; how then can "God exact *day*-labour, *light* deny'd?":

When I consider how my light is spent,
E're half my days, in this dark world and wide,
And that one talent which is death to hide,
Lodg'd with me useless, though my soul more bent
To serve therewith my Maker, and present 5
My true account, lest he returning chide,
"Doth God exact day-labour, light deny'd?"
I fondly ask.

Then Milton answers his own question by showing how a person whose one great talent has been removed may still serve God by doing His will. One serves Him best by bearing His yoke, that is, by accepting whatever task He has providentially assigned. Hence, the question—"Doth God exact day-labour?" . . . —is answered. No, He does not; but He does ask for patience.

But Patience, to prevent
That murmur, soon replies, "God doth not need
Either man's work or his own gifts. Who best 10
Bear his mild yoke, they serve him best. His state
Is kingly: thousands at his bidding speed,
And post o'er land and ocean without rest;
They also serve who only stand and wait."

Whatever the design of a poem—and there are as many designs as there are genuine poems—design it must have. Otherwise a poem would be a mere jumble of unrelated ideas, a collection of words and sounds without reference to a meaningful context.

STYLE: THE PATTERN OF WORDS AND SOUNDS

Design, structure, pattern are terms that we apply primarily to the coherent development of the images, ideas, and emotional elements of a poem, as we have shown above. But a good poem also contains an unusually effective arrangement of language, that is, a good style. Although a poem uses the same words as prose, it uses them in a special context—a context that at once controls their meaning and establishes a new and often different set of meanings. Hence, the diction of a poem is marked by the choice of words that are just as precise as those of prose, but more suggestive. For example, in Wordsworth's sonnet, the word "beauteous" (line 1) simultaneously characterizes the evening and suggests sublimity. In line 2 the expression "holy time" evokes a tone of awe, especially when it is drawn into the context of the expressions "calm and free" and "a Nun breathless with adoration." Too, words are arranged in a different way, as in the inverted order of the adjectives in "calm and free" in line 1.

Moreover, the words in a poem respond to a definite *rhythm*. In one sense rhythm means simply a recurrent stress on certain syllables in words, often indicated thus:

> Todáy we líve
> Tomórrow díe.

In another sense rhythm may be considered not as a mechanical series of regularly recurrent stresses, but as the life-giving pulse of the poem, the beat that emphasizes the feeling, thought, and imagery. Thus, while the rhythm in Wordsworth's sonnet is predominantly iambic, as in

> The holy time is quiet as a Nun

it frequently changes its beat, in response to excitement, to something like this:

> Dear Child! dear Girl! that walkest with me here

Note, too, that apparently identical rhythms may differ because of the length of syllables and the number of pauses within the line. Thus, in its context,

> They also serve who only stand and wait

is solemn and slow, whereas, in *its* context,

> And many goodly states and kingdoms seen

is lighter and more rapid.

In addition to its special diction and rhythm, a good poem is often melodious. *Melody,* an agreeable succession of vowel or consonant sounds, includes rhyme, alliteration, assonance and onomatopoeia.* In successful poems these and other devices often create patterns of sound that are intimately connected with the sense. Note how, in Wordsworth's sonnet, the sounds are inseparable from the meaning of the poem.

In lines 1-5, where the poet wishes to suggest tranquillity, the consonants are mostly soft liquids (*l* and *r* sounds), low hums (*m*'s and *n*'s) and gentle sibilants; the vowel sounds are hushed, short, and low in pitch. But in lines 6-8, where the poet wishes to suggest the majesty of mighty Being, he combines the long vowels, *i* and *a,* with consonants, pauses, and full stops to form sounds like thunder. Moreover, the various end rhymes, assonances, and alliterations delight the ear as they serve also to bind together emotion, thought, image, and feeling. Thus, the melody is a distinct aid in conveying the emotions, ideas, and images, indeed, the total experience of the poem.

We know now in a general way why we read a poem. We read a poem because it presents a total experience that is accompanied by and results in delight. That total experience consists of several closely related elements: *emotional* activity motivated by an *intellectual* grasp of a situation that is *imaginatively* realized. Moreover, the total experience of a poem is presented in an artistic way, that is, in an appropriate design and style.

In the succeeding chapters we will examine in detail each of the elements that contributes to the formation of a poem.

* For definitions of these terms consult the Glossary. They are treated in detail in Chapter XIII.

CHAPTER II

Emotion in Poetry

FROM EARLY times critics have agreed that emotion, understood as intense feeling, is a predominant characteristic of poetry—indeed, the hallmark that distinguishes it from ordinary discourse. Hence, the term emotion—or terms conveying a similar import, like pleasure, feeling, delight, charm or inspiration—occur in many classic descriptions of poetry. Even tragic poetry, as we shall see, is accepted as a source of intellectual or aesthetic pleasure.

Aristotle (*Poetics,* IV) claimed that poetry originates in the natural pleasure of learning by means of imitation. "Everybody takes pleasure in imitation," that is, in the arts, painting, dancing, music and poetry. Another classic writer, Horace, wrote: "The poet's aim is either to profit or to please, or to blend in one the delightful and the useful. . . . The man who mingles the useful with the sweet carries the day by charming his reader and at the same time instructing him." (*Ars Poetica,* 333.) Literary excellence, according to Longinus, flowed from several sources. The first was the gift of genius; the second, vigorous and inspired emotion. Feeling of a high order, he claimed (*On the Sublime,* VIII, 16), when it is called out by the occasion, "seems to issue from a sort of divine rapture and enthusiasm and fills the words with inspiration."

EMOTION CHARACTERISTIC OF POETRY

Since those early times new views on poetry have developed. Although emphasis shifted from one element in poetry to another, emotion of some kind continued to be demanded as one of the characteristics of poetry. Thus, in the seventeenth century Dryden wrote, "Delight is the chief, if not the only, end of poesy; instruction can be admitted but in the second place; for poesy only instructs as it delights."

A century later Wordsworth wrote, "Poetry is the spontaneous overflow of powerful feelings: it takes its origin from emotion recollected in tranquillity. . . whatever passions [the poet] communicates to his reader, those passions, if his reader's mind be sound and vigorous, should always be accompanied by an overbalance of pleasure." Coleridge's statement also testifies to the predominance of the emotional element in poetry: Poetry is a "species of composition, opposed to science, as having intellectual pleasure for its object, and as attaining its end by the use of language natural to us in a state of excitement. . . ."

In more recent times, too, despite the conflicting claims of various schools of poetry, there is common agreement that, whatever else poetry does, it moves, excites, and inspires. "The poet takes note of nothing that he cannot feel emotionally," says Thomas Hardy. "A poem begins in delight and ends in wisdom," Robert Frost writes. We might fill many pages with similar quotations all to the effect that poetry expresses feeling, and that, if it does not, no matter how witty its thought or brilliant its style, it lacks an essential poetic characteristic.

Despite this testimony as to the necessity of emotion in poetry, many critics today regard the term *emotion* with disfavor. They have good reasons for this attitude, as we may judge from the statements below.

1. In too many discussions the term emotion shifts its meaning. When it is said that poetry is emotional it may refer to the emotional effect on the reader, the emotional state of the poet, or the emotional attitude presented within the poem itself.
2. The term *emotion* connotes pleasure, delight, charm, and so on. But poetry frequently expresses emotions that are not pleasant or delightful in any usual sense.

While these objections are directed against misuse of the term *emotion* rather than against the necessity of emotion in poetry, they should be examined carefully. Moreover, by answering these objections we may define more precisely our own sense of the term emotion.

EMOTION: IN THE READER, THE WRITER, THE POEM

Many readers think that emotion in poetry refers exclusively to their own emotional attitudes rather than to those that are directly connected with the poem. Thus we may hear a woman say: "When I read, in Tennyson's 'Lullaby,'

> 'Rest, rest, on mother's breast,
> Father will come to thee soon,'

I feel like weeping. It is so beautiful. It reminds me of my baby falling asleep in his cradle."

Another reaction goes like this. "I have just read *Romeo and Juliet* and it left me cold. The characters lack common sense. Imagine anyone saying, as Romeo does,

> ' Heaven is here
> Where Juliet lives . . .
> More validity,
> More honourable state, more courtship lives
> In carrion-flies than Romeo; they may seize
> On the white wonder of dear Juliet's hand
> And steal immortal blessings from her lips . . .'

I have never experienced such far-fetched emotion. I don't believe any real man has."

In both cases the speakers regard the emotion in a poem in terms of their own feelings. The mother is not thinking of the poem, but of her baby. Her real affection for the baby is the true cause of her feeling; the poem itself is merely an occasion that reminds her of that affection. In the second instance the speaker fails to respond to the romantic tragedy of Romeo and Juliet because of his expectation that tragic characters must possess, as he feels he does, common sense and emotional maturity.

Many additional examples could be presented to show how, for one reason or another, a reader confuses his own emotions with those circulating within the poem itself. A reader's physical condition, his mental attitude, his previous education, his habits of behavior, his linguistic preferences—all these may interfere with or qualify his participation in the emotional excitement intrinsic to the poem.

Just as some readers confuse the emotion intrinsic to the poem with their own purely personal feelings, so others regard *emotion* as the poet's personal feelings. Hence, some readers tend to interpret a poem in terms of the poet's biography. They may discover for instance that Byron wrote the lines cited below shortly after he had attended an evening party at which he first met Lady Wilmot Horton, his cousin by marriage.

SHE WALKS IN BEAUTY

She walks in beauty, like the night
Of cloudless climes and starry skies;
And all that's best of dark and bright
Meet in her aspect and her eyes:
Thus mellow'd to that tender light 5
Which heaven to gaudy day denies.

One shade the more, one ray the less,
Had half impar'd the nameless grace
Which waves in every raven tress,
Or softly lightens o'er her face; 10
Where thoughts serenely sweet express
How pure, how dear their dwelling-place.

And on that cheek, and o'er that brow,
So soft, so calm, yet eloquent,
The smiles that win, the tints that glow, 15
But tell of days in goodness spent,
A mind at peace with all below,
A heart whose love is innocent!

GEORGE GORDON, LORD BYRON

The fact that the poem was suggested by an actual meeting, however, is no reason to conclude that Byron was describing his own personal feelings toward Lady Horton. The emotion intrinsic to the poem transcends the occasion that inspired it. It is no longer a purely personal feeling.

Now, it is true that the personal emotions of the poet and of the reader are connected with the reading and writing of a poem. What the poet felt as he wrote the poem, and how we feel as we read it, are parts of the total process of writing and reading poetry. Yet, strictly speaking, emotion in poetry refers less to personal, or so-called real emotions, of the poet or the reader than to *aesthetic* emotions, that is, to emotions intrinsic to the poem itself.

EMOTIONS INTRINSIC TO THE POEM

In real life emotions or feelings are aroused by an actual concrete situation that provokes feelings of love or hate, desire or aversion. We feel joy in the presence of someone we love, hatred or indignation in the presence of a crime or an act of malice. We hope for the possession of things that may help us, or fear some evil in the presence of danger.

These emotions are sometimes pleasurable, sometimes harrowing. Love and hope, together with kindred feelings of joy, admiration, and awe, are expansive feelings that range in intensity from satisfaction to exalted joy. Hate and fear, on the other hand, together with *their* kindred feelings of envy, contempt, dismay, are depressing feelings that range in intensity from mere dissatisfaction to acute despair. These emotions are responses to an actual situation. They are often accompanied by physical sensations of heat or cold, rigidity or trembling. Moreover, they manifest themselves in words, in facial expressions, in gestures, and occasionally motivate specific actions, sometimes, indeed, a whole human life.

A poetic emotion, on the other hand, is a response to an imagined or fictitious situation. Although sensitive persons, A. E. Housman for instance, sometimes identify such emotion by a tingling sensation in the spine, many readers feel no bodily sensation at all, even when they are deeply moved by reading a poem or looking at a picture or hearing music. When they see a play in which a villain attempts to kill the hero they do not start or cry out a warning, nor do they confuse the actor in his role as a villain with the actor's personal character. They recognize, in short, that the play, or the poem or novel, is not life itself, not even an attempted reproduction of the real thing, but an *imaginative representation* of life, a *fiction* embodying a general truth rather than actual events, an *imitation* of human actions and thoughts by means of language. Hence, the emotional response to an imaginative representation is *aesthetic* rather than real, the result of contemplation rather than actual involvement.

Since emotion is reflected through the medium of thought and language, it is, therefore, in some degree detached from the particular life both of the poet and of the reader. "It is not in his personal emotions, the emotions provoked by the particular events in his life, that the poet is in any way remarkable or interesting," writes T. S. Eliot. Rather, "the emotion in his poetry will be a very complex thing. . . a concentration of a very great number of experiences. . ."

Ideally, the poet cannot let his private emotions get in the way of the emotion of the poem. So, too, should it be with the reader. Ideally, he will not regard the emotion in the poem merely as a description of the poet's personal mental state, a case history, so to speak; nor will he impose his own personal emotional attitudes on the poem. Rather, he will see the emotional experience in the poem objectively, or, to use a convenient phrase, "at an aesthetic distance."

HOW "UNPLEASANT" EMOTIONS MAY BE PLEASING

Aesthetic distance, or detachment, explains why a poet and a reader can delight in feelings that, in real life, give pain. Thus, in Thomas Hardy's "The Man He Killed," we read of an experience that in real life could only result in dismay. The speaker is an imaginary soldier:

"Had he and I but met
By some old ancient inn,
We should have sat us down to wet
Right many a nipperkin!

"But ranged as infantry, 5
And staring face to face,
I shot at him as he at me,
And killed him in his place.

"I shot him dead because—
Because he was my foe, 10
Just so: my foe of course he was;
That's clear enough; although

"He thought he'd 'list, perhaps,
Off-hand like—just as I;
Was out of work, had sold his traps— 15
No other reason why.

"Yes; quaint and curious war is!
You shoot a fellow down
You'd treat if met where any bar is,
Or help to half-a-crown." 20

The situation described in "The Man He Killed," if real, would sadden the normal reader. Yet, since the poet is presenting the experience imaginatively, most readers do enjoy the vivid portrayal of the incident. Moreover, recognition of the irony of the situation satisfies the reader's desire to understand a tragic predicament, and to share in an experience that would otherwise be denied him. Furthermore, if the reader appreciates literary skill, he will delight in Hardy's dramatic contrast between the ways of peace and war and his adroit handling of the soldier's speech. In other words, since actual danger is out of the question, the poet and reader enjoy, within limits of good sense, the aesthetic freedom to experience all the emotions connected with vivid sensation, passionate thought, and active sympathy.

PROPRIETY AND PROPORTION

We have said above that the emotions connected with poetry are limited by good sense. Just how does good sense limit our enjoyment of a poem? Good sense demands propriety and proportion. *Propriety* means that the emotions contained in a poem should be appropriate to the situation presented in that poem. Propriety demands certain *kinds of emotion* in certain represented situations. Thus, we expect that a normal soldier will not take pleasure in killing an enemy. He responds to such an event, as does the soldier in "The Man He Killed," by a bewildered regret that gives rise to reflections about the irony of war. On the other hand, we would call inappropriate, if not irrational, an emotion of exalted joy in response to a description of the dropping of the atom bomb on Hiroshima, or to the moral collapse of a rival nation. Attitudes of this kind may be appropriately ascribed only to evil or ignorant men, not to normal men or to that class we call man in general. Thus, propriety closely resembles a sense of justice since it demands a just, that is, a decently human response to a particular situation.

Proportion, the second characteristic of good sense, means that the *degree* or intensity of the emotion should be relative to the situation presented in the poem. A matter-of-fact speaker, like the soldier in Hardy's poem, in the context of that poem, exhibits just the right proportion of feeling—sincere, ironic, low-pitched, puzzled regret—a feeling perfectly matched by the colloquial diction and rhythm. The emotion would be disproportionate if Hardy, speaking in the person of his imaginary character, burst out in the intense grief of Shelley's ornamental lament in "Adonais" for his dead friend, John Keats.

Note how the emotional responses in the poems that appear earlier in this book are both appropriate and proportionate. For instance, in "Lark" (p. 3), the speaker responds with a mild astonishment, as if just awakened to a quickened sense of life by the lark's song. This is as it should be, since the situation presented in the poem does not call for great joy, or another strong kind of emotion, or for a more intense emotional expression. On the other hand, in "On First Looking into Chapman's Homer" (p. 4), the speaker's emotional response is an exalted sense of wonder, suggested by the words "wild surmise." Moreover, the intensity of the emotional expression is proportionate to the situation that evokes it, namely the discovery of new planets and new kingdoms of the mind.

Similarly, in "A Red, Red Rose" (p. 6), "Evening on Calais Beach" (p. 7), and "On His Blindness" (p. 10), the several emotional responses of tender regret, reverent awe, and devoted resignation are all exactly appropriate to the situations presented in each of the poems. Note, too, that the degree of the emotion is neither too high nor too low. Each poem has avoided the pitfalls of excess and defect.

To take another example, consider this poem, "With Rue My Heart Is Laden," by A. E. Housman.

With rue my heart is laden
  For golden friends I had,
For many a rose-lipt maiden
  And many a lightfoot lad.

By brooks too broad for leaping (5)
  The lightfoot boys are laid;
The rose-lipt girls are sleeping
  In fields where roses fade.

Here the emotional response is suggested by the first line. The speaker's heart is laden not with sorrow, or wild grief or tearful memory, but with *rue*. *Rue* is regret, a regret that leaves a bitter taste in the mouth, like the herb of the same name. Rue, then, is the exact kind of feeling, a general, almost impersonal, regret for the loss of friends. Moreover, the emotion is expressed with just the right degree of intensity. It is quiet, ironic, wearily sad. The poem does complete justice to the situation.

Propriety and proportion—these terms suggest that the emotion in a successful poem is *just*, both in kind and in degree. We say of Shakespeare's *Hamlet*, for instance, that, whether it ranges in kind from despair to love, or in degree from the utmost pitch of sorrow to a delicate fanciful melancholy, its emotions are appropriate and proportionate. Propriety and proportion account for the perfection of "simple" poems that reflect with uncomplicated joy the beauty of nature, and of "difficult" poems that reflect a clouded situation in the ambiguous tones of loving hate or hopeful fear.

But in some attempted poems the emotion is neither appropriate nor proportionate. Shelley, for instance, expresses his grief in "A Lament" with great verbal intensity.

> Oh world! O life! O time!
> On whose last steps I climb,
>   Trembling at that where I had stood before;
> When will return the glory of your prime?
>   No more—Oh, never more! 5
>
> Out of the day and night
> A joy has taken flight;
>   Fresh spring, and summer, and winter hoar,
> Move my faint heart with grief, but with delight
>   No more—Oh, never more! 10

The grief expressed in these lines is appropriate to a tragic hero who comes home defeated in war to find his wife and children dead and his home in ashes. But here the emotion appears in a void. We do not know why the speaker is sad. Hence, we tend to suspect his sorrow is disproportionate. Shelley's biographers tell us that Shelley is grieving because Emilia Viviani, his friend, has married. If we accept this biographical fact as an element in interpreting the poem we still must conclude that the speaker's emotion is excessive, not to say inappropriate.

But few will question the propriety or proportion of the grief expressed in the passages from Shelley's "Adonais" below. Here Shelley does not merely grieve; he also presents the context, and hence the motives for grief—the tragic situation of the poet, John Keats, "A pardlike Spirit beautiful and swift," but one like himself already marked for death

ADONAIS

A pardlike Spirit beautiful and swift— 280
A Love in desolation masked;—a Power
Girt round with weakness;—it can scarce uplift
The weight of the superincumbent hour;
It is a dying lamp, a falling shower,
A breaking billow;—even whilst we speak 285
Is it not broken? On the withering flower
The killing sun smiles brightly: on a cheek
The life can burn in blood, even while the heart may break . . .

He has outsoared the shadow of our night;
Envy and calumny and hate and pain,
And that unrest which men miscall delight,
Can touch him not and torture not again; 355
From the contagion of the world's slow stain
He is secure, and now can never mourn
A heart grown cold, a head grown gray in vain;
Nor, when the spirit's self has ceased to burn,
With sparkless ashes load an unlamented urn. . . . 360

The relative success of "Adonais," as opposed to the relative failure of "A Lament," may be traced to the fact that Shelley established the just grounds or motives for the emotion in "Adonais," whereas he failed to do so in "A Lament." The failure in "A Lament" is closely related to the poet's sensibility.

DEFECTIVE SENSIBILITY

Sensibility is the capacity to feel and to render the emotion appropriate to a given situation. Death calls for sadness; a marriage feast normally evokes joy; misfortune elicits compassion. A poem fails in sensibility, and thus clearly fails as a poem, when it does not convey the appropriate response to the situation it presents.

In T. L. Peacock's "The Grave of Love" the speaker describes an incident at the burial place of his faithless sweetheart. He digs a small grave for the "pledges," presumably letters and trinkets, that she had given him. In a parody of the burial service he presses down the sod and places a faded wreath of roses on a small stone. In the concluding stanza the poet moralizes on the contrasting symbols of the dead roses, signs of his sweetheart's faithlessness, and the spreading cypress, the sign of his eternal regret.

THE GRAVE OF LOVE

I dug, beneath the cypress shade,
  What well might seem an elfin's grave;
And every pledge in earth I laid,
  That erst thy false affection gave.

I pressed them down the sod beneath; 5
  I placed one mossy stone above;
And twined the rose's fading wreath
  Around the sepulchre of love.

Frail as thy love, the flowers were dead,
  Ere yet the evening sun was set: 10
But years shall see the cypress spread,
  Immutable as my regret.

THOMAS L. PEACOCK

The situation presented in these lines allows for many appropriate responses. The speaker could mourn the frailty of women, or the imperfection of human love in general, or the irony of fate. But he responds to the situation, or rather fails to respond to it, by stressing a self-centered regard for his own person. We feel, with some justice, that the speaker's sensibility is as shallow as the elfin grave he dug. Since he was not moved himself, or simply moved to self-pity, he fails to stir his readers.

SENTIMENTALITY

Nothing has contributed more to the disrepute of the term emotion than its confusion with that excess of sensibility we call sentimentality. Whereas a genuine poetic emotion derives from a vital experience newly imaged, freshly felt, originally expressed, mere sentiment resides in worn-out emotions and conventional thoughts. The sentimental poem often pretends intense feelings without grounds to support them. Thus, it plasters the word *bliss* on a scene of mere domestic contentment, the word *tragedy* on a passing lovers' quarrel, the word *sublime* on the expression of commonplace ideals, the word *eternal* on trite platitudes. It commands the reader to be indignant when he can only feel annoyance, or ecstatic when he can only acknowledge a mild exhilaration.

The sentimental poem may be subjectively sincere in that it does express the writer's actual feeling. But, in another sense, sentimentality is insincere because it is fundamentally an exaggerated response. Thus, in William Cowper's *The Task*, the poet's subjectively sincere love of animals objectively may well be mere squeamishness. Note how the speaker in the poem refuses friendship to the insensitive because they do not share his own sentiments.

> I would not enter on my list of friends,
> Though graced with polished manners and fine sense,
> Yet wanting sensibility, the man
> Who needlessly sets foot upon a worm.
> An inadvertent step may crush the snail
> That crawls at evening in the public path;
> But he that has humanity, forewarned,
> Will tread aside and let the reptile live.

Sentimentality appears, too, in exaggerated or mawkish expression. Many poems on fervent subjects, such as patriotism, hero-worship, and partisan ideals, are notoriously extravagant. Patriotism's ruddy glow turns into the hectic fever of jingoism in W. E. Henley's lines from "England, My England."

> England, my own,
> Chosen daughter of the Lord, 40
> Spouse-in-Chief of the ancient Sword,
> There's the menace of the Word
> In the Song of your bugles blown,
> England—
> Out of heaven on your bugles blown! . . . 45

Love, too, is a tender trap into which amateur versifiers often fall. Conscious of the sincerity of their love, they sometimes express that love in the fatuous banality of sub-literary popular songs ("Baby mine, be my baby fine"). But even reputable poets can write sentimental poetry. Frederick Locker-Lampson's poem, "At Her Window," while not without merit, sinks beneath tenderness to an insipidly soft sweetness.

Beating Heart! we come again
 Where my Love reposes:
This is Mabel's window-pane;
 These are Mabel's roses.

Is she nested? Does she kneel 5
 In the twilight stilly,
Lily clad from throat to heel,
 She, my virgin Lily?

Soon the wan, the wistful stars,
 Fading, will forsake her; 10
Elves of light, on beamy bars,
 Whisper then, and wake her.

Let this friendly pebble plead
 At her flowery grating;
If she hear me will she heed? 15
 Mabel, I am waiting.

Mabel will be deck'd anon,
 Zoned in bride's apparel;
Happy zone! O hark to yon
 Passion-shaken carol! 20

Sing thy song, thou trancèd thrush,
 Pipe thy best, thy clearest;—
Hush, her lattice moves, O hush—
 Dearest Mabel!—dearest. . . .

Even great poets, Tennyson among them, are unconscious victims of sentimentality. In the poem below a genuine fancy falls into a decline, thence a swoon, and thence "a sickness." The repeated feminine intensives like "so dear," stock epithets like "balmy bosom," the artificial personifications of the earrings, girdle, and necklace, the expectedness of the rhymes, all these proclaim the superficiality of the emotion.

THE MILLER'S DAUGHTER

It is the miller's daughter,
  And she is grown so dear, so dear,
That I would be the jewel
  That trembles at her ear:
For hid in ringlets day and night, 5
I'd touch her neck so warm and white.

And I would be the girdle
  About her dainty dainty waist,
And her heart would beat against me,
  In sorrow and in rest: 10
And I should know if it beat right,
I'd clasp it round so close and tight.

And I would be the necklace,
  And all day long to fall and rise
Upon her balmy bosom, 15
  With her laughter or her sighs:
And I would lie so light, so light,
I scarce should be unclasp'd at night.

ALFRED, LORD TENNYSON

Emotion, mood, or intense feeling, is an essential element in all poetry. But emotion as an element in poetry must be distinguished from the "private" or real emotions of the reader and the writer. "Poetic" emotion is aesthetic. It is the feeling produced by the incidents or the situation presented in the poem itself. Because poetic emotion is aesthetic rather than real, the reader may enjoy "unpleasant" emotions.

Poetic emotion is characterized by propriety and proportion; it is a just response to the situation presented in the poem. The two chief errors of poems that lack propriety and proportion are a defective sensibility and sentimentality.

POEMS FOR DISCUSSION

OZYMANDIAS

I met a traveller from an antique land
Who said: Two vast and trunkless legs of stone
Stand in the desert. Near them, on the sand,
Half sunk, a shatter'd visage lies, whose frown,
And wrinkled lip, and sneer of cold command, 5
Tell that its sculptor well those passions read
Which yet survive, stamp'd on these lifeless things,
The hand that mock'd them and the heart that fed:
And on the pedestal these words appear:
"My name is Ozymandias, king of kings: 10
Look on my works, ye Mighty, and despair!"
Nothing beside remains. Round the decay
Of that colossal wreck, boundless and bare
The lone and level sands stretch far away.

PERCY BYSSHE SHELLEY

1. What details in the description of the statue point up the ironic character of the inscription?
2. In your own words describe the predominant feeling evoked by this poem. How is that feeling connected with the thought of the poem? Is the thought implied or stated explicitly? How is the thought connected with the concrete situation presented in the poem?
3. Is the predominant emotion appropriate? proportionate? Why or why not?
4. Does this poem present a universal rather than a particular experience? Explain.
5. How may this poem be said to evoke delight when it so clearly emphasizes death and decay?
6. In what sense do the details of this poem "speak for themselves?"

SOLILOQUY OF THE SPANISH CLOISTER

I

Gr-r-r—there go, my heart's abhorrence!
  Water your damned flower-pots, do!
If hate killed men, Brother Lawrence,
  God's blood, would not mine kill you!
What? your myrtle-bush wants trimming? 5
  Oh, that rose has prior claims—

Needs its leaden vase filled brimming?
  Hell dry you up with its flames!

II

At the meal we sit together;
  Salve tibi! I must hear 10
Wise talk of the kind of weather,
  Sort of season, time of year:
Not a plenteous cork-crop: scarcely
  Dare we hope oak-galls, I doubt;
What's the Latin name for "parsley"? 15
What's the Greek name for Swine's Snout?

III

Whew! We'll have our platter burnished,
  Laid with care on our own shelf!
With a fire-new spoon we're furnished,
  And a goblet for ourself, 20
Rinsed like something sacrificial
  Ere 'tis fit to touch our chaps—
Marked with L. for our initial!
  (He—he! There his lily snaps!)

IV

Saint, forsooth! While brown Dolores 25
  Squats outside the Convent bank
With Sanchicha, telling stories,
  Steeping tresses in the tank,
Blue-black, lustrous, thick like horsehairs,
  —Can't I see his dead eye glow, 30
Bright as 'twere a Barbary corsair's?
  (That is, if he'd let it show!)

V

When he finishes refection,
  Knife and fork he never lays
Cross-wise, to my recollection, 35
  As do I, in Jesu's praise.
I the Trinity illustrate,
  Drinking watered orange-pulp—

10. *Salve tibi:* Hail to thee

In three sips the Arian frustrate;
  While he drains his at one gulp! 40

VI

Oh, those melons? If he's able
  We're to have a feast; so nice!
One goes to the Abbot's table,
  All of us get each a slice.
How go on your flowers? None double? 45
  Not one fruit-sort can you spy?
Strange!—And I, too, at such trouble,
  Keep them close-nipped on the sly!

VII

There's a great text in Galatians,
  Once you trip on it, entails 50
Twenty-nine distinct damnations,
  One sure, if another fails;
If I trip him just a-dying,
  Sure of heaven as sure can be,
Spin him round and send him flying 55
  Off to hell, a Manichee?

VIII

Or, my scrofulous French novel
  On grey paper with blunt type!
Simply glance at it, you grovel
  Hand and foot in Belial's gripe; 60
If I double down its pages
  At the woeful sixteenth print,
When he gathers his greengages,
  Ope a sieve and slip it in't?

IX

Or, there's Satan!—one might venture 65
  Pledge one's soul to him, yet leave

39. Arian: a heretic who denied the Trinity
49. Gal. 3:10-11
51. Deut. 28:16-24
56. Manichee: a heretic who regarded matter as evil
60. Belial: the name of the devil

Such a flaw in the indenture
  As he'd miss till, past retrieve,
Blasted lay that rose-acacia
  We're so proud of! *Hy, Zy, Hine. . . .* 70
'St, there's Vespers! *Plena gratia*
  Ave, Virgo! Gr-r-r—you swine!

ROBERT BROWNING

70. *Hy, Zy, Hine*: Nonsense words
71-2. *Plena . . . Virgo*: Hail, Virgin full of grace

1. Who is the speaker in the poem? To whom does he speak? Where does the incident occur? What is Brother Lawrence doing there? What is the speaker doing?
2. Why does the speaker hate Brother Lawrence? Does he have solid reasons for his hate? Why or why not?
3. Although Brother Lawrence does not speak directly, his speech is suggested. Where? How does that suggested speech characterize him?
4. How has the speaker attempted to harass Brother Lawrence? to tempt him?
5. What lines suggest that the speaker is willing to contract with the devil to bring about Brother Lawrence's defeat?
6. Hate is the predominant emotion of the speaker in this poem. But what is the predominant emotion expected of the reader? Explain.
7. Is the emotion expressed by the speaker appropriate? proportionate? Explain.
8. Is the situation presented in this poem believable? Why or why not?
9. Read the parody on this poem below. Why does Chesterton object to "Soliloquy of the Spanish Cloister?" Are his objections valid? Why or why not?

FROM THE SPANISH CLOISTER

Grrrr—what's that? A dog? A poet?
  Uttering his damnations thus—
If hate killed things, Brother Browning,
  God's Word, would not hate kill us?

If we'd ever meet together, 5
  Salve tibi! I might hear
How you know poor monks are really
  So much worse than they appear.

There's a great text in Corinthians
  Hinting that our faith entails 10
Something else, that never faileth,
  Yet in you, perhaps, it fails.

But if *plena gratia* chokes you,
  You at least can teach us how
To converse in wordless noises, 15
  Hy, zi; hullo!—Grrrr—Bow-wow!

GILBERT KEITH CHESTERTON

GO, LOVELY ROSE

Go, lovely rose—
Tell her that wastes her time and me,
That now she knows,
When I resemble her to thee,
How sweet and fair she seems to be. 5

Tell her that's young,
And shuns to have her graces spied,
That hadst thou sprung
In deserts where no men abide,
Thou must have uncommended died. 10

Small is the worth
Of beauty from the light retired:
Bid her come forth,
Suffer herself to be desired,
And not blush so to be admired. 15

Then die—that she
The common fate of all things rare
May read in thee;
How small a part of time they share
That are so wondrous sweet and fair! 20

EDMUND WALLER

1. Explain the points in which the rose resembles the woman of this poem.
2. Show how the identification of the rose and the woman evoke a mood or feeling of love *and* sorrow. Which emotion predominates? Why?
3. In what sense does this poem have a universal application? Explain.

4. Much of the success of this poem depends on the overtones created by expressions that contain several meanings. Show how "wastes" (line 2), "shuns" (line 7), "suffer" (line 14) possess several meanings within the context of the poem.
5. Show how the rose, as a personification of beauty, becomes a more important symbol as the poem progresses.

MAN'S BEST FRIEND

When false friends seek to use you,
Gaining wealth at your expense,
Turn to one who'll ne'er abuse you,
Who'll always rise to your defence.

She it is who'll smooth your brow, 5
Bring you another cup of tea,
Softly tell you, "Easy now!
Bring your worries home to me."

Bring your worries home to mother.
She will soothe your cares away, 10
She will go to any bother
Just to hear her dear one say—
"Search the world from end to end,
A Mother is a man's best friend."

1. What grounds are there for saying that this verse is deficient in sensibility? Explain.
2. Find several attempted poems that are lacking in emotional power. Find several that are sentimental. Explain how they lack emotional power or how they are oversentimental.

❋ CHAPTER III ❋

How Emotion Is Expressed

THUS FAR we have seen that emotion in poetry, although derived from a vital experience, is aesthetic, that it is appropriate, and that it is proportionate in its response to the situation presented in a poem. We may now examine the various ways the poet expresses emotion, remembering that emotional effects are not separable from the thought, the imagery, the total structure of the poem, the diction and rhythm.

We must remember, too, that some aspects of poetic experience will always lie mysteriously beyond analysis. No one has yet explained in logical fashion just why a great poem is great or just how a great poet uses the strategies of thought and language to evoke profound and meaningful emotional experiences. But our humility in the face of the creative process does not prevent the use of analysis in considering those elements of poetry, and they are many, that yield to explanation.

Unanalyzable "inspiration" does play a part in the creation of a poem. So, too, does unanalyzable luck—the luck of being born in a creative era, of being born to, or trained in, the use of a natively poetic habit of speech, of experiencing early those tests of soul and mind that flower into knowledge, understanding, and wisdom. But art, the habit of composition, plays its part, too, and this part is to some extent analyzable.

Like the musician, the painter, or the sculptor, the poet is a composer; that is, he, like them, achieves his emotional effects by the right use of age-old habits of his particular art. Those habits, sometimes deliberately learned, sometimes instinctively discovered, are most simply named selection, amplification, compression, and variation. Each of these terms describes one aspect of the poet's total function; each of the functions contributes directly or indirectly to the expression of feeling.

SELECTION

Selection is the art of choosing details that, properly expressed, will result in a unified emotional impression. By selecting telling details the poet focuses his observations, images, incidents, or thoughts on one central emotion. We have already seen how Robert Burns's "A Red, Red Rose" (p. 6) does just this. Each detail in his poem—the likening of his beloved to a rose and to a melody, the comparison between the perfection of her beauty and the proportionate depth of his own love—unites to convey a deeply personal feeling of love. So, too, the details of Wordsworth's "It Is a Beauteous Evening" (p. 7) contribute to an emotion of awe. But the choice of exact and harmonious details is not as easy as it may appear.

What do we mean when we say that in poetry a detail is *exact*? In prose a detail is exact when it corresponds to an objective fact. Exactness of this kind occurs in a proposition such as: Shakespeare was a playwright, or George Washington was the first president of the United States. Here exactness is scientifically measurable, precise, unequivocal. But exactness in poetry is measured by the correspondence of the detail with the emotional state or impression the poet is attempting to convey. The critical reader, and not the dictionary, the encyclopedia or the informed witness, is the judge of the exactness of the poet's details. Thus, the critical reader will accept Keats's use of Cortez instead of Balboa in the poem on p. 4, even though the reference is historically inexact. Moreover, the critical reader may decide that, while Wordsworth may have drawn his detail from observation, and may have intended to convey an impression of pastoral peace, nevertheless the lines

> Green pastures she views in the midst of the dale
> Down which she so often has tripped with her pail

merely sound funny. The rhythm is inappropriate, the word "tripped" is awkward; the detail itself contributes little to the desired impression.

On the other hand, the reader is likely to agree that in "A Birthday" Christina Rossetti has chosen details that do evoke a woman's feeling of joy occasioned by the coming of her lover.

My heart is like a singing bird
  Whose nest is in a water'd shoot;
My heart is like an apple-tree
  Whose boughs are bent with thick-set fruit;
My heart is like a rainbow shell 5
  That paddles in a halcyon sea;
My heart is gladder than all these,
  Because my love is come to me.

In the second stanza she describes that joy in terms of the dais that symbolizes the joyful occasion. Note how the last two lines justify the opulent details she has selected.

Raise me a daïs of silk and down;
  Hang it with vair and and purple dyes; 10
Carve it in doves and pomegranates,
  And peacocks with a hundred eyes;
Work it in gold and silver grapes,
  In leaves and silver fleur-de-lys;
Because the birthday of my life 15
  Is come, my love is come to me.

10. Vair: a fur used for trimming

One test of a well-chosen detail is that it speaks for itself. Or, to put it otherwise, the emotion is present in the image; interpretative comment, like that in the last two lines in the stanzas above, is an aid rather than a necessity. We could know, even without those lines, that the poet was expressing a jubilant feeling of love.

Indeed, some poets actually present exact details without comment, as does Walter de la Mare in "Winter." Here the poet conveys the loneliness, bleakness, and moon-blanched chill of winter without ever stating how you should feel.

WINTER

Clouded with snow
The cold winds blow,
And shrill on leafless bough
The robin with its burning breast
Alone sings now. 5

The rayless sun,
Day's journey done,
Sheds its last ebbing light
On fields in leagues of beauty spread
Unearthly white. 10

Thick draws the dark,
And spark by spark
The frost-fires kindle, and soon
Over that sea of frozen foam
Floats the white moon. 15

WALTER DE LA MARE

An even more conspicuous example of the inherent emotional quality of exact details occurs in John Masefield's "Cargoes"; the title merely hints that the cargoes will themselves explain the poet's emotional impression.

Quinquireme of Nineveh from distant Ophir
Rowing home to haven in sunny Palestine,
With a cargo of ivory,
And apes and peacocks,
Sandalwood, cedarwood, and sweet white wine.

Masefield pictures an ancient quinquireme with its five tiers of oarsmen rowing home to Nineveh after a voyage to Ophir, in southern Arabia. The time is the distant past, the place is the remote mysterious east, the cargo consists of objects that are valuable because they can be enjoyed rather than be put to familiar use. These details arouse in us a romantic sense of the rich, mysterious beauty of the ancient east.

Stately Spanish galleon coming from the Isthmus,
Dipping through the Tropics by the palm-green shores,
With a cargo of diamonds,
Emeralds, amethysts,
Topazes, and cinnamon, and gold moidores.

The second stanza presents another group of details that center upon a stately Spanish galleon. The time is the less-distant past, the place is the exotic Spanish Main, the cargo consists of precious stones, valuable spices and gold coins. Already the quinquireme and the galleon, together with their cargoes, have common characteristics: remoteness, splendor and romance. It is with a certain shock then that we read the third stanza, with its realistic details of the contemporary British coaster.

> Dirty British coaster with a salt-caked smoke stack
> Butting through the Channel in the mad March days,
> With a cargo of Tyne coal,
> Road-rail, pig-lead,
> Firewood, iron-ware, and cheap tin trays.

We are doused with the salt water of modern actuality. The time is the present, the place is industrial England, and the cargo, carried in an ugly old freighter, consists not of beautiful objects, or precious stones, but ugly useful things. Our first impression may well be that the present is ugly in contrast to the romantic past.

Here, then, are three separate stanzas devoted in turn to the quinquireme, the galleon, and the coaster. There is no transitional link, no interpretative comment, not even a complete sentence in the whole poem, yet the details are so exact that the verbless sentences do predicate an emotional judgment.

The ships and their cargoes reveal the author's feelings about the romantic past and the realistic present. In the past men stowed rich material rather than cheap manufactured things; their ships were designed for beauty as well as for use. Yet the mood of the poem, as a whole, is not a longing for the past and contempt for the present. The poem is not reducible to such logical terms. It is rather an expression of feeling about the differences between the past and the present.

HARMONIOUS DETAILS

In "A Birthday," "Winter," and "Cargoes" we have seen how exact details help to express the feeling of the poet. But all these poems are comparatively simple, that is, they express relatively unmixed feelings of jubilation, of bleakness, of disenchantment. Other poems, however, are concerned with complex emotions, involving many intensely remembered experiences, or with discordant emotions, born of conflicting experiences, in which hope mingles with fear, joy with sorrow. In these situations the poet still selects the exact details that will recreate the desired emotion. But details will be more complex, and the poet must relate them, bind them together and established a basis for their presence in the poem. In short, he must harmonize complex details to create a unified impression. Let us see how several poets have done just this.

SONNET 43

How do I love thee? Let me count the ways.
I love thee to the depth and breadth and height
My soul can reach, when feeling out of sight
For the ends of Being and ideal Grace.
I love thee to the level of everyday's 5
Most quiet need, by sun and candle-light.
I love thee freely, as men strive for Right;
I love thee purely, as they turn from Praise.
I love thee with the passion put to use
In my old griefs, and with my childhood's faith. 10
I love thee with a love I seemed to lose
With my lost saints—I love thee with the breath,
Smiles, tears, of all my life!—and, if God choose,
I shall but love thee better after death.

ELIZABETH BARRETT BROWNING

The speaker is in a sense cataloguing the various ways she loves her husband, but her love is not a simple one, like that of Christina Rossetti in "A Birthday." No one kind of detail, however multiplied, can indicate the quality of her affection. She needs details that will express at once the range and intensity of her emotion. To indicate the range of her feeling she selects seven details to show that her love is of several kinds; ethereal yet familiar, free, pure, passionate, holy and, in hope at least, eternal. Yet these different kinds of love have one common characteristic—each is in its way superlative. Together they represent the highest, widest, deepest and fullest stretch of human affection. Thus, all her details are interrelated and all contribute to the central feeling.

Let us consider another poem that presents a complex emotion.

SPRING

Nothing is so beautiful as spring—
When weeds, in wheels, shoot long and lovely and lush;
Thrush's eggs look like low heavens, and thrush

Through the echoing timber does so rinse and wring
The ear, it strikes like lightning to hear him sing; 5
  The glassy peartree leaves and blooms, they brush
  The descending blue; that blue is all in a rush
With richness; the racing lambs too have fair their fling.
What is all this juice and all this joy?
  A strain of the earth's sweet being in the beginning 10
In Eden garden.—Have, get, before it cloy,
  Before it cloud, Christ, lord, and sour with sinning,
Innocent mind and Mayday in girl and boy,
Most, O maid's child, thy choice and worthy the winning.

GERARD MANLEY HOPKINS

Indeed, a first reading leaves some readers baffled. What is the central emotion? Joy, fear, hope or love? Is Hopkins really talking about spring, or about the Garden of Eden, or about the Fall of Man and the Redemption? It appears the poet is talking about all of these subjects. Moreover, each is represented by exact details, and these details do evoke a variety of emotions. Does he relate these subjects, details, and emotions so as to form an harmonious whole? Let us see.

In the first eight lines every detail supports the general statement in the opening line. The lush growth, the thrush's song, the pear tree in bloom, the rich blue sky, the racing lambs, all are exuberant emblems of the joy and vigor of spring. The language, too, throbs with joy as it races along in vivid accompaniment to the thought.

Then the subject, if not the emotion, changes. "What is all this juice and all this joy?" It is a strain, that is, an inheritance, of the beauty and innocence of Paradise. The poet has perceived a relation between the springtime in nature and the springtime of creation in the Garden of Eden.

He is suggesting, too, that sin ruined the Garden of Eden. That he is thinking of Adam's fall, of man's inheritance of sin, that other strain of the Garden, and of the subsequent redemption of man by Christ, is immediately evident in the succeeding lines. He has perceived a further relation, that between spring and youth. Like spring, youth is innocent—yet another "strain of earth's sweet being in the beginning." But, again like spring, youth is the inheritor of sin and ruin. His joy now shades into fear that youth may lose its innocence. Hence, he begs Christ to "Have, get," that is, to preserve youth's springtime innocence before it is soured with sinning.

To save youth from corruption, the lines imply, is Christ's own choice, since Christ chose once and forever to drive sin out of the world. It is most worthy of Christ's effort, because Christ, the Son of the most pure Virgin, is eternal innocence. Thus, the poem ends on a note of confidence.

"Spring," then, has introduced several subjects through various details and the poet has evoked an impression of mingled joy, fear, and confidence. But the subjects, the details, and the emotions these details evoke are all of a piece. Spring—joy—the Garden—innocent youth, these suggest another set of ideas, namely—sin—ruin—redemption—preservation of innocent youth. There is a discernible unity of impression throughout the poem even though some details are submerged and some are elided.

Selection of unified details focuses on the emotion at the center of the poem and is therefore a means of intensification. Invariably, the poet finds that, in choosing the exact details that will best convey the feeling in a poem, he must also decide to expand some details and to compress others. Just as a storyteller summarizes those incidents that form the background of his story, and magnifies other incidents that are crucial to the development of character or to the resolution of plot, so the poet compresses some details and expands others the better to achieve a precise, a more intense, emotional effect.

Amplification and compression, then, are ways of intensifying details, or, to put it in terms of our previous discussion, of giving a more emphatic expression to exact details. Both of them work hand in hand, but, for the sake of convenience, let us examine *amplification* first.

AMPLIFICATION

The poet magnifies the emotion in his poem in several ways; by his choice of words, by repetition, by the use of contrast and comparison, by a climactic arrangement. The use of any one of these means of amplification does not exclude the others. A long poem is likely to employ all of them.

The first two ways, choice of words and repetition, will be discussed elsewhere (p. 262). Here, let us simply point out that vivid language and some form of repetition are essential to the creation and reinforcement of poetic feeling. We may illustrate this by turning for a moment to stanzas 6-10 and 13 from Part II of Coleridge's "The Rime of the Ancient Mariner." These stanzas describe the fatal calm that struck the ship after the Mariner had shot the albatross.

PART II

6

Down dropt the breeze, the sails dropt down,
'Twas sad as sad could be;
And we did only speak to break
The silence of the sea! 110

7

All in a hot and copper sky,
The bloody Sun, at noon,
Right up above the mast did stand,
No bigger than the Moon.

8

Day after day, day after day, 115
We stuck, nor breath nor motion;
As idle as a painted ship
Upon a painted ocean.

9

Water, water, everywhere,
And all the boards did shrink; 120
Water, water, everywhere
Nor any drop to drink.

10

The very deep did rot: O Christ!
That ever this should be!
Yea, slimy things did crawl with legs 125
Upon the slimy sea. . . .

13

And every tongue, through utter drought,
Was wither'd at the root;

We could not speak, no more than if
We had been choked with soot. 130

Coleridge has chosen exact details to impress us with the unnatural silence, motionlessness, heat, thirst, and desolation. Everything is dead save the capacity to suffer. But he renders these details even more emphatic by using words like "bloody sun" instead of red sun, "stuck" instead of stood; so, too, in the context of the poem, the expressions "painted ship" and "painted ocean," "the very deep did rot," "slimy things did crawl with legs," "withered at the root," "choked with soot," make us see, feel, even taste what happens and thus share in the experience of the Mariner's physical and mental torment.

Repetition, too, works its spell. Coleridge emphasizes the silence, stillness, thirst, and sadness again and again. We are saturated with a feeling of desolation. Moreover, he repeats many expressions several times. This combination of vivid diction and reiteration, together with the rhythm and rhyme, explains why these stanzas are intense and therefore unforgettable.

AMPLIFICATION BY COMPARISON

Comparison is a means of increasing emotional intensity. To relate one image, thought, or feeling to another helps the reader to see vividly, to think deeply, to feel intensely. Notice how Shakespeare does this in "That time of year . . . ." The speaker pleads with his beloved "To love that well which thou must leave ere long," asking her compassion because he soon must die. His plea is justified by the thought alone. But how much more vividly we appreciate the speaker's situation when he associates it with an early winter scene, then with sunset, finally with a dying fire—all vivid emblems of change, decay, and death.

SONNET 73

That time of year thou mayst in me behold
When yellow leaves, or none, or few, do hang
Upon those boughs which shake against the cold,
Bare ruin'd choirs where late the sweet birds sang.
In me thou see'st the twilight of such day 5
As after sunset fadeth in the west,

Which by and by black night doth take away,
Death's second self, that seals up all in rest.
In me thou see'st the glowing of such fire
That on the ashes of his youth doth lie, 10
As the death-bed whereon it must expire,
Consum'd with that which it was nourish'd by.
This thou perceiv'st, which makes thy love more strong,
To love that well which thou must leave ere long.

WILLIAM SHAKESPEARE

Why are the three comparisons between the speaker's state and winter, sunset and a dying fire effective? Let us examine the first one. In the explicit language of paraphrase the poet is saying, "You may see me, that is, understand my situation, by visualizing an early winter scene. That scene is desolate and my state is very much like it." Note, too, how Shakespeare establishes the exact correspondence between early winter and the speaker's situation. The bare boughs shaking against the cold imply that the speaker has reached the early winter of life. The bare boughs suggest, too, a resemblance to the bare ruined choir in a devastated church. The two scenes of desolation also recall two scenes of earlier happiness—the time when sweet birds sang in the summer trees and when choristers chanted in the once beautiful temple. Through these implied comparisons or metaphors* Shakespeare greatly extends the range and vigor of his feeling. A lost but poignantly remembered youth, associated with the dying year and the ruined church, echoes a world woe universal in its application.

This feeling of desolation is further developed by the sunset metaphor in the second stanza. The speaker's situation is now likened to a twilight deepening into night, itself a symbol of death. A third metaphor, even more daring, compares his present state to a fire that is consumed by the very principle that gives it life.

All three metaphors serve to expand the emotional range by identifying the poet's situation with similar situations. Yet this amplification costs but few words.

* For more detailed treatment of metaphor and other figures of speech see pp. 141ff. Here we are merely concerned with figurative language as a means of amplification and compression.

AMPLIFICATION BY CONTRAST

Contrast is a kindred method of intensification. Sometimes the poet builds up a strong feeling by opposing one image, thought or feeling to its contrary. Let us turn again to Shakespeare. In his sonnet, "Tired with all these . . .", his imaginary speaker is worn out by life's miseries and disgusted with its inequitable rewards and punishments. He would prefer a restful death save that it would separate him from his beloved. Many poets have dramatized similar attitudes by comparing the miseries and injustices of life to a stage of fools, a tale told by an idiot, an empty bubble, a mad-house, a withered waste and so on. Equally effective, perhaps more so because of its sustained irony, is the method of contrast that appears in the sonnet below:

SONNET 66

Tired with all these, for restful death I cry:
As, to behold desert a beggar born,
And needy nothing trimm'd in jollity,
And purest faith unhappily forsworn,
And gilded honour shamefully misplac'd,
And maiden virtue rudely strumpeted,
And right perfection wrongfully disgrac'd,
And strength by limping sway disabled,
And art made tongue-tied by authority,
And folly, doctor-like, controlling skill,
And simple truth miscall'd simplicity,
And captive good attending captain ill:
Tired with all these, from these would I be gone,
Save that, to die, I leave my love alone.

WILLIAM SHAKESPEARE

Shakespeare develops the reasons for this world weariness by ten contrasts, each emphasizing vain hope of happiness in a world that has turned all values upside-down. He further emphasizes these contrasts by his language. The ten *ands* moan. The parallel structure of balanced sentences, the seesaw of alliterated nouns and adjectives, the heavy verse stress now on one opposite, then on the other, all these amplify the feeling of disillusion.

In longer narrative poems a poet expands the climactic details of his story. Thus, in *Sohrab and Rustum* Matthew Arnold focuses on the battle scene between father and son and on the recognition that is the emotional climax. But even in shorter lyric poems, a poet tends to expand and thus to intensify his main point. Note, for instance, how in "The Pulley" George Herbert enlarges the main feeling of the poem, God's love for man, by developing the last and best gift, Rest.

When God at first made Man,
Having a glass of blessings standing by—
Let us (said He) pour on him all we can;
Let the world's riches, which dispersèd lie,
Contract into a span. 5

So strength first made a way,
Then beauty flow'd, then wisdom, honour, pleasure:
When almost all was out, God made a stay,
Perceiving that, alone of all His treasure,
Rest in the bottom lay. 10

For if I should (said He)
Bestow this jewel also on My creature,
He would adore My gifts instead of Me,
And rest in Nature, not the God of Nature:
So both should losers be. 15

Yet let him keep the rest,
But keep them with repining restlessness;
Let him be rich and weary, that at least,
If goodness lead him not, yet weariness
May toss him to My breast. 20

Amplification in all good poetry is not mere enlargement or useless repetition. Rather, the development and intensification of feeling is accomplished by saying a great deal briefly. In "Spring," for instance, Hopkins crams words and phrases together, often with some violence to normal syntax. Here, and in other poems, he drops definite articles, omits verbs, prepositions and conjunctions, leaps over relatives, presses adjectives into service as nouns because they are a syllable shorter, distorts the order of sentences in the interest of brevity and elides the obvious. Like a lover mounting two steps at a time to meet his beloved, he rushes, but with an efficient haste, to his main point. All his compression, telescoping, and fusion serve to stress or amplify the essential feeling.

Thus, amplification and compression are necessary opposites; their functions are reciprocal rather than contradictory, like those of inhaling and exhaling, charging and discharging.

COMPRESSION

In the first stanza of Shakespeare's "That time of year . . ." the images of leaves, boughs, wind, choir, and birds *depict* the scene of early winter, embody the *thought* that death is near, and discharge a *feeling* of desolation. The experiences of sensation, reflection, and feeling are all compressed in one utterance.

This kind of compression is often achieved by metaphorical or figurative expression. Metaphor, indeed figurative language in general, describes one thing in terms of another because of a common quality that links them together. In Shakespeare's sonnet (p. 130), leafless boughs are described metaphorically in terms of the choirs of a church because, despite the fact that trees and churches are separate kinds of reality, both objects happen to be bare and ruined. Like other good metaphors, this one makes us see things in a new light. Winter is more desolate for its association with the picture of the ruined church. Moreover, by relating the winter scene to the ruined church, the poet widens our mental horizon. We begin to sense that man, nature, and all things created are doomed to decay. Thus, one brief, vivid metaphor, "bare ruined choirs," compresses two worlds of experience, the physical and moral, in three words.

Similarly, in Hopkins's "Spring" (p. 38) metaphors compress several worlds together, the outer world of things and the inner world of sensation; the world of nature and the world of spirit. "Thrush's eggs look [like] little low heavens." We are aware at once of the shape, size and blue color of the eggs, and the shape, size and color of the heavens. When the thrush *rinses* and *wrings* the ear we sense the clear, clean ring of his song and also its vivid cleansing effect. The substance and the quality of the spring scene are associated with similar scenes of refreshment and joy. By grace of metaphor we see the nest and hear the song and feel the cleansing effect of water, imagine the sudden flash of lightning.

At the same time we know that all these experiences are in some way connected with a spring-time of the spirit.

The emotional experience of poetry is intensified by metaphorical expressions. Other figurative devices also help to concentrate much emotional experience in a few lines. Thus, by a paradoxical use of *ascended* and *descent,* W. H. Davies in his "Ambition" secures greater intensity in his contrast between pride and humility:

> I had Ambition, by which sin
> The angels fell;
> I climbed and, step by step, O Lord,
> Ascended into Hell . . .
> Let my descent and fall, O Lord,
> Be into Paradise.

And, in "Eight O'Clock," A. E. Housman expresses with utmost intensity the feelings of a condemned man through a clock that personifies or symbolizes his fate.

> He stood, and heard the steeple
> Sprinkle the quarters on the morning town.
> One, two, three, four, to market-place and people,
> It tossed them down.
> Strapped, noosed, nighing his hour, 5
> He stood and counted them and cursed his luck;
> And the clock collected in the tower
> Its strength, and struck.

But figurative language is not always or necessarily direct or emphatic as it is in Davies' "Ambition" and Housman's "Eight O'Clock." Often the poet achieves emotional effects by quiet allusion or quotation from the well-known legends or poems of the past. Thus, Poe depends upon our already formulated impressions of classic beauty to evoke in us the impact of a beauty that recalls him

> To the glory that was Greece,
> And the grandeur that was Rome.

Walter Savage Landor expects that, in comparing his beloved to Helen of Troy and Queen Alcestis, we will remember Homer's *Iliad* and Euripides' *Alcestis* and thus feel more poignantly the proud profession of his love:

Past ruin'd Ilion Helen lives,
  Alcestis rises from the shades;
Verse calls them forth; 'tis verse that gives
  Immortal youth to mortal maids.

Soon shall Oblivion's deepening veil
  Hide all the peopled hills you see,
The gay, the proud, while lovers hail
  These many summers you and me.

Nor should we ever forget that the quiet eloquence of understatement is frequently as moving as the fretted emphasis of overstatement and elaboration. No poem is more essentially emotional than Wordsworth's poem on the dead Lucy where the poet expresses a profound sorrow briefly, simply, reticently.

She dwelt among the untrodden ways
  Beside the springs of Dove,
A Maid whom there were none to praise
  And very few to love:

A violet by a mossy stone 5
  Half hidden from the eye!
Fair as a star, when only one
  Is shining in the sky.

She lived unknown, and few could know
  When Lucy ceased to be; 10
But she is in her grave, and oh,
  The difference to me!

UNITY AND VARIETY OF EMOTIONS

How a poet achieves emotional intensity is closely related to the means he uses to sustain that intensity. For in a poem emotion is intense, not only in certain key lines but throughout. The pleasure of poetry, as Coleridge noted, is both in the whole and in the parts. It follows then that if the emotion loses its intensity the poem is faulty. Although successful poems may falter, for even Homer nods, they never fail to sustain the live emotional current that is the source of their poetic strength.

The poet's creative energy, plus his willingness to criticize and to revise his own verse, is one explanation of sustained emotional intensity. From the manuscript revisions of Keats, Tennyson, Yeats, and A. E. Housman, we know that these poets worked with unflagging zeal to find the exact word, or rhythm, or figure of speech necessary to maintain the emotional unity and intensity of a poem. Thus, in composing "Eight O'Clock" (p. 47), Housman, as his notebooks reveal, searched long for the exact word to suggest the condemned man's impression of the bell's sounding the hours. Before he chose the word *tossed* in the line, "It tossed them down," he had fumbled with *pitched, dealt, cast,* and *spilt.* All of them were effective but none of them expressed as well as *tossed* the convict's grim sense of the ironic indifference of fate.

The unremitting concern for the charged word, however, merely explains how the poet sustains emotional intensity line by line. This is a matter of diction. Maintaining emotional interest is indeed a matter of diction and other verbal strategies, but it also involves a larger element, which may be summed up under the term *variety.* By variety we mean the presentation of the predominant emotion or idea in the context of subordinate emotions and of subordinate degrees of emotion. Variety accounts for the richness of emotional response, the range of feeling, the suggestiveness in a poem.

A simple, intense emotion, a feeling of ecstasy, for instance, can rarely be maintained, either in poetry or in life, beyond a brief lyric moment. Ecstasy is rare and should be rare. Few readers can endure to live continuously at the highest stretch of sensation and feeling, even though the poet may exclaim—

> If I could only live at the pitch that is near madness,
> When everything is as it was in my childhood,
> Violent, vivid and of infinite possibility.
>
> RICHARD EBERHART

Moreover, our emotions are rarely simple. In sympathizing with a leper, for instance, we do not feel simple, isolated pity; nor is pity an unbroken feeling. Rather, it is mixed with kindred feelings of fear; it shifts in intensity from mere sympathy to blinding compassion; often it blends into opposite feelings of revulsion.

So, too, in a poem, the one predominant emotion embraces a variety of similar and contrasting emotions. In long poems this variety is clearly demanded. The Inferno section of Dante's *The Divine Comedy*, for instance, evokes a predominant feeling of horror. But the horror is neither unrelieved nor monotonous. As we circle down the mountain of hell our terror is partly relieved by Dante's recollection of life on earth, by his awareness of a contrasting purgatory and heaven, and by the detachment of Vergil, Dante's guide, who stands apart from the scenes of torture. Neither is our horror of one kind. Sometimes it approaches contempt, as in the case of the trimmers; sometimes it is tinged with pathos, as in the case of the guilty lovers, Paolo and Francesca. We feel many varieties of horror—horror combined with loathing, or contempt, or indignation, or anxiety.

Moreover, our horror mounts in intensity. At the beginning it resembles superficial, agitated shock. As we descend to the solitary, icy abyss where Satan sits in the utter loneliness of fire and ice, the accumulated horror leaves us speechless. We are paralyzed and silent. Dilation of horror alone could not have produced this final total experience; rather it is the sum of many different emotions.

VARIETY IN LONGER POEMS

Dramatic poetry, too, illustrates how variety contributes to the emotional effect. In Shakespeare's *Romeo and Juliet* the main theme is tragic—"A pair of star-cross'd lovers take their life." Yet, in this tale of multiple deaths and multiplied sorrows, almost grotesque in its tearful imagery, the variety in the kind of emotion and the variety in the degree of the same emotion help to sustain a tension that might otherwise collapse.

First of all, there is the element of comic relief. The servants joke in an atmosphere of tragedy; Mercutio jests at Romeo's love and later at Tybalt's fury; the nurse cracks coarse jokes when Juliet is most seriously troubled. These comic moments are still directly related to the tragic emotions in the play. The servants, mindless of civil disorder, point up the judicial wrath of the Prince of Verona; Mercutio's buoyant optimism makes his accidental death more tragic, and also underlines Romeo's seriousness and melancholy; the nurse's coarse good humor, self-seeking common sense, and corrupt worldliness are the base from which we view Juliet's aspiration, generosity, and self-sacrifice. Thus, here, as in many of Shakespeare's plays, laughter and tears, two opposite kinds of emotion, complement each other.

The same emotion, too, may be varied in the development of the play, and this variety helps to sustain emotional intensity. Thus, Romeo's love for Juliet begins as a kind of distant infatuation. At the Capulet party she is a "Beauty too rich for use, for earth too dear." Later, in the Capulet orchard, he sees her as a somewhat less fantastic figure, but she still resembles a sun, a bright angel, an incarnation of that ideal lady dreamed of by lunatics, lovers, and poets. In Friar Laurence's cell prior to their marriage, Romeo's love is that of an eager bridegroom for a flesh and blood bride. After the duel, Romeo agonizes for a lost wife. From this point on Romeo's love grows with his own experience. Thus, the emotion of love is presented in all its degrees from infatuation to tragic involvement. Romeo's love is not a simple feeling, but a complex, shifting, total experience.

Even within the same series of speeches the emotion of love assumes a different shape under the pressure of the dramatic situation. Thus, in the orchard scene, Juliet's simplicity nevertheless allows for complex feelings. First, speaking in a soliloquy, Juliet is shamelessly importunate. She speaks like any love-stricken girl. Then, abashed by Romeo's sudden appearance below the balcony, she is alarmed. Fear mingles with her love as she warns him of danger. "If they do see thee they will murder thee." Her fears overcome by Romeo's eloquence, she admits her love and begs for his. Suddenly a word—"swear"—fills her with a presentiment of disaster. This contrast is "too rash, too unadvised, too sudden,/Too like the lightning, which doth cease to be/Ere one can say it lightens." In a moment this cloud passes and she impetuously repeats her love, and, with innocent candor, courts Romeo's, and elicits a proposal of marriage. When she returns to the balcony a second time her love is playful, gentle, whimsical.

Thus, the scene sounds many variations on the theme of love; it shows love as fantastic, daring, fearful, practical, triumphant, tender and playful. Each variation of feeling, in conjunction with the suspenseful action, sustains the emotional interest of the scene.

VARIETY IN SHORTER POEMS

What is true of longer poems, like *The Divine Comedy* and *Romeo and Juliet,* is proportionately true of many shorter poems where emotional intensity is maintained by discriminating among the various shades of the same emotion, or by using contrasting emotions, or by the dramatic use of suspense. If we look for a second time at "The Man He Killed" (p. 18), we will note how adroitly Thomas Hardy has modulated his feeling of pity in a scale that ranges from a quizzical wonder to a sense of uncomprehending tragic irony. This variation is partly the result of the tragic contrast between the natural good-fellowship in the tavern and the artificial animosities of the battlefield. Suspense, too, plays a part in the total effect. We are in no doubt that the speaker killed a man, but we do not know what is the speaker's response to that action. The answer to the question "Why?" is suspended until the last stanza.

Note, too, the variety of feeling in G. M. Hopkins's "Spring" (p. 38). The poet expresses joy in the different manifestations of spring. This joy contrasts with anxiety for the loss of innocence in the last four lines. Moreover, as in the case of "The Man He Killed," and indeed of most poems, the situation is dramatized. In "Spring," the poet speaks in his own person rather than as an imagined character, perceives a situation, appraises it, reacts to it and addresses a second person in a climactic utterance.

Or, to take a fresh example, consider Robert Burns's "To a Mouse." Here is variation of the comic and tragic, the light and dark. At first the poem is sentimentally humorous. The "Wee, sleekit, cow'rin, tim'rous beastie" is addressed with childlike simplicity. Gradually the parallel between man and mouse is hinted at. Burns then compares the two, ending with a climactic and tragic contrast.

> But, Mousie, thou art no thy lane,
> In proving foresight may be vain:
> The best laid schemes o' mice an' men
>   Gang aft agley, 40
> An' lea'e us naught but grief an' pain
>   For promis'd joy.
> Still, thou art blest compar'd wi' me!

The present only toucheth thee:
But och! I backward cast my e'e 45
    On prospects drear!
An' forward, tho' I canna see,
    I guess an' fear!

SUMMARY

In this chapter we have indicated that emotion is essential to poetry. We have seen, too, some of the processes the poet employs to present a situation that will evoke an emotional response, namely, selection, amplification, compression, and variation. In the course of this discussion we have been constantly aware of the fact that the situation presented in the poem provides an adequate motive, that is, a reason for sharing the emotion of the poem. This in turn leads us to consider more carefully the element of thought in poetry. For poetry, as we have already seen, is emotional only in the sense that it is meaningful. And, since it is meaningful, poetry embodies thought.

POEMS FOR DISCUSSION

RICHARD CORY

Whenever Richard Cory went down town,
  We people on the pavement looked at him:
He was a gentleman from sole to crown,
  Clean favored, and imperially slim.

And he was always quietly arrayed, 5
  And he was always human when he talked;
But still he fluttered pulses when he said,
  Good-morning, and he glittered when he walked.

And he was rich—yes, richer than a king,
  And admirably schooled in every grace: 10
In fine, we thought that he was everything
  To make us wish that we were in his place.

So on we worked, and waited for the light,
  And went without the meat, and cursed the bread;

And Richard Cory, one calm summer night, 15
Went home and put a bullet through his head.

EDWIN ARLINGTON ROBINSON

1. Judging from the first three stanzas in this poem what do you expect to happen in this poem?
2. How are your expectations reversed in the last stanza?
3. What is the proper emotional response to the situation presented in this poem?
4. How does the contrast in the last stanza contribute to the emotional effect of the poem? Explain.
5. Show how this poem illustrates the processes of amplification and compression as described in this chapter.
6. Is this poem enjoyable? How? Why or why not? (See Chapter I.)
7. Point out some similarities between this poem and "The Man He Killed," p. 18, and "Ozymandias," p. 27.
8. How does this poem differ from a newspaper account of a similar tragedy?
9. Does the poem contain any truth of human nature? Explain.

PROUD MAISIE

Proud Maisie is in the wood,
Walking so early;
Sweet Robin sits on the bush,
Singing so rarely.

"Tell me, thou bonny bird, 5
When shall I marry me?"
—"When six braw gentlemen
Kirkward shall carry ye."

"Who makes the bridal bed,
Birdie, say truly?" 10
—"The grey-headed sexton
That delves the grave duly.

"The glow-worm o'er grave and stone
Shall light thee steady;
The owl from the steeple sing, 15
'Welcome, proud lady!' "

SIR WALTER SCOTT

1. What attitudes in the dialogue of Maisie justifies the adjective "proud?"
2. What attitudes are presented in the dialogue of Sweet Robin?
3. Show how the attitudes of the two speakers represent an ironic contrast.
4. Compare the methods used to express irony in this poem with those used in "Richard Cory."
5. How does the irony illustrated in this poem differ from contrast?
6. What is the difference between an ironic statement and an ironic situation? (For additional discussion of irony see p. 176.)

LYCIDAS

Yet once more, O ye laurels, and once more,
Ye myrtles brown, with ivy never sear,
I come to pluck your berries harsh and crude,
And with forced fingers rude
Shatter your leaves before the mellowing year. 5
Bitter constraint and sad occasion dear
Compels me to disturb your season due;
For Lycidas is dead, dead ere his prime,
Young Lycidas, and hath not left his peer.
Who would not sing for Lycidas? He knew 10
Himself to sing, and build the lofty rime.
He must not float upon his watery bier
Unwept, and welter to the parching wind,
Without the meed of some melodious tear.
  Begin, then, Sisters of the sacred well, 15
That from beneath the seat of Jove doth spring;
Begin, and somewhat loudly sweep the string.
Hence with denial vain and coy excuse;
So may some gentle muse
With lucky words favor my destined urn, 20
And as he passes turn
And bid fair peace be to my sable shroud!
  For we were nursed upon the selfsame hill,
Fed the same flock, by fountain, shade, and rill;
Together both, ere the high lawns appeared 25
Under the opening eyelids of the Morn,
We drove afield, and both together heard

8. Lycidas: a traditional name for a shepherd. Here it refers to Milton's friend, Edward King

15. Sisters: the muses
Sacred well: the source of poetic inspiration

What time the gray-fly winds her sultry horn,
Battening our flocks with the fresh dews of night,
Oft till the star that rose at evening, bright, 30
Toward heaven's descent had sloped his westering wheel.
Meanwhile the rural ditties were not mute,
Tempered to the oaten flute;
Rough Satyrs danced, and Fauns with cloven heel
From the glad sound would not be absent long; 35
And old Damoetas loved to hear our song.
  But, oh! the heavy change, now thou art gone,
Now thou art gone, and never must return!
Thee, Shepherd, thee the woods and desert caves,
With wild thyme and the gadding vine o'ergrown, 40
And all their echoes, mourn.
The willows, and the hazel copses green,
Shall now no more be seen
Fanning their joyous leaves to thy soft lays.
As killing as the canker to the rose, 45
Or taint-worm to the weanling herds that graze,
Or frost to flowers, that their gay wardrobe wear,
When first the white-thorn blows—
Such, Lycidas, thy loss to shepherd's ear.
  Where were ye, Nymphs, when the remorseless deep 50
Closed o'er the head of your loved Lycidas?
For neither were ye playing on the steep
Where your old Bards, the famous Druids, lie,
Nor on the shaggy top of Mona high,
Nor yet where Deva spreads her wizard stream: 55
Ay me! I fondly dream!
Had ye been there, for what could that have done?
What could the Muse herself that Orpheus bore,
The Muse herself for her enchanting son,
Whom universal nature did lament, 60
When by the rout that made the hideous roar,
His gory visage down the stream was sent,
Down the swift Hebrus to the Lesbian shore?
  Alas! what boots it with uncessant care
To tend the homely slighted shepherd's trade, 65
And strictly meditate the thankless Muse?
Were it not better done as other use,

36. Damoetas: a traditional name, referring possibly to a teacher of Milton and King

To sport with Amaryllis in the shade,
Or with the tangles of Neaera's hair?
Fame is the spur that the clear spirit doth raise 70
(That last infirmity of noble mind)
To scorn delights, and live laborious days:
But the fair guerdon when we hope to find,
And think to burst out into sudden blaze,
Comes the blind Fury with the abhorrèd shears, 75
And slits the thin-spun life. "But not the praise,"
Phoebus replied, and touched my trembling ears:
"Fame is no plant that grows on mortal soil,
Nor in the glistering foil
Set off to the world, nor in broad rumor lies, 80
But lives and spreads aloft by those pure eyes
And perfect witness of all-judging Jove;
As he pronounces lastly on each deed,
Of so much fame in Heaven expect thy meed."
O fountain Arethuse and thou honored flood, 85
Smooth-sliding Mincius, crowned with vocal reeds,
That strain I heard was of a higher mood.
But now my oat proceeds,
And listens to the herald of the sea,
That came in Neptune's plea. 90
He asked the waves, and asked the felon winds,
What hard mishap hath doomed this gentle swain?
And questioned every gust of rugged wings
That blows from off each beakèd promontory;
They knew not of his story, 95
And sage Hippotades their answer brings,
That not a blast was from his dungeon strayed;
The air was calm, and on the level brine
Sleek Panope with all her sisters played.
It was that fatal and perfidious bark, 100
Built in the eclipse, and rigged with curses dark,
That sunk so low that sacred head of thine.
Next Camus, reverend sire, went footing slow,
His mantle hairy, and his bonnet sedge,
Inwrought with figures dim, and on the edge 105
Like to that sanguine flow'r inscribed with woe.
"Ah! Who hath reft" (quoth he) "my dearest pledge?"
Last came, and last did go,

103. Camus: the River Cam; a figure of speech for Cambridge

The pilot of the Galilean lake.
Two massy keys he bore of metals twain, 110
(The golden opes, the iron shuts amain)
He shook his mitred locks, and stern bespake,
"How well could I have spared for thee, young swain,
Enow of such as for their bellies' sake
Creep, and intrude, and climb into the fold! 115
Of other care they little reckoning make,
Than how to scramble at the shearer's feast,
And shove away the worthy bidden guest;
Blind mouths! that scarce themselves know how to hold
A sheep-hook, or have learned aught else the least 120
That to the faithful herdman's art belongs!
What recks it them? What need they? They are sped;
And when they list, their lean and flashy songs
Grate on their scrannel pipes of wretched straw;
The hungry sheep look up, and are not fed, 125
But swoln with wind, and the rank mist they draw,
Rot inwardly, and foul contagion spread;
Besides what the grim wolf with privy paw
Daily devours apace, and nothing said;
But that two-handed engine at the door 130
Stands ready to smite once, and smite no more."
  Return, Alpheus, the dread voice is past,
That shrunk thy streams; return, Sicilian Muse,
And call the vales, and bid them hither cast
Their bells, and flow'rets of a thousand hues. 135
Ye valleys low, where the mild whispers use
Of shades, and wanton winds, and gushing brooks,
On whose fresh lap the swart-star sparely looks:
Throw hither all your quaint enamelled eyes,
That on the green turf suck the honied showers, 140
And purple all the ground with vernal flowers.
Bring the rathe primrose that forsaken dies,
The tufted crow-toe, and pale jessamine,
The white pink, and the pansy freaked with jet,
The glowing violet, 145
The musk-rose, and the well-attired woodbine,
With cowslips wan that hang the pensive head,
And every flower that sad embroidery wears.

109. Pilot: St. Peter
130. Two-handed engine: the avenging sword of the Archangel Michael

Bid amaranthus all his beauty shed,
And daffadillies fill their cups with tears, 150
To strew the laureate hearse where Lycid lies.
For so to interpose a little ease,
Let our frail thoughts dally with false surmise.
Ay me! whilst thee the shores and sounding seas
Wash far away, where'er thy bones are hurled, 155
Whether beyond the stormy Hebrides,
Where thou perhaps under the whelming tide
Visit'st the bottom of the monstrous world;
Or whether thou, to our moist vows denied,
Sleep'st by the fable of Bellerus old, 160
Where the great vision of the guarded mount
Looks toward Namancos and Bayona's hold;
Look homeward, Angel, now, and melt with ruth;
And, O ye dolphins, waft the hapless youth.
 Weep no more, woeful shepherds, weep no more, 165
For Lycidas, your sorrow, is not dead,
Sunk though he be beneath the watery floor;
So sinks the day-star in the ocean bed,
And yet anon repairs his drooping head,
And tricks his beams, and with new-spangled ore 170
Flames in the forehead of the morning sky:
So Lycidas, sunk low, but mounted high,
Through the dear might of him that walked the waves,
Where, other groves and other streams along,
With nectar pure his oozy locks he laves, 175
And hears the unexpressive nuptial song,
In the blest kingdoms meek of joy and love.
There entertain him all the saints above,
In solemn troops and sweet societies
That sing, and singing in their glory move, 180
And wipe the tears for ever from his eyes.
Now, Lycidas, the shepherds weep no more;
Henceforth thou art the Genius of the shore,
In thy large recompense, and shalt be good
To all that wander in that perilous flood. 185
 Thus sang the uncouth swain to the oaks and rills,
While the still morn went out with sandals gray;
He touched the tender stops of various quills,

161. Guarded mount: Mount Bellerium in Cornwall where, according to legend, the Archangel Michael stood guard

With eager thought warbling his Doric lay.
And now the sun had stretched out all the hills, 190
And now was dropped into the western bay;
At last he rose, and twitched his mantle blue:
To-morrow to fresh woods, and pastures new.

JOHN MILTON

1. The emotion of this poem is one of sorrow for the death of a friend. In what specific lines is that theme announced? Show how the theme is repeated throughout the poem.
2. How is the emotion of the poem varied?
3. Are the details of this poem harmonious throughout? Consider especially the mingling of Christian and pagan elements.
4. Is the ornate, learned style in harmony with the professed intention of the poem—lament for the death of a friend? Why or why not?
5. An elegy is a lyric poem that expresses the poet's reflections on some aspect of death. Most frequently it laments the death of a friend. The pastoral elegy, a special form of the elegy derived from the Sicilian Greek poet, Theocritus, employs numerous artificial conventions. In "Lycidas" most of these conventions appear. The dead friend, Edward King, is called Lycidas, a traditional name for a shepherd. The poem begins with a statement of grief. This is followed by an invocation of the Muses, the inspirers of poetry, to assist in the composition. There follows a reminiscence of the happy days spent with the dead friend. This is followed by a climactic expression of grief. The last phase usually meditates on the consolations of religion or philosophy.
   Is this formal, stylized expression of emotion convincing to a contemporary audience? Why or why not?

ELEGY WRITTEN IN A COUNTRY CHURCH-YARD

The curfew tolls the knell of parting day,
  The lowing herd wind slowly o'er the lea,
The plowman homeward plods his weary way,
  And leaves the world to darkness and to me.

Now fades the glimmering landscape on the sight, 5
  And all the air a solemn stillness holds,
Save where the beetle wheels his droning flight,
  And drowsy tinklings lull the distant folds;

Save that from yonder ivy-mantled tow'r
  The moping owl does to the moon complain 10
Of such as, wand'ring near her secret bow'r,
  Molest her ancient solitary reign.

Beneath those rugged elms, that yew-tree's shade,
  Where heaves the turf in many a mould'ring heap,
Each in his narrow cell for ever laid, 15
  The rude Forefathers of the hamlet sleep.

The breezy call of incense-breathing Morn,
  The swallow twitt'ring from the straw-built shed,
The cock's shrill clarion, or the echoing horn,
  No more shall rouse them from their lowly bed. 20

For them no more the blazing hearth shall burn,
  Or busy housewife ply her evening care:
No children run to lisp their sire's return,
  Or climb his knees the envied kiss to share.

Oft did the harvest to their sickle yield, 25
  Their furrow oft the stubborn glebe has broke:
How jocund did they drive their team afield!
  How bow'd the woods beneath their sturdy stroke!

Let not Ambition mock their useful toil,
  Their homely joys, and destiny obscure; 30
Nor Grandeur hear with a disdainful smile
  The short and simple annals of the poor.

The boast of heraldry, the pomp of pow'r,
  And all that beauty, all that wealth e'er gave,
Await alike th' inevitable hour: 35
  The paths of glory lead but to the grave.

Nor you, ye Proud, impute to these the fault,
  If Memory o'er their Tomb no Trophies raise,
Where through the long-drawn aisle and fretted vault
  The pealing anthem swells the note of praise. 40

Can storied urn or animated bust
  Back to its mansion call the fleeting breath?

Can Honour's voice provoke the silent dust,
  Or Flatt'ry soothe the dull cold ear of death?

Perhaps in this neglected spot is laid 45
  Some heart once pregnant with celestial fire;
Hands, that the rod of empire might have sway'd,
  Or waked to ecstasy the living lyre.

But Knowledge to their eyes her ample page
  Rich with the spoils of time did ne'er unroll; 50
Chill Penury repress'd their noble rage,
  And froze the genial current of the soul.

Full many a gem of purest ray serene
  The dark unfathom'd caves of ocean bear:
Full many a flower is born to blush unseen, 55
  And waste its sweetness on the desert air.

Some village Hampden that with dauntless breast
  The little tyrant of his fields withstood,
Some mute inglorious Milton here may rest,
  Some Cromwell guiltless of his country's blood. 60

Th' applause of list'ning senates to command,
  The threats of pain and ruin to despise,
To scatter plenty o'er a smiling land,
  And read their history in a nation's eyes,

Their lot forbade: nor circumscribed alone 65
  Their growing virtues, but their crimes confined;
Forbade to wade through slaughter to a throne,
  And shut the gates of mercy on mankind,

The struggling pangs of conscious truth to hide,
  To quench the blushes of ingenuous shame, 70
Or heap the shrine of Luxury and Pride
  With incense kindled at the Muse's flame.

Far from the madding crowd's ignoble strife
  Their sober wishes never learn'd to stray;
Along the cool sequester'd vale of life 75
  They kept the noiseless tenor of their way.

Yet ev'n these bones from insult to protect
  Some frail memorial still erected nigh,
With uncouth rhymes and shapeless sculpture deck'd,
  Implores the passing tribute of a sigh. 80

Their name, their years, spelt by th' unletter'd muse,
  The place of fame and elegy supply:
And many a holy text around she strews,
  That teach the rustic moralist to die.

For who, to dumb Forgetfulness a prey, 85
  This pleasing anxious being e'er resign'd,
Left the warm precincts of the cheerful day,
  Nor cast one longing ling'ring look behind?

On some fond breast the parting soul relies,
  Some pious drops the closing eye requires; 90
E'en from the tomb the voice of Nature cries,
  E'en in our Ashes live their wonted Fires.

For thee, who, mindful of th' unhonour'd dead,
  Dost in these lines their artless tale relate;
If chance, by lonely contemplation led, 95
  Some kindred spirit shall inquire thy fate,

Haply some hoary-headed Swain may say,
  "Oft have we seen him at the peep of dawn
Brushing with hasty steps the dews away
  To meet the sun upon the upland lawn. 100

"There at the foot of yonder nodding beech
  That wreathes its old fantastic roots so high,
His listless length at noontide would he stretch,
  And pore upon the brook that babbles by.

"Hard by yon wood, now smiling as in scorn, 105
  Mutt'ring his wayward fancies he would rove,
Now drooping, woeful wan, like one forlorn,
  Or crazed with care, or cross'd in hopeless love.

"One morn I miss'd him on the custom'd hill,
  Along the heath and near his fav'rite tree; 110

Another came, nor yet beside the rill,
  Nor up the lawn, nor at the wood was he;

"The next with dirges due in sad array
  Slow through the church-way path we saw him borne.
Approach and read (for thou canst read) the lay 115
  Graved on the stone beneath yon aged thorn."

THE EPITAPH

Here rests his head upon the lap of Earth
  A Youth to Fortune and to Fame unknown.
Fair Science frown'd not on his humble birth,
  And Melancholy mark'd him for her own. 120

Large was his bounty, and his soul sincere,
  Heav'n did a recompense as largely send:
He gave to Mis'ry all he had, a tear,
  He gain'd from Heav'n, ('twas all he wish'd) a friend.

No farther seek his merits to disclose, 125
  Or draw his frailties from their dread abode,
(There they alike in trembling hope repose,)
  The bosom of his Father and his God.

THOMAS GRAY

1. What lines in this poem suggest that it is about death in general rather than about the death of an individual?
2. Do all the details contribute to a unified emotional effect? Explain.
3. What means does the poet employ to amplify "the short and simple annals of the poor" (line 32)?
4. How does the poet achieve variety of emotional feeling in this poem?
5. Is the concluding epitaph a summary of the poem? Why or why not?
6. Is Gray's "Elegy" more or less intense in its feeling than "Lycidas?" Why or why not?
7. "Richard Cory," "Proud Maisie," "Lycidas" and this poem are all concerned with death. Do they also arouse similar emotions? Explain.

DOVER BEACH

The sea is calm to-night.
The tide is full, the moon lies fair
Upon the straits;—on the French coast the light
Gleams and is gone; the cliffs of England stand,
Glimmering and vast, out in the tranquil bay. 5
Come to the window, sweet is the night air!
Only, from the lone line of spray
Where the sea meets the moon-blanch'd land,
Listen! you hear the grating roar
Of pebbles which the waves draw back, and fling, 10
At their return, up the high strand,
Begin, and cease, and then again begin,
With tremulous cadence slow, and bring
The eternal note of sadness in.

Sophocles long ago 15
Heard it on the Ægæan, and it brought
Into his mind the turbid ebb and flow
Of human misery; we
Find also in the sound a thought,
Hearing it by this distant northern sea. 20

The Sea of Faith
Was once, too, at the full, and round earth's shore
Lay like the folds of a bright girdle furl'd.
But now I only hear
Its melancholy, long, withdrawing roar, 25
Retreating, to the breath
Of the night wind, down the vast edges drear
And naked shingles of the world.

Ah, love, let us be true
To one another! for the world, which seems 30
To lie before us like a land of dreams,
So various, so beautiful, so new,
Hath really neither joy, nor love, nor light,
Nor certitude, nor peace, nor help for pain;
And we are here as on a darkling plain 35
Swept with confused alarms of struggle and flight,
Where ignorant armies clash by night.

MATTHEW ARNOLD

1. What is the predominant feeling of this poem? What details support that feeling?
2. Is there a progressive intensification of feeling? If there is, show how it is achieved.
3. Does the introduction of a hearer in line 29 change the tone of this poem? Why or why not?
4. Is the shift from the sea imagery to that of the darkling plain warranted in this poem? Why?
5. Many thoughts and feelings are compressed in this poem. Cite several ways in which the poet has achieved compression.

✣ CHAPTER IV ✣

Thought in Poetry: Psychological and Logical Structure

In our previous discussion we said that emotion is central and essential to a poem. At the same time, we stressed the fact that in poetry emotion is not an end in itself, nor is it isolated from the other elements in a poem; rather it arises from, and is always associated with, thought and imagination.

In this chapter, and in the two that follow, we will deal with thought in poetry. In its largest sense thought is knowledge—the power of conceiving ideas, of framing judgments, or of reasoning from judgments to conclusions. Now, common sense tells us that poetry does contain ideas, judgments, and reasoning, often of a very high order. Milton's *Paradise Lost,* for instance, embodies a scholar's knowledge of philosophy, theology, biblical history, and literature. Moreover, his knowledge is presented in a thoughtful way; in an orderly sequence of incidents, in a logical display of argument or reasoning, in a masterly choice and arrangement of diction. Even the short lyric, Keats's "On First Looking into Chapman's Homer" (p. 4) clearly embodies an idea—the relationship between a poet's discovery of a great writer, Homer, and the explorer's discovery of a new ocean.

To assert the contrary—that poetry is only concerned with emotions, attitudes, and images, not with any kind of knowledge—is to suggest that the poet (and the reader) may ignore reason when they write or read a poem. Archibald MacLeish seems to argue for this view in his "Ars Poetica."

A poem should be palpable and mute
As a globed fruit

Dumb
As old medallions to the thumb

Silent as the sleeve-worn stone 5
Of casement where the moss has grown—

A poem should be wordless
As the flight of birds

* * * * *

A poem should be motionless in time
As the moon climbs 10

Leaving, as the moon releases
Twig by twig the night-entangled trees,

Leaving, as the moon behind the winter leaves,
Memory by memory the mind—

A poem should be motionless in time 15
As the moon climbs

* * * * *

A poem should be equal to:
Not true

For all the history of grief
An empty doorway and a maple leaf 20

For love
The leaning grasses and two lights above the sea—

A poem should not mean
But be.

Even a casual reading of the poem reveals that, in arguing against the presence of thought in poetry, Mr. MacLeish himself presents his view in a logical order—clearly, a kind of thought. A poem he says should be silent, motionless, and meaningless. If we may take meaningless to mean absence of thought, the poem may be said to be contradictory, for the generalization that appears in the last two lines is an inference developed from the preceding statements.

As Donald Stauffer remarked, "Mr. MacLeish's argument, of course, is all on the side of concreteness; but the mere fact that it is an argument points the arrow back toward a rational significance. . . . And do not the final famous two lines contradict in practice, because of their explicit intellectual statement, the very point that they are making?"

If the theory that thought has no place in poetry were consistently applied, it would exclude many of the world's great poems. But the place of thought in poetry is by no means settled completely by an appeal to common sense. The poet thinks, but thought in poetry is not identical to thought in science. The abstract, scientific thinking of the philosopher, or the astronomer, for instance, is largely concerned with the cold analysis of measurable facts. The less emotional and the less subjective is scientific thought, the more accurate and objective it is likely to be.

The poet's thought, on the other hand, is emotional and personal. For him the stars are not so much gaseous objects of a certain mass, position, and energy that exist wholly outside himself. They are that, but much more; they are light in darkness; they are evidence of order, splendor, harmony, intuitively comprehended; they are evidence that evokes in him thoughts and impressions that cannot be shredded into the exact formulations of science.

In Walt Whitman's poem, "When I Heard the Learn'd Astronomer," he suggests one respect in which thought in poetry differs from thought in science.

When I heard the learn'd astronomer,
When the proofs, the figures, were ranged in columns before me
When I was shown the charts and diagrams, to add, divide, and
  measure them,
Where I sitting heard the astronomer where he lectured with much
  applause in the lecture room,
How soon unaccountable I became tired and sick,
Till rising and gliding out I wander'd off by myself,
In the mystical moist night-air; and from time to time
Look'd up in perfect silence at the stars.

For the poet, stars are both objects and symbols; they are themselves, but they help express some deeply personal meanings, as in G. M. Hopkins's

> I kiss my hand
> To the stars, lovely-asunder
> Starlight, wafting him out of it . . .

or in Francis Thompson's

> Across the margent of the world I fled,
> And troubled the gold gateway of the stars,
> Smiting for shelter on their clangéd bars . . .

or in Shakespeare's references to star-crossed lovers, or in Wordsworth's lines on Lucy

> Fair as a star, when only one
> Is shining in the sky.

In short, when we ask what poetic thought is, we may answer by saying that it is a personal, intuitive vision rather than impersonal, scientific knowledge. But when we ask how the poet presents that vision, we discover that the poet avails himself of all the mind's resources to make sure that that vision is as vivid, as intelligible, indeed as logical, as his particular subject allows. This is to say that the poet gives form, shape, or structure to his vision in language. He does not merely say, "I have a vision . . . isn't it beautiful . . . see it there . . . pathetic . . . terrifying . . ." Nor does he say, "Laugh with me . . . Weep with me . . ." without presenting or suggesting the motives for laughter or tears. Rather, he creates a verbal object, just as a sculptor creates a spatial object, that will make you see, even without pointers and exclamations, something approximating his own vision, and will convince you of the rightness of his feeling in the presence of that vision.

The poet's knowledge is not simply a vision of reality. It is a knowledge of how to express his vision of that reality. Poetic thought then includes both the *what* and the *how*. But the *what*, namely, the vision itself, is knowable only through the *how*, namely, the structure of language in which it is embodied. Note below how W. B. Yeats expresses his vision in "The Lake Isle of Innisfree."

I will arise and go now, and go to Innisfree,
  And a small cabin build there, of clay and wattles made;
Nine bean rows will I have there, a hive for the honey bee,
  And live alone in the bee-loud glade.

And I shall have some peace there, for peace comes dropping slow, 5
  Dropping from the veils of the morning to where the cricket sings;
There midnight's all a-glimmer, and noon a purple glow,
  And evening full of linnet's wings.

I will arise and go now, for always night and day
  I hear lake water lapping with low sounds by the shore; 10
While I stand on the roadway, or on pavements gray,
  I hear it in the deep heart's core.

In the first stanza Yeats dreams of a cabin he proposed to build in his native Sligo. The vision is extended in the next stanzas where the separate images of sight and sound cluster around the magnetic center of a wished-for peace, a land of content, soothing in contrast to the city's roar which is implied by the word "roadway," and beautiful in contrast to the ugliness implied by the words "pavements gray." At the poem's end we have *seen* Yeats's vision because the vision is presented, objectified, imagined and intelligible. Moreover, the presentation is convincing, not in the manner of the real estate advertisement for a dream-house, but in the manner of a work of art. Every word tells. Even the *ands* serve not merely to connect the sentence grammatically, but also to emphasize the forward movement of the poet's dream.

WHAT STRUCTURE MEANS

In general, structure is the order, organization or design of any written composition. One kind of structure is often described in familiar terms of beginning, middle, and end. A poem, no less than a prose composition, starts with a question, a meaningful situation, an event, a scene or a puzzling thought, and then proceeds to answer the question, to explain the situation, to render some meaning from the event, to give an impression of the scene or to examine the implications of a thought. Like prose, but more intensely, a poem excites attention in its beginning lines, satisfies our curiosity by the succession of events or ideas in the middle and comes to a fitting conclusion. In a successful poem the beginning, middle, and end are not detachable parts. As in "The Lake Isle of Innisfree" every line moves toward the next, and all toward the last completing line, so that the poem is all of a piece, each word indispensable.

Structure—the organized movement of language to a definite end—differs from poem to poem. A simple descriptive lyric like William Allingham's "Four Ducks on a Pond," for instance, requires a less intricate structure than Matthew Arnold's "The Scholar-Gipsy," a poem that combines descriptive, narrative, and expository elements to achieve a great variety of tones. A tight "metaphysical" poem, a sonnet of Donne or Shakespeare, for instance, is more rigorously logical than a simple song, such as Burns's "A Red, Red Rose."

Extended narrative and dramatic poems by their very nature require the complex interweaving of parts we call plot. An epic, for instance, develops a theme—in the *Iliad* how Achilles' wrath affected the Trojan War; in the *Aeneid* how great a task it was for Aeneas to found the Roman State; in *Beowulf* how the hero saved his people by struggle with a monster. The various episodes are artfully arranged to portray the several heroes in significant actions. In dramatic poetry, the incidents flow from initial complication to turning point to resolution, following the order that best exploits the tragic death of a Hamlet or the happy fate of a Prospero. In short, every living poem will have its own special structure, that is, an animating principle that causes it to be this poem and not any other poem.

Hence, poem differs from poem in structure; not only will epic differ from lyric but sonnet will differ from sonnet, even when both sonnets employ the same number of lines, the same meter, and the same rhyme scheme to talk about the same general subject. But if there is no single structure that is appropriate for every poem, there are certain interrelated principles of structure. For purposes of our discussion we may identify these three principles as psychological, logical, and symbolic.

PSYCHOLOGICAL STRUCTURE

We may call the principle of poetic structure psychological when it imitates the normal movement of the human mind from sense perception to understanding and emotional response. Let us illustrate this process in a very simple poem—one that at first may seem a fragment rather than a complete poem.

FOUR DUCKS ON A POND

Four ducks on a pond,
A grass-bank beyond,
A blue sky of spring,
White clouds on the wing;
What a little thing
To remember for years—
To remember with tears!

WILLIAM ALLINGHAM

In the first four lines the speaker sketches four sense impressions—the ducks, the bank, the sky, the cloud. Each detail, however, blends into the other, the ducks on the pond into the background of the bank's green grass, the blue sky above into the wandering white clouds. Taken together, these sense perceptions form one vivid composite image of spring—an essential spring vital in its movement and its striking primary colors.

This image of spring stirs a thought full of quiet wonder. "What a little thing/To remember for years." There is an instant's pause, marked by the dash, between the swift recollection and the caught breath—"To remember with tears!" This natural progression from image to thought to sigh, from sense perception to understanding to emotional response, imitates the way man comes to know reality. It is at once organic and climactic.

We may judge the effectiveness of this structure by attempting to alter the present order of the poem. We are not, in Wordsworth's language, "surprised by joy" to read the poem in the order below:

To remember with tears!
To remember for years—
White clouds on the wing
A blue sky in spring;
A grass bank beyond
Four ducks on a pond;
What a little thing.

Psychological structure as we have described it above may be found in more elaborate poems, either as a principle that underlies the main movement, as in Wordsworth's *The Prelude,* or a subordinate movement of the poem, as in the soliloquies of *Hamlet.*

LOGICAL STRUCTURE

We may call the principle of structure logical when a poem is developed by logical analysis or reasoning. For, as we observed above (p. 70), the fact that a poem presents an intuitive vision of truth rather than a scientific understanding of it does not mean that a poet cannot avail himself of the resources and strategies of logical expression. In Chapter III we observed how the poet achieved emotional impact by the use of comparison and contrast —both of them logical modes of analysis. Often the poet expresses his intuition (the beauty of a snowflake, for instance) by appropriating and transforming logical modes of reasoning.* In Francis Thompson's "To a Snowflake," note how in stanza one the speaker asks who could have caused the effect of intricate beauty. In stanza two the snowflake supplies an answer.

TO A SNOWFLAKE

What heart could have thought you?—
Past our devisal
(O filigree petal!)
Fashioned so purely,
Fragilely, surely, 5
From what Paradisal
Imagineless metal,
Too costly for cost?
Who hammered you, wrought you,
From argentine vapor?— 10

"God was my shaper.
Passing surmisal,

* As Sir Herbert J. C. Grierson remarked, "Passionate thinking is always apt to become metaphysical, probing and investigating the experience from which it takes rise." Herbert J. C. Grierson, *Metaphysical Lyrics and Poems of the Seventeenth Century* (New York, 1921), p. xvi.

He hammered, He wrought me,
From curled silver vapor,
To lust of his mind:— 15
Thou couldst not have thought me!
So purely, so palely,
Tinily, surely,
Mightily, frailly,
Insculped and embossed, 20
With His hammer of wind,
And His graver of frost."

FRANCIS THOMPSON

The poem is clearly fictitious, since the speaker in this context is not actually addressing a snowflake, nor does the snowflake actually respond, nor should we suppose that God immediately or directly creates each snowflake. Nevertheless, the poem employs several devices normally used in strict logical argument. One such device is a philosophical analysis of cause and effect. Note how in stanza one the effect, namely, the snowflake, is described. In stanza two the nature of the cause proportionate to that effect is analyzed in terms of the efficient, material, instrumental, and final cause. The *efficient* cause (God) is the person who brings the snowflake into being; the *material* cause ("curled silver vapor") is the substance out of which the snowflake was made; the *instrumental* causes ("hammer of wind, . . . graver of frost") are the means used to fashion the snowflake; the *final* cause ("lust [that is, pleasure] of his mind") is the purpose for which the snowflake was created.

Many poems, particularly those written in times when philosophy was widely studied and enjoyed, are constructed in the manner of a fictitious disputation, in which a thesis is announced and proved. John Donne's "Death, Be Not Proud," for instance, is a refutation of the implied arguments of Death, personified as a boastful soldier reciting his victories over mankind.

Death, be not proud, though some have callèd thee
Mighty and dreadful, for thou are not so:
For those whom thou think'st thou dost overthrow
Die not, poor Death; nor yet canst thou kill me.
From Rest and Sleep, which but thy pictures be, 5
Much pleasure; then from thee much more must flow;
And soonest our best men with thee do go—

Rest of their bones and souls' delivery!
Thou art slave to fate, chance, kings, and desperate men,
And dost with poison, war, and sickness dwell; 10
And poppy or charms can make us sleep as well
And better than thy stroke. Why swell'st thou then?
One short sleep past, we wake eternally,
And Death shall be no more: Death, thou shalt die!

Here the speaker argues that Death's pride is unreasonable. The argument may be outlined as follows:

THEME Although some have called you mighty, you have no reason for pride, lines 1-2.

PROOF Those whom you think you kill do not die; neither can you kill me, lines 3-4.

SUPPORTING REASONS: Since rest and sleep, mere counterfeits of death, bring pleasure, Death itself, the reality, will bring more pleasure, lines 5-6. The good die young and go to heaven, lines 7-8. Death itself is subject to other forces, lines 9-10. Death is less effective than other forces that produce sleep, lines 11-12. In eternity there is no death, lines 13-14.

Often the argument in a poem takes the form of a dialogue between the poet and his soul. In this dialogue the poet poses a question that has aroused his anxiety and then attempts to discover an answer. Thus, in his sonnet, "Poor soul, the center of my sinful earth," Shakespeare considers the paradox of the sovereign soul's captivity to the rebellious flesh and asks ruefully why this is so and what should be done about it.

SONNET 146

Poor soul, the centre of my sinful earth,
Thrall to these rebel powers that thee array,
Why dost thou pine within and suffer dearth,
Painting thy outward walls so costly gay?
Why so large cost, having so short a lease, 5
Dost thou upon thy fading mansion spend?
Shall worms, inheritors of this excess,
Eat up thy charge? Is this thy body's end?
Then, soul, live thou upon thy servant's loss,
And let that pine to aggravate thy store; 10

Buy terms divine in selling hours of dross
Within be fed, without be rich no more:
So shalt thou feed on Death, that feeds on men,
And Death once dead, there's no more dying then.

WILLIAM SHAKESPEARE

The poem supposes that the soul, an immortal element, is and should be the master, while the body, a mortal element, is and should be the servant. The speaker then deliberates on this anomaly in which the body is master and the soul the servant. Just as a tenant wastes his money painting and decorating a house that he has leased for a short time, so the soul wastes its substance when it spends its energies on the body.

Rather, the soul should live at the expense of the sinful body, buy the eternal lease on heaven by "selling hours of dross." Death is sin. The soul feeds on death, then, in proportion to the defeat of sin.

This argument on the soul's struggle against the inherent rebellion of the flesh presents a thesis and a solution. In a series of analogies the problem is first reduced to an absurdity—the soul's subjection to the body. This absurdity, it is argued, must be reversed, whereupon the soul will free itself from death and sin.

The two sonnets we have just examined have the structure of fictitious arguments, the one presented as a dialogue between the speaker and death, the other as a dialogue between the speaker and his own conscience. Neither sonnet would make sense without the framework of reasoning that it contains. But logical structure is not confined to poems that philosophize on life and death.

THE LOGIC OF IMAGINATION

Consider, for example, a poem like John Keats's "To Autumn." At first glance we may regard this vivid description of a season as a spontaneous rush of visual, tactile and auditory impressions. This is no argument, we may say. See, it merely tells us how autumn looks, how it feels and tastes, and how it sounds. Here no general truth proceeds to its concrete illustration. Keats does not say autumn is rich, and then enumerate the details of its wealth; nor does he link a series of particulars in a march toward a universal truth. Keats is attempting to evoke a mood rather than to reason; to share with the reader his own responses to the sights and sounds and impressions of the season.

Yet these responses are carefully selected and arranged so that each stanza has its own center of gravity and is linked to the other stanzas to form a logical whole.

No less than the sonnets of Shakespeare and Donne, "To Autumn" is an imaginative argument designed to persuade the reader to share Keats's attitude toward the season. (The italics are supplied.)

> Season of mists and *mellow fruitfulness,*
> Close bosom-friend of the *maturing sun;*
> Conspiring with him how *to load and bless*
> *With fruit* the vines that round the thatch-eaves run;
> To *bend with apples* the moss'd cottage-trees, 5
> And *fill all fruit with ripeness to the core;*
> To *swell the gourd* and *plump the hazel shells*
> With a sweet kernel; *to set budding more,*
> And still more, later flowers for the bees,
> Until they think warm days *will never cease,* 10
> For Summer has *o'er-brimm'd* their clammy cells.

Notice how the first stanza describes autumn as a season of mists and mellow fruitfulness. Here "mellow fruitfulness," the *ripeness* of autumn, is its essential characteristic. Hence autumn is personified as a close friend of the "maturing sun," a conspirer in producing abundance. Note, too, that the series of italicized expressions ascend to a climax.

> Who hath not seen thee oft amid thy store?
> Sometimes whoever seeks abroad may find
> Thee *sitting careless* on a granary floor,
> Thy hair *soft-lifted* by the winnowing wind; 15
> Or on a half-reap'd furrow *sound asleep,*
> *Drowsed with the fume of poppies,* while thy hook
> Spares the next swath and all its twinèd flowers;
> And sometimes like a gleaner thou dost keep
> Steady thy laden head across a brook; 20
> Or by a cider-press, *with patient look,*
> Thou watchest the last oozings *hours by hours.*

The second stanza has its center in a series of personifications announced by a question in the first line. Autumn is seen as a careless, that is, a carefree, figure on the granary floor, as a drowsy reaper, as a gleaner carrying a burden across a brook, as a contented countryman standing beside a cider-press. These four figures suggest the country tasks of the autumn season—the reaping and winnowing and storing of grain and the harvesting and pressing of apples. Yet these tasks are peaceful, carefree, slumbrous. A drowsy peace born of warm days and rich harvests soaks each detail and rhythm in delicious languor. Thus the second stanza has its own center of gravity, the mood of languor that we have marked by the italicized expressions. But it is also related to the first stanza, more or less as an effect is related to a cause. In the first stanza we saw what autumn did: it ripened and brought increase. In the second stanza we experience the effects of that fruitfulness: harvest and satisfaction and peace.

The third stanza begins with an abrupt transition that shifts from the sights of autumn to its sounds, from the topics of fruitfulness and peace to the topic of music.

> Where are the *songs* of Spring? Aye, where are they?
>   Think not of them, thou hast *thy music too,*—
> While barrèd clouds bloom the soft-dying day, 25
>   And touch the stubble-plains with rosy hue;
> Then in a *wailful choir* the small gnats *mourn*
>   Among the river sallows, borne aloft
>   Or sinking as the *light wind lives* or dies;
> And full-grown lambs *loud bleat* from hilly bourn; 30
>   Hedge-crickets *sing;* and now with treble soft
>   The redbreast *whistles* from a garden-croft;
>   And gathering swallows *twitter* in the skies.

As you were reading you may have agreed that the italicized expressions clearly indicate the burden of the stanza—autumn song. But how is this topic related to the two preceding stanzas? Is this stanza merely tagged on, as a kind of afterthought, or is there a natural connection between the topics of fruitfulness, peace and song? The key to the problem is in the first two lines of the stanza.

There is a connection between the stanzas, implied rather than fully expressed. "Where are the *songs* of spring?" seems to be a new and perhaps irrelevant topic. Yet, in terms of the imaginative logic of this poem, the question is natural. That argument, we have seen, first imagined autumn as a figure of increase, then as a figure of peace, first as an action, then as an effect. Now the poet turns as if to an objector who says to him, "What you say of autumn is true, but spring has its songs. That element of beauty autumn surely lacks." To this the poet replies, "Aye, where are they?" as if to say, "They are gone, but what of it? Think not of them, for autumn has another kind of music." Whereupon he sounds the autumnal songs of gnats, lambs, hedge crickets, robins and swallows. Thus the third stanza is a natural development of the argument of the poem, a refutation of the view that the season is deficient in comparison with spring.

But there are still further connections between the last stanza and the two preceding stanzas. If we reread the poem carefully we can see that it reveals two closely related secondary movements. In addition to moving from action to effect to refutation, it also moves in a more or less chronological order, from early to middle to late autumn, and from morning to afternoon to evening. The details of the first stanza clearly suggest the characteristics of early autumn. Nature is still growing, about to burst in her plenty. Moreover, some of these details—the mists, the maturing sun—may suggest morning. In the second stanza the harvest activities belong to mid-autumn; the attitudes of the reaper, the winnower, and the figure at the press suggest afternoon drowsiness. The third stanza evokes a picture of late autumn when harvest is over, the fields are reduced to stubble, the new lambs are full grown, and the swallows are gathering in the sky to migrate south. Moreover, it is evening, we know, from the references to the "soft-dying day," the gnat's mournful hum and the rising swallows.

In "To Autumn" we see, then, a poem that is not about abstract ideas, but about impressions. Yet we see, too, as the diagram suggests, that these impressions are organized in a kind of imaginative argument that justifies the poet's attitude.

THEME: Autumn evokes a feeling of joy.
STRUCTURE: Stanza I, Early Autumn—Morning
Stanza II, Mid-Autumn—Afternoon
Stanza III, Late Autumn—Evening

We note, too, that each stanza not only develops an aspect of autumn, but is closely related to the other stanzas. Taken together they justify the poet's exuberant joy in all aspects of autumn, its days, its months, its activities and its essential character—mellowness and fulfillment.

POEMS FOR DISCUSSION

THIS LIFE

This Life, which seems so fair,
Is like a bubble blown up in the air
By sporting children's breath,
Who chase it everywhere
And strive who can most motion it bequeath. 5
And though it sometimes seem of its own might,
Like to an eye of gold, to be fix'd there,
And firm to hover in that empty height,
That only is because it is so light.
—But in that pomp it doth not long appear; 10
For even when most admired, it in a thought,
As swelled from nothing, doth dissolve in nought.

WILLIAM DRUMMOND

1. Is the structure of this poem primarily logical or psychological? Explain.
2. Show how the words "seems" (line 1), "seem" (line 6), "appear" (line 10), "dissolve" (line 12), each in its local context, help to establish the coherence of the poem.

SIASCONSET SONG

The girls
of golden summers whirl
through sunsprung
bright Julys
with born right 5
sky-bright
star-night
eyes;

everywhere
their tennis twirl 10
of young gold

legs and arms,
they singsong
summer-long
I-belong 15
charms;

and through
the summer sailing swirl
they cut like
shining knives 20
in sun-told
never old
ever gold
lives.

PHILIP BOOTH

1. What is the main impression of this poem?
2. What details contribute to the impression?
3. Are the details related to the main impression logically? Why or why not?

LOVE'S PHILOSOPHY

I

The fountains mingle with the river
And the rivers with the Ocean,
The winds of Heaven mix for ever
With a sweet emotion;
Nothing in the world is single; 5
All things by a law divine
In one spirit meet and mingle.
Why not I with thine?—

II

See the mountains kiss high Heaven
And the waves clasp one another; 10
No sister-flower would be forgiven
If it disdained its brother;
And the sunlight clasps the earth
And the moonbeams kiss the sea:
What is all this sweet work worth 15
If thou kiss not me?

PERCY BYSSHE SHELLEY

1. What is the argument proposed by the speaker in this poem?
2. Is his argument logical? Why or why not?
3. If it is not may the poem be considered defective? Why or why not?

FERN HILL

Now as I was young and easy under the apple boughs
About the lilting house and happy as the grass was green,
  The night above the dingle starry,
    Time let me hail and climb
  Golden in the heydays of his eyes, 5
And honoured among wagons I was prince of the apple towns
And once below a time I lordly had the trees and leaves
    Trail with daisies and barley
  Down the rivers of the windfall light.

And as I was green and carefree, famous among the barns 10
About the happy yard and singing as the farm was home,
  In the sun that is young once only,
    Time let me play and be
  Golden in the mercy of his means,
And green and golden I was huntsman and herdsman, the calves 15
Sang to my horn, the foxes on the hills barked clear and cold,
    And the sabbath rang slowly
  In the pebbles of the holy streams.

All the sun long it was running, it was lovely, the hay-
Fields high as the house, the tunes from the chimneys, it was air 20
  And playing, lovely and watery
    And fire green as grass.
  And nightly under the simple stars
As I rode to sleep the owls were bearing the farm away,
All the moon long I heard, blessed among stables, the night-jars 25
  Flying with the ricks, and the horses
    Flashing into the dark.

And then to awake, and the farm, like a wanderer white
With the dew, come back, the cock on his shoulder: it was all
  Shining, it was Adam and maiden, 30
    The sky gathered again
  And the sun grew round that very day.
So it must have been after the birth of the simple light

In the first, spinning place, the spellbound horses walking warm
  Out of the whinnying green stable 35
  On to the fields of praise.

And honoured among foxes and pheasants by the gay house
Under the new made clouds and happy as the heart was long,
  In the sun born over and over,
    I ran my heedless ways, 40
  My wishes raced through the house-high hay
And nothing I cared, at my sky blue trades, that time allows
In all his tuneful turning so few and such morning songs
  Before the children green and golden
    Follow him out of grace, 45

Nothing I cared, in the lamb white days, that time would take me
Up to the swallow thronged loft by the shadow of my hand,
  In the moon that is always rising,
    Nor that riding to sleep
  I should hear him fly with the high fields 50
And wake to the farm forever fled from the childless land.
Oh as I was young and easy in the mercy of his means,
    Time held me green and dying
  Though I sang in my chains like the sea.

DYLAN THOMAS

1. What is the dominant impression in this poem?
2. Do the main details contribute to the impression?
3. What principle of organization underlies the poem? Explain.
4. Are all the details of this poem intelligible? If not, is the structure of the poem defective? Explain.

IS MY TEAM PLOUGHING

"Is my team ploughing,
  That I was used to drive
And hear the harness jingle
  When I was man alive?"

Aye, the horses trample, 5
  The harness jingles now;
No change though you lie under
  The land you used to plough.

"Is football playing
  Along the river shore, 10
With lads to chase the leather,
  Now I stand up no more?"

Ay, the ball is flying,
  The lads play heart and soul,
The goal stands up, the keeper 15
  Stands up to keep the goal.

"Is my girl happy,
  That I thought hard to leave,
And has she tired of weeping
  As she lies down at eve?" 20

Ay, she lies down lightly,
  She lies not down to weep:
Your girl is well contented.
  Be still, my lad, and sleep.

"Is my friend hearty, 25
  Now I am thin and pine,
And has he found to sleep in
  A better bed than mine?"

Yes, lad, I lie easy,
  I lie as lads would choose; 30
I cheer a dead man's sweetheart.
  Never ask me whose.

A. E. HOUSMAN

1. Is the structure of this poem adequately described in the statement below? Say why or why not. "In this poem a dead man asks four questions; the answers progressively reveal that life goes on without him."

2. If you are dissatisfied with the description of the structure above, how would you describe it? Give reasons for your answer.

AN ESSAY ON MAN

EPISTLE II

Know then thyself, presume not God to scan;
The proper study of mankind is man.
Placed on this isthmus of a middle state,
A being darkly wise, and rudely great:
With too much knowledge for the sceptic side, 5
With too much weakness for the stoic's pride,
He hangs between, in doubt to act, or rest;
In doubt to deem himself a god, or beast;
In doubt his mind or body to prefer;
Born but to die, and reasoning but to err; 10
Alike in ignorance, his reason such,
Whether he thinks too little, or too much:
Chaos of thought and passion, all confused;
Still by himself abused, or disabused;
Created half to rise and half to fall; 15
Great lord of all things, yet a prey to all;
Sole judge of truth, in endless error hurled:
The glory, jest, and riddle of the world!
Go, wondrous creature! mount where science guides,
Go, measure earth, weigh air, and state the tides; 20
Instruct the planets in what orbs to run,
Correct old time, and regulate the sun;
Go, soar with Plato to the empyreal sphere,
To the first good, first perfect, and first fair;
Or tread the mazy round his followers trod, 25
And quitting sense call imitating God;
As Eastern priests in giddy circles run,
And turn their heads to imitate the sun.
Go, teach Eternal Wisdom how to rule—
Then drop into thyself, and be a fool! 30
Superior beings, when of late they saw
A mortal man unfold all nature's law,
Admired such wisdom in an earthly shape,
And showed a Newton as we show an ape.
Could he whose rules the rapid comet bind, 35
Describe or fix one movement of his mind?
Who saw its fires here rise, and there descend,
Explain his own beginning, or his end?
Alas what wonder! man's superior part

Unchecked may rise, and climb from art to art; 40
But when his own great work is but begun,
What reason weaves, by passion is undone.
  Trace science then, with modesty thy guide;
First strip off all her equipage of pride;
Deduct what is but vanity, or dress, 45
Or learning's luxury, or idleness;
Or tricks to show the stretch of human brain,
Mere curious pleasure, or ingenious pain;
Expunge the whole, or lop the excrescent parts
Of all our vices have created arts; 50
Then see how little the remaining sum,
Which served the past, and must the times to come!

. . . .

ALEXANDER POPE

1. What is the main argument or theme of this passage?
2. What are the supporting reasons or methods of development?
3. Is the thought of this passage abstract and scientific? Explain.

✠ CHAPTER V ✠

Thought in Poetry: Symbolic Structure

WE MAY call the structure of a poem symbolic when it is specifically designed to convey more than one meaning. In a sense Dante attempts that in his *The Divine Comedy*. Of that poem he wrote, "The sense of the work is not simple, but on the contrary, it may be called polysemous, that is to say, of more senses than one." In the literal sense Dante's poem recounts the hero's visit to Hell, Purgatory and Heaven and describes the state of men's souls after death. But, in a symbolic sense, *The Divine Comedy* shows how, "by good or ill deserts, in the exercise of freedom of his choice, he [man] becomes liable to rewarding or punishing justice." Milton's structure in *Paradise Lost* is also symbolic in that the literal story of the fall is, on another level, an argument that justifies God's punishment of Adam and Eve. So, too, Browning's dramatic monologue "Fra Lippo Lippi" is literally the story of an escapade, and symbolically a drama of the dilemma of the artist, while Tennyson's "The Holy Grail" is not just a medieval adventure, but a symbolic representation of the "reality of the unseen."

It is easy to grasp the broad outlines of symbolic structure, but difficult to see exactly how the many details of a particular poem are interconnected. Where does Dante's description of an individual scene manifest a secondary meaning? At what point can we say that Milton has left his story of Adam and Eve to justify God's way to man? Does the symbolic meaning in "Fra Lippo Lippi" accompany the story step by step, developing an aura of suggestion around a clear center of incident, or does it suddenly appear, as an inevitable comment on the action, in the moralizing lines

> God's works—paint anyone, and count it crime
> To let a truth slip . . .
>   Art was given for that;

God uses us to help each other so,
Lending our minds out . . . .

These questions remind us again that the design of each poem is different. To know one design, then, is not to know all designs, but simply to know that there is some principle of design in all successful poems. With these preliminaries in mind let us look at Matthew Arnold's "The Scholar-Gipsy," a poem that in telling a story of a legendary scholar also shows how modern man differs from an ideal representative of the past.

THE SCHOLAR-GIPSY

I

Go, for they call you, shepherd, from the hill;
Go, shepherd, and untie the wattled cotes!
No longer leave thy wistful flock unfed,
Nor let thy bawling fellows rack their throats,
Nor the cropped herbage shoot another head. 5
But when the fields are still,
And the tired men and dogs all gone to rest,
And only the white sheep are sometimes seen,
Cross and recross the strips of moon-blanch'd green,
Come, shepherd, and again begin the quest! 10

II

Here, where the reaper was at work of late—
In this high field's dark corner, where he leaves
His coat, his basket, and his earthen cruse,
And in the sun all morning binds the sheaves,
Then here, at noon, comes back his stores to use— 15
Here will I sit and wait,
While to my ear from uplands far away
The bleating of the folded flocks is borne,
With distant cries of reapers in the corn—
All the live murmur of a summer's day. 20

III

Screen'd is this nook o'er the high, half-reap'd field,
And here till sun-down, shepherd! will I be.
Through the thick corn the scarlet poppies peep,
And round green roots and yellowing stalks I see

Pale pink convolvulus in tendrils creep; 25
And air-swept lindens yield
Their scent, and rustle down their perfum'd showers
Of bloom on the bent grass where I am laid,
And bower me from the August sun with shade;
And the eye travels down to Oxford's towers. 30

In the first three stanzas the speaker addresses a shepherd in a language that, at once familiar and formal, free and conventional, colloquial and archaic, establishes a mood of pastoral calm. It is noon; the shepherd is about to lead his flocks to pasture in the hills; the reaper has left his work for dinner, and the speaker plans to remain here, under the linden tree, looking down at the towers of Oxford until sundown. The speaker, stimulated by Glanvil's account* of the legendary scholar-gypsy, relives the story in the second section of the poem, stanzas IV-XIV.

IV

And near me on the grass lies Glanvil's book—
Come, let me read the oft-read tale again!
The story of the Oxford scholar poor,
Of pregnant parts and quick inventive brain,
Who, tired of knocking at preferment's door, 35
One summer-morn forsook

* In the first appearance of "The Scholar-Gipsy" in *Poems,* 1853, Arnold supplied the following passage from Joseph Glanvil's *Vanity of Dogmatizing,* 1661: "There was very lately a lad in the University of Oxford, who was by his poverty forced to leave his studies there; and at last to join himself to a company of vagabond gypsies. Among these extravagant people, by the insinuating subtlety of his carriage, he quickly got so much of their love and esteem as that they discovered to him their mystery. After he had been a pretty while exercised in the trade, there chanced to ride by a couple of scholars, who had formerly been of his acquaintance. They quickly spied out their old friend among the gypsies; and he gave them an account of the necessity which drove him to that kind of life, and told them that the people he went with were not such impostors as they were taken for, but that they had a traditional kind of learning among them, and could do wonders by the power of imagination, their fancy binding that of others: that himself had learned much of their act, and when he had compassed the whole secret, he intended, he said, to leave their company, and give the world an account of what he had learned."

His friends, and went to learn the gipsy-lore,
And roam'd the world with that wild brotherhood,
And came, as most men deem'd, to little good,
But came to Oxford and his friends no more. 40

V

But once, years after, in the country-lanes,
Two scholars, whom at college erst he knew,
Met him, and of his way of life enquired;
Whereat he answer'd that the gipsy-crew,
His mates, had arts to rule as they desired 45
The workings of men's brains,
And they can bind them to what thoughts they will.
"And I," he said, "the secret of their art,
When fully learn'd, will to the world impart;
But it needs heaven-sent moments for this skill." 50

VI

This said, he left them, and return'd no more.—
But rumors hung about the country-side,
That the lost Scholar long was seen to stray,
Seen by rare glimpses, pensive and tongue-tied,
In hat of antique shape, and cloak of grey, 55
The same the gipsies wore.
Shepherds had met him on the Hurst in spring;
At some lone alehouse in the Berkshire moors,
On the warm ingle-bench, the smock-frock'd boors
Had found him seated at their entering, 60

VII

But, 'mid their drink and clatter, he would fly.
And I myself seem half to know thy looks,
And put the shepherds, wanderer! on thy trace;
And boys who in lone wheatfields scare the rooks
I ask if thou hast pass'd their quiet place; 65
Or, in my boat I lie
Moor'd to the cool bank in the summer-heats,
'Mid wide grass meadows which the sunshine fills,
And watch the warm, green-muffled Cumner hills,
And wonder if thou haunt'st their shy retreats. 70

VIII

For most, I know, thou lov'st retired ground!
Thee at the ferry Oxford riders blithe,

Returning home on summer-nights, have met
Crossing the stripling Thames at Bablock-hithe,
Trailing in the cool stream thy fingers wet, 75
As the punt's rope chops round;
And leaning backward in a pensive dream,
And fostering in thy lap a heap of flowers
Pluck'd in shy fields and distant Wychwood bowers,
And thine eyes resting on the moonlit stream. 80

IX

And then they land, and thou art seen no more!—
Maidens, who from the distant hamlets come
To dance around the Fyfield elm in May,
Oft through the darkening fields have seen thee roam,
Or cross a stile into the public way. 85
Oft thou hast given them store
Of flowers—the frail-leaf'd, white anemony,
Dark bluebells drench'd with dews of summer eves,
And purple orchises with spotted leaves—
But none hath words she can report of thee. 90

X

And, above Godstow Bridge, when hay-time's here
In June, and many a scythe in sunshine flames,
Men who through those wide fields of breezy grass
Where black-wing'd swallows haunt the glittering Thames,
To bathe in the abandon'd lasher pass, 95
Have often pass'd thee near
Sitting upon the river bank o'ergrown;
Mark'd thine outlandish garb, thy figure spare,
Thy dark vague eyes, and soft abstracted air—
But, when they came from bathing, thou wast gone! 100

XI

At some lone homestead in the Cumner hills,
Where at her open door the housewife darns,
Thou hast been seen, or hanging on a gate
To watch the threshers in the mossy barns.
Children, who early range these slopes and late 105
For cresses from the rills,
Have known thee eying, all an April-day,
The springing pastures and the feeding kine;
And mark'd thee, when the stars come out and shine,
Through the long dewy grass move slow away. 110

XII

In autumn, on the skirts of Bagley wood—
Where most the gipsies by the turf-edged way
Pitch their smoked tents, and every bush you see
With scarlet patches tagg'd and shreds of grey,
Above the forest-ground called Thessaly— 115
The blackbird, picking food,
Sees thee, nor stops his meal, nor fears at all;
So often has he known thee past him stray,
Rapt, twirling in thy hand a wither'd spray,
And waiting for the spark from heaven to fall. 120

XIII

And once, in winter, on the causeway chill
Where home through flooded fields foot-travellers go,
Have I not pass'd thee on the wooden bridge,
Wrapped in thy cloak and battling with the snow,
Thy face tow'rd Hinksey and its wintry ridge? 125
And thou hast climb'd the hill,
And gain'd the white brow of the Cumner range;
Turn'd once to watch, while thick the snowflakes fall,
The line of festal light in Christ-Church hall—
Then sought thy straw in some sequester'd grange. 130

XIV

But what—I dream! Two hundred years are flown
Since first thy story ran through Oxford halls,
And the grave Glanvil did the tale inscribe
That thou wert wander'd from the studious walls
To learn strange arts, and join a gipsy tribe; 135
And thou from earth art gone
Long since, and in some quiet churchyard laid—
Some country-nook, where o'er thy unknown grave
Tall grasses and white flowering nettles wave,
Under a dark, red-fruited yew-tree's shade. 140

The scholar-gypsy's tale is, we see readily, a legend shot through with magical elements. This we discover in the idyllic tone continued from the opening stanzas and in the explicit references to the secret arts of the gypsies and to the alleged immortality of the scholar-gypsy. An apparition, dressed in a "hat of antique shape, and cloak of grey" (line 55), he is seen only in rare glimpses by shepherds, Oxford boatmen, country maidens, bathers in the Thames, housewives and children, sometimes in April, or in autumn, and once in winter. His magical character is further suggested by the fact that the speaker, two hundred years his junior, seems to have seen him too:

Have I not pass'd thee on the wooden bridge . . . (line 123)

Then, in stanza xiv, the speaker wakes from his reverie. The scholar-gypsy, he realizes, is long dead.

In the third section of the poem, stanzas xv-xxv, Arnold abruptly shifts from dream-haunted pastoral reverie to clear, precise, explicit, moral judgments.

XV

—No, no, thou hast not felt the lapse of hours!
For what wears out the life of mortal men?
'Tis that from change to change their being rolls;
'Tis that repeated shocks, again, again,
Exhaust the energy of strongest souls 145
And numb the elastic powers.
Till having used our nerves with bliss and teen,
And tired upon a thousand schemes our wit,
To the just-pausing Genius we remit
Our worn-out life, and are—what we have been. 150

XVI

Thou hast not lived, why should'st thou perish, so?
Thou hadst *one* aim, *one* business, *one* desire;
Else wert thou long since number'd with the dead!
Else hadst thou spent, like other men, thy fire!
The generations of the peers are fled, 155
And we ourselves shall go;
But thou possessest an immortal lot,
And we imagine thee exempt from age
And living as thou liv'st on Glanvil's page,
Because thou hast—what we, alas! have not. 160

XVII

For early didst thou leave the world, with powers
Fresh, undiverted to the world without,

147. Teen: sorrow

Firm to their mark, not spent on other things;
Free from the sick fatigue, the languid doubt,
Which much to have tried, in much been baffled, brings. 165
O life unlike to ours!
Who fluctuate idly without term or scope,
Of whom each strives, nor knows for what he strives,
And each half lives a hundred different lives;
Who wait like thee, but not, like thee, in hope. 170

XVIII

Thou waitest for the spark from heaven! and we,
Light half-believers of our casual creeds,
Who never deeply felt, nor clearly will'd,
Whose insight never has borne fruit in deeds,
Whose vague resolves never have been fulfill'd; 175
For whom each year we see
Breeds new beginnings, disappointments new;
Who hesitate and falter life away,
And lose to-morrow the ground won to-day—
Ah! do not we, wanderer! await it too? 180

XIX

Yes, we await it!—but it still delays,
And then we suffer! and amongst us one,
Who most has suffer'd, takes dejectedly
His seat upon the intellectual throne;
And all his store of sad experience he 185
Lays bare of wretched days;
Tells us his misery's birth and growth and signs,
And how the dying spark of hope was fed,
And how the breast was soothed, and how the head,
And all his hourly varied anodynes. 190

XX

This for our wisest! and we others pine,
And wish the long unhappy dream would end,
And waive all claim to bliss, and try to bear;
With close-lipp'd patience for our only friend,
Sad patience, too near neighbour to despair— 195
But none has hope like thine!
Thou through the fields and through the woods dost stray,
Roaming the country-side, a truant boy,

Nursing thy project in unclouded joy,
And every doubt long blown by time away. 200

XXI

O born in days when wits were fresh and clear,
And life ran gayly as the sparkling Thames;
Before this strange disease of modern life,
With its sick hurry, its divided aims,
Its heads o'ertax'd, its palsied hearts, was rife— 205
Fly hence, our contact fear!
Still fly, plunge deeper in the bowering wood!
Averse, as Dido did with gesture stern
From her false friend's approach in Hades turn,
Wave us away, and keep thy solitude! 210

XXII

Still nursing the unconquerable hope,
Still clutching the inviolable shade,
With a free, onward impulse brushing through,
By night, the silver'd branches of the glade—
Far on the forest-skirts, where none pursue, 215
On some mild pastoral slope
Emerge, and resting on the moonlit pales
Freshen thy flowers as in former years
With dew, or listen with enchanted ears,
From the dark dingles, to the nightingales! 220

XXIII

But fly our paths, our feverish contact fly!
For strong the infection of our mental strife,
Which, though it gives no bliss, yet spoils for rest;
And we should win thee from thy own fair life,
Like us distracted, and like us unblest. 225
Soon, soon thy cheer would die,
Thy hopes grow timorous, and unfix'd thy powers,
And thy clear aims be cross and shifting made;
And then thy glad perennial youth would fade,
Fade, and grow old at last, and die like ours. 230

XXIV

Then fly our greetings, fly our speech and smiles!
—As some grave Tyrian trader, from the sea,
Descried at sunrise an emerging prow

Lifting the cool-hair'd creepers stealthily,
The fringes of a southward-facing brow 235
Among the Ægæan isles;
And saw the merry Grecian coaster come,
Freighted with amber grapes, and Chian wine,
Green, bursting figs, and tunnies steep'd in brine—
And knew the intruders on his ancient home, 240

XXV

The young light-hearted masters of the waves—
And snatch'd his rudder, and shook out more sail;
And day and night held on indignantly
O'er the blue Midland waters with the gale,
Betwixt the Syrtes and soft Sicily, 245
To where the Atlantic raves
Outside the western straits; and unbent sails
There, where down cloudy cliffs, through sheets of foam,
Shy traffickers, the dark Iberians come;
And on the beach undid his corded bales. 250

In the third section the scholar-gypsy has become a symbolic opposite of the modern man as Arnold conceived him in 1853. He is timeless, whereas modern man wears himself out in constant change; he is immortal, firm in his beliefs, single in his aims and fresh in his hopes, whereas modern man is sick from languid doubt, from divided aims, and from hopeless waiting. The wanderer, inspired by heaven, sees vividly, feels deeply, and commits himself to his goal, while modern man at best reaps the bitter wisdom of suffering; at worst, withers in despair. Modernity is a disease, a contagion. Hence the speaker bids the scholar-gypsy fly to the freedom of his solitude, his unconquerable hopes, and his dreams of immortal beauty. The two final stanzas repeat the central idea of the whole poem, this time in an elaborate similitude. The scholar is compared to a grave Tyrian trader who shuns the light-minded Greeks, the modern men of their time, to traffic with the distant Iberians, the protoypes of the shy, mysterious, nature-loving gypsies.

The foregoing comment on the structure of the poem suggests that Matthew Arnold was in complete command of his material: that, in the first section, he evokes a mood of reverie; in the second section, he envisions the symbolic figure of the scholar.

Then, suddenly emerging from the dream, he contrasts the scholar with essential types or symbols of the modern generation—a contrast that rises in intensity with his warning to the wanderer to flee, and then dissolves in a picturesque simile that recaptures the dream-like mood of the beginning.

Many critics, however, object to this reading of the poem. The structure, they say, is imperfect because the third section alters the tone of the poem, and, worse still, imputes to the wandering scholar a symbolic value that his earlier characterization does not warrant. The present structure, they suggest, is imperfectly imposed on recalcitrant material. In considering these objections we shall have a chance further to test the strength of Arnold's symbolic design.

But does Arnold alter the tone of his poem in stanzas xii-xxiii or xxv? From the romantic atmosphere evoked by the depiction of wistful flocks crossing strips of "moon-blanch'd green," of quiet meadows in "green-muffled" hills, of rural figures that move in a frieze-like trance, he does shift suddenly—"But what—I dream! . . . —No, no . . ." (lines 131 and 141), to a realistic mood. The joyous imagery of nature dwindles; the imagery of disease, strife, distraction takes its place. The glowing lines are few, and these few (117-202 and 211-220, for instance) hark back to the wandering gypsy. But the change in tone is *warranted.* The subject of this poem is not the historical scholar-gypsy alone, but the symbolic scholar-gypsy too, a figure who is especially meaningful against the background of nineteenth-century attitudes. The speaker in the poem is simultaneously aware of the past and the present, of romance and reality, of the holiness of nature and the impiety of extreme rationalism. Hence, the change in tone is simply an accommodation to the manifold implications of the subject. The critical reader may object that modern (*circa* 1853) man is not as divided as Arnold claims. But this objection is addressed to the validity of the evidence rather than to the rightness of the structure, to thought in its scientific sense, rather than to thought as structure, or design.

The figure of the scholar-gypsy is consistent throughout. Indeed we may even claim that his role in the third section has been carefully anticipated in the second section. In the earlier section, (lines 44-50) the wanderer told his former college mates that he wished to learn the art of ruling men's brains, a secret art that comes only in "heaven-sent moments." Later, in line 171, we are reminded that, in contrast to the modern half-belief in casual creeds, the wanderer waits "for the spark from heaven." The scholar-gypsy has always been in contact with an inner truth. Moreover, his powers, described in the third section as "undiverted to the world without," are anticipated in the second where he shuns the society of the shepherds who found him seated in a lonely ale-house. "But, 'mid their drink and clatter, he would fly." The incident suggests self-reliance, the concentration rather than dissipation of spiritual resources. Finally, the unconquerable hope of lines 211-220 in the third section is foreshadowed by the courageous optimism in lines 118-120 in the second, where the blackbird fears his presence not at all.

> So often has he known thee past him stray,
> Rapt, twirling in thy hand a wither'd spray,
> And waiting for the spark from heaven to fall.

We see, then, a structure that harmonizes, by contrast, foreshadowing and repetition, the attitude of the speaker toward the scholar-gypsy in the various sections of the poem.

There remains one further objection, namely, that the last two stanzas are unnecessary, and in a perfect structure no part can be unnecessary. We may note at once that they are unnecessary to complete the literal meaning of the poem. When the speaker bids the wanderer avoid "our feverish contact" lest he, too, become distracted and hopeless and exchange his glad perennial youth for death, he has summarized the prose message of the poem. The similitude of the Tyrian trader (line 232) adds nothing to this statement. But it does complete the poem in other important ways. It re-establishes the mood of the beginning by returning to a romantic reverie, rich in metaphor, confident in rhythm and opulent in melody. It rescues the poem, too, from the corrosive emotions of the third section, restoring an aesthetic distance almost lost in describing the immediacies of squalid nineteenth-century doubt. The scholar-gypsy is a symbol of positive hope rather than of mere escape to the past. Hence, the comparison to a Tyrian trader who sailed day and night to the farthest limits of the ancient world, daring to be himself and successful in his daring, is necessary to complete the symbolic structure of the poem.

POEMS FOR DISCUSSION

A DIRGE

The glories of our blood and state
  Are shadows, not substantial things;
There is no armour against fate;
  Death lays his icy hand on kings:
    Sceptre and Crown 5
    Must tumble down,
And in the dust be equal made
With the poor crooked scythe and spade.

Some men with swords may reap the field,
  And plant fresh laurels where they kill: 10
But their strong nerves at last must yield;
  They tame but one another still:
    Early or late
    They stoop to fate,
And must give up their murmuring breath 15
When they, pale captives, creep to death.

The garlands wither on your brow;
  Then boast no more your mighty deeds;
Upon Death's purple altar now
  See where the victor-victim bleeds: 20
    Your heads must come
    To the cold tomb;
Only the actions of the just
Smell sweet, and blossom in their dust.

JAMES SHIRLEY

1. Show how the statements and incidents in this poem support the conclusion in the last two lines. In so far as they do support the conclusion, may one describe the structure of this poem as logical? Explain.
2. Show how death is presented in a dramatic way in each stanza. In so far as the poem has an implicitly dramatic structure, may one also describe the structure of this poem as imaginative? Explain.

3. Is the structure of this poem simultaneously logical and imaginative? Explain.

TO A SKYLARK

Ethereal minstrel! pilgrim of the sky!
Dost thou despise the earth where cares abound?
Or, while the wings aspire, are heart and eye
Both with thy nest upon the dewy ground?
Thy nest which thou canst drop into at will, 5
Those quivering wings composed, that music still!

Leave to the nightingale her shady wood;
A privacy of glorious light is thine,
Whence thou dost pour upon the world a flood
Of harmony, with instinct more divine; 10
Type of the wise, who soar, but never roam,
True to the kindred points of Heaven and Home!

WILLIAM WORDSWORTH

1. What does the skylark symbolize? Explain.
2. Presuming that the skylark is a symbol, may we describe the structure of this poem as symbolic? Why or why not?

TO A SKYLARK

Hail to thee, blithe Spirit!
Bird thou never wert,
That from Heaven, or near it,
Pourest thy full heart
In profuse strains of unpremeditated art. 5

Higher still and higher
From the earth thou springest
Like a cloud of fire;
The blue deep thou wingest,
And singing still dost soar, and soaring ever singest. 10

In the golden lightning
Of the sunken sun,
O'er which clouds are bright'ning,
Thou dost float and run;
Like an unbodied joy whose race is just begun. 15

The pale purple even
  Melts around thy flight;
Like a star of Heaven,
  In the broad daylight
Thou art unseen, but yet I hear thy shrill delight, 20

Keen as are the arrows
  Of that silver sphere,
Whose intense lamp narrows
  In the white dawn clear
Until we hardly see—we feel that it is there. 25

All the earth and air
  With thy voice is loud,
As, when night is bare,
  From one lonely cloud
The moon rains out her beams, and Heaven is overflowed. 30

What thou art we know not;
  What is most like thee?
From rainbow clouds there flow not
  Drops so bright to see
As from thy presence showers a rain of melody. 35

Like a Poet hidden
  In the light of thought,
Singing hymns unbidden,
  Till the world is wrought
To sympathy with hopes and fears it heeded not: 40

Like a high-born maiden
  In a palace-tower,
Soothing her love-laden
  Soul in secret hour
With music sweet as love, which overflows her bower: 45

Like a glow-worm golden
  In a dell of dew,
Scattering unbeholden
  Its aëreal hue
Among the flowers and grass, which screen it from the view! 50

Like a rose embowered
  In its own green leaves,

By warm winds deflowered,
  Till the scent it gives
Makes faint with too much sweet those heavy-wingéd thieves: 55

Sound of vernal showers
  On the twinkling grass,
Rain-awakened flowers,
  All that ever was
Joyous, and clear, and fresh, thy music doth surpass: 60

Teach us, Sprite or Bird,
  What sweet thoughts are thine:
I have never heard
  Praise of love or wine
That panted forth a flood of rapture so divine. 65

Chorus Hymeneal,
  Or triumphal chant,
Matched with thine would be all
  But an empty vaunt,
A thing wherein we feel there is some hidden want. 70

What objects are the fountains
  Of thy happy strain?
What fields, or waves, or mountains?
  What shapes of sky or plain?
What love of thine own kind? what ignorance of pain? 75

With thy clear keen joyance
  Languor cannot be:
Shadow of annoyance
  Never came near thee:
Thou lovest—but ne'er knew love's sad satiety. 80

Waking or asleep,
  Thou of death must deem
Things more true and deep
  Than we mortals dream,
Or how could thy notes flow in such a crystal stream? 85

We look before and after,
  And pine for what is not:
Our sincerest laughter

With some pain is fraught;
Our sweetest songs are those that tell of saddest thought. 90

Yet if we could scorn
Hate, and pride, and fear;
If we were things born
Not to shed a tear,
I know not how thy joy we ever should come near. 95

Better than all measures
Of delightful sound,
Better than all treasures
That in books are found,
Thy skill to poet were, thou scorner of the ground! 100

Teach me half the gladness
That thy brain must know,
Such harmonious madness
From my lips would flow
The world should listen then—as I am listening now. 105

PERCY BYSSHE SHELLEY

1. This ode may be divided into three parts: (1) a description of the lark's flight and song, lines 1-30; (2) comparison of the lark with a poet, a "high-born maiden," a "glow-worm," a "rose," and "vernal showers," lines 31-60; (3) the poet's plea for the wisdom of the lark, lines 61-105. Does this division suggest that the structure of the poem is symbolic? Why or why not?
2. Compare and contrast the structure of this poem with that of Wordsworth's "To a Skylark."

THE BEE

A zig-zag bee, zzz and zzz-ing, came
Out of the flowers in my room; his claim
For being there was he had been carried there
While he worked in a flower, unaware.

He swayed, buzzed toward a window where a screen 5
Stopped him, sieved the universe between
A green beyond and his desire for
A green beyond: he was neither/nor.

From flowers to screen, he hummed a sort of thunder—
Nothing, yet olympic to my wonder; 10
His song stopped when the network stopped the bee.
He inspected man's ingenuity.

The screen was there to keep him out, not in.
I wanted to let his ecstasy begin
Again—to let it continue as it was. 15
Let a bee have his summer: what he does

With his brief season is a song for hours;
Let a bee have his privilege of flowers,
I thought. Therefore, I took an envelope
(He did not know this was his one white hope) 20

And tried to maneuver him to crawl inside.
Something, maybe fear or maybe pride,
Prompted him to be difficult:
He had his bee-wise reason to consult

Whether this should be or should not be. 25
I learned some independence from the bee.
Yet, because I could not watch him strive
Futilely, and wanted him alive—

I could not let him die, with honeysuckle
Just in view—I nudged him with my knuckle, 30
Then carried him outside like a note for mailing.
I opened the envelope, and the bee went sailing

Into his freedom as his thunder began
Again. I felt aliveness as a man
Should. I felt the summer rise in me. 35
I saw a million flowers for the bee.

JOHN FANDEL

1. Is this poem simply concerned with the story of the bee's liberation? If not, what other meaning is suggested? Explain.
2. How does the structure of this poem differ from that of the two preceding poems? Explain.

✤ CHAPTER VI ✤

Thought and Truth in Poetry

IN THE previous chapter we found that thought in poetry consists (1) in the poet's vision of reality, and (2) in his presentation of that vision in a unified structure of language. There we took for granted that his vision, or thought, was true. Now we must inquire just how the thought in a poem may be said to be true. For manifestly the thoughts that some poems contain are not truths in every sense of the term. Death in Donne's sonnet, autumn in Keats's ode, the scholar-gypsy in Arnold's narrative, are fictions rather than literal truths. Francis Thompson's portrayal of God as the artificer of snowflakes clearly does not correspond to the theological understanding of God as pure spirit.

Often a poem contains factual error, as we observed in the case of Keats's sonnet, "On First Looking into Chapman's Homer," where Cortez is mistaken for Balboa. Yet we are certain that there is an essential truth in Donne's thoughts on death, in Keats's thoughts on autumn, in Arnold's view of the state of man, and in Thompson's image of God as a divine artisan.

An even greater problem arises when we consider extended philosophical poems, such as Shelley's *Prometheus Unbound.* The underlying theme of that dramatic poem is the perfectibility of mankind, that is, man's ability to achieve complete perfection by his own unaided strength. In Prometheus himself, a figure of the perfectible man, we find an expression of that theme, as the speech below indicates:

> To suffer woes which Hope thinks infinite;
> To forgive wrongs darker than death or night;
> To defy Power, which seems omnipotent;
> To love, and bear; to hope till Hope creates

From its own wreck the thing it contemplates;
Neither to change, nor falter, nor repent;
This . . . is to be
Good, great and joyous, beautiful and free;
This is above Life, Joy, Empire, and Victory . . .

Suppose one were to say: "But I do not accept the theory of human perfectibility. The thoughts expressed in the lines above are false. It is mere wishful thinking to suggest that Hope alone can create the thing it contemplates. Shelley is eloquent, but irrationally optimistic about the power of humanity to hope itself to perfection. This is sheer romantic idealism."

Suppose further that the reader feels the objection stated above applies not to a few lines but to the whole poem. Let us suppose, too, for the sake of argument, that the theory of human perfectibility is objectively false—even though Shelley himself sincerely felt it to be true. Is *Prometheus Unbound* then an unsuccessful poem? May we say that Shelley's lines are eloquent, sincere, stylistically admirable, but that, since his view of the truth is false, they fail to elicit the emotion he intended? To answer affirmatively means that, whatever else it does, *Prometheus Unbound* fails as a poem. Or contrariwise, may we say that, in a poem, the objective truth of thought is irrelevant; what matters is the clarity and persuasiveness of the expression? To say this is to suggest that poetry is language alone.

Is the truth of thought irrelevant? If so, in what respects? Are some general attitudes repugnant to poetry? If we are to explore this question—and to shirk that exploration is impossible—we must first know what men commonly mean by truth in ordinary discourse.

TRUTH IN ORDINARY DISCOURSE

What do men commonly mean by the term *truth?* One common sense view is that truth is *real* and falsity is *unreal.* Thus, we say that the *truth of things* is in their existence. The tree standing in my garden exists; it is actually there; it is not a chimera. A lake exists; it is a true lake, not a mirage. To emphasize our sense of the truth of things, we often say, "But this is actually true; I do have a tree in my garden."

Common sense also recognizes another kind of truth—*a truth of thought,* that is, the conformity of knowledge or ideas with the thing known. Thus we say that Newton's idea of gravitation corresponds to an operation of nature, or that our mental certainty of the inevitability of death corresponds to reality. Our common expression has it—"Your ideas make sense, that is, they represent mentally an objective fact or event or operation."

We speak, too, of *truth of words,* that is, the conformity of our words with what we think. "Is that what you really think? Are you talking the exact truth?" These common-sense expressions reflect our ordinary concern for truth-telling.

Finally there is *truth of conduct*—that is, the conformity of our acts to the requirements of human nature. Thus, we say of a neglectful mother that she is not a true or a real mother, or of an unjust or ignorant judge that he is not a true or a real judge, meaning thereby that they are false to the general dictates of human nature or to the particular laws of moral conduct.

Common sense then considers truth to be reality itself, or the agreement of mind with reality.

Now we may ask: Are these statements about truth relevant to poetry? *Under some circumstances they are.* We expect the poet, as we do any honest man, to speak the truth contained in the subject he professes to set forth. If he professes to write seriously about truth of things, an actual historical event like World War II, for instance, his poem should manifest the substantial truth of that event. The poet could not situate the main action in the Himalayas, or describe the causes of the war as a feud between sheep-herders and farmers. Nor could he characterize a man who ruthlessly murdered his enemies as a just man. So, too, if in *Paradise Lost* Milton actually violated an essential truth of Adam's history, by omitting the temptation scene, his poem would be untrue in that respect. To do any of these would *revolt* our sense of the truth of things, of thought, and of conduct. We would reject a poem of this sort as unreal, untrue, absurd.

In short, truth, of things or thoughts or words or conduct, is relevant to poetry *when the poet is professedly concerned with these kinds of truth.* The poet has the same obligations to truth as the historian, the philosopher, the moralist, or the man in the street. But, as we shall see, he is principally concerned with another kind of truth.

TRUTH IN POETRY

Normally, a poet's purpose is not to describe actual incidents, or to offer scientific proofs, but to draw from his own imagination ideas, events, or objects that will best express his own vision. To say this is to say again that poetry is essentially an art; it creates its own imaginary world, an illusion of reality that must not be confused with the actual world. But the imaginary world of a poem is not therefore an absurd world. It has its own kind of truth.

It is true to human nature *in general.* Just as human nature is rational, so, too, a poem is rational in that it proposes for contemplation something essentially true. Thus, we cherish as a masterpiece of the human mind a poem like Homer's *Iliad.* Despite the fact that Homer's *Iliad* includes some ridiculous activities by sportive gods and goddesses, it reveals, with unsurpassed clarity, the way men live, love, fight, and die. It delves beneath mere appearances or surface details to reveal the universal truth that underlies individual human experiences. It is, in short, essentially true and essentially reasonable even though some incidents appear to be false.

The truth of poetry, then, is the fidelity of the *imagined* situation to a *general* truth of human nature. The poet establishes this kind of truth, not by reference to the facts of history or science, or to the theories of philosophy, but by making his fiction plausible. Thus, we may hear the poet say, "I ask you to accept my truth as a probable truth of human nature. This probability I will establish by creating an image of human life that you will believe. To induce you to believe it, my poem will be consistent, reasonable, and natural." *Consistency* means that the separate elements in the poem, the details of a description, the incidents of a narrative, the ideas in an exposition or an argument, will unite in a meaningful whole. Even a fantasy about elves and dwarfs is consistent, once the right to create an imaginary world is granted, provided the elves and dwarfs do not suddenly become ordinary Jacks and Janes.

In constructing a poem the poet is also *reasonable.* What happens in the poem will be acceptable in the sense that the poem presents adequate motives for action, adequate reasons for a conclusion and adequate details to support an impression.

A poem is also *natural*. The language must be appropriate to the speaker, the subject, and the audience. Moreover, the action of the poem reflects the truths of human conduct. It will "hold as 'twere, the mirror up to Nature—to show Virtue her own feature, scorn her own image, and the very age and body of the time his form and pressure."

By being consistent, reasonable and natural, the poet may hope to induce in his readers that "willing suspension of disbelief" that allows them to accept for the moment at least the complete rightness of Hamlet's doubt, Lear's madness, and Prospero's magic. Thus, the vision made public in a poem is as meaningful in its own way as reason itself.

WISDOM AND THE GREATNESS OF POETRY

If vision is essential to a poem then we may say that a great poem is the manifestation in language of a great vision. Here the term *great* does not refer to physical size or number, but to a quality of mind. A great vision ranges from the minute observation of four ducks on a pond to the audacious report of angels in celestial debate. Above all, a great vision is informed by wisdom, the spirit that guides men to the proper understanding of truth and the proper use of that understanding.

In the past most educated readers treasured their classics for their wisdom. They read the ancient writers, Vergil and Horace, the medieval poets of Christendom, Dante and Chaucer, the Renaissance Englishmen, Shakespeare and Milton, not only for their style, or for the rational pleasures that great art always affords. They read and reread these poets chiefly because each of them had penetrated, in his own fashion, the central mysteries of human existence. In all these poets readers found wisdom: in Vergil and Horace the chaste wisdom embodied in the key words *pietas, gravitas and urbanitas;** in Dante and Chaucer, the wisdom of the just man with the *cuore gentile*, the gentle heart, who portrayed humanity struggling to be or not to be divine; in Shakespeare and Milton, the moral wisdom of humanists who saw in unweeded gardens, unpurged souls, and civil anarchy the tragic reversal of the intended order of the universe.

Nor were poets and their readers less concerned with wisdom in

* Piety, seriousness and urbanity.

later ages, even during those times when systematic philosophies of life were dissolving and religious convictions were becoming attenuated. When Coleridge wrote his appreciation of Wordsworth's *The Prelude,* ("To W. W."), he did not emphasize the merely technical accomplishments of the poem, but its wisdom, and the effects of that wisdom upon himself, as the lines below suggest:

Friend of the Wise! and Teacher of the Good! . . . thy work
Makes audible a linked lay of Truth,
Of Truth profound a sweet continuous lay,
Not learnt, but native, her own natural notes! . . . For Peace is nigh
Where Wisdom's voice has found a listening heart.

Closer to our own times, Browning also emphasized that poetry possesses a double truth, the truth of thought that makes the poem a poem, that is, the thought embodied in its literary structure, and the larger truth we have called wisdom. Thus, near the end of his poem, *The Ring and the Book,* he reminds us that the purpose of art is not simply to construct an image but to "save the soul beside," a phrase that hints at one of the meanings of wisdom—the proper use of truth.

So may you paint your picture, twice show truth,
Beyond mere imagery on the wall,—
So note by note bring music from your mind
Deeper then ever e'en Beethoven dives,—
So write a book shall mean beyond the facts,
Suffice the eye and save the soul beside.

ROBERT BROWNING
(From Book XII, *The Ring and The Book*)

The great poem does satisfy the eye; indeed, all the senses and the intelligence as well. It does not save the soul in the strict theological sense of the word, but it uplifts the soul and entices it, through its appeal to the senses and feelings, to consider the central mysteries and values of human life and directs it to contemplate truth for the sake of the poem and for the sake of the reader, too. At its best, a great poem is a just criticism of life—the utterance of a great mind pronouncing judgment on the affairs of men. The informing spirit of this judgment is the poet's wisdom—

his intense and passionate realization of the range and value of the realities his poem embodies.

Dante often appealed explicitly to the readers to contemplate the wisdom within the poem. He warned them—

"O ye of sound understanding, consider well the doctrine that lurks behind the veil of strange poetry." (Inferno, XX, 61)

"Reader, sharpen here your vision of the truth for the veil is now so fine it is easy to pierce." (Purgatorio, VIII, 19)

Modern poets are not usually so explicit in their references to the wisdom that underlies their imagery and word play. But, in one fashion or another, by allusion or quotation, by irony or paradox, they give testimony to their belief in the wisdom of poetry.

POEMS FOR DISCUSSION

IT WAS A BEAUTY THAT I SAW

It was a beauty that I saw
So pure, so perfect, as the frame
Of all the universe was lame,
To that one figure, could I draw,
Or give least line of it a law! 5

A skein of silk without a knot,
A fair march made without a halt,
A curious form without a fault,
A printed book without a blot,
All beauty, and without a spot! 10

BEN JONSON

8. Curious: elegant

1. In what sense is the beauty referred to in this poem poetic? In what sense actual? Explain.
2. How does stanza two complement stanza one?

A VALEDICTION: FORBIDDING MOURNING

As virtuous men pass mildly away,
And whisper to their soules to goe,
While some of their sad friends doe say,
The breath goes now, and some say, no:

So let us melt, and make no noise, 5
  No teare-floods, nor sigh-tempests move,
T'were prophanation of our joyes
  To tell the layetie our love.

Moving of th'earth brings harms and fearses;
  Men reckon what it did and meant, 10
But trepidation of the spheares,
  Though greater farre, is innocent.

Dull sublunary lovers love
  (Whose soule is sense) cannot admit
Absence, because it doth remove 15
  Those things which elemented it.

But we by a love so much refin'd,
  That ourselves know not what it is,
Inter-assuréd of the mind,
  Care lesse, eyes, lips, and hands to misse. 20

Our two souls therefore, which are one,
  Though I must goe, endure not yet
A breach, but an expansion,
  Like gold to ayery thinnesse beate.

If they be two, they are two so 25
  As stiffe twin compasses are two;
Thy soule the fixt foot, makes no show
  To move, but doth, if the other doe.

And though it in the center sit,
  Yet when the other far doth rome, 30
It leanes, and hearkens after it,
  And growes erect, as that comes home.

Such wilt thou be to mee, who must
  Like th'other foot, obliquely runne;
Thy firmnes makes my circle just, 35
  And makes me end, where I begunne.

JOHN DONNE

1. Show how the first two stanzas propose the general truth that is developed in the succeeding stanzas. Is the development reasonable in the sense that the term is used in this chapter? Why or why not?

2. Is the image of the compasses developed in the last three stanzas consistent with the emotion suggested in the first two stanzas? Explain.
3. Is the language of this poem natural? Why or why not?

JOHN ANDERSON MY JO

John Anderson my jo, John,
  When we were first acquent,
Your locks were like the raven,
  Your bonie brow was brent;
But now your brow is beld, John, 5
  Your locks are like the snow;
But blessings on your frosty pow,
  John Anderson, my jo.

John Anderson my jo, John,
  We clamb the hill thegither; 10
And mony a canty day, John,
  We've had wi' ane anither:
Now we maun totter down, John,
  And hand in hand we'll go,
And sleep thegither at the foot, 15
  John Anderson, my jo.

ROBERT BURNS

1. Jo: sweetheart
4. Brent: smooth
7. Pow: head
11. Canty: jolly

1. In what sense is this poem comparable to "A Valediction: Forbidding Mourning"? Why? In what senses is it not comparable? Why?

TITHONUS

The woods decay, the woods decay and fall,
The vapours weep their burthen to the ground,
Man comes and tills the field and lies beneath,
And after many a summer dies the swan.
Me only cruel immortality 5
Consumes: I wither slowly in thine arms,
Here at the quiet limit of the world,
A white-hair'd shadow roaming like a dream
The ever-silent spaces of the East,

Far-folded mists, and gleaming halls of morn. 10
  Alas! for this gray shadow, once a man—
So glorious in his beauty and thy choice,
Who madest him thy chosen, that he seem'd
To his great heart none other than a God!
I asked thee, "Give me immortality." 15
Then didst thou grant mine asking with a smile,
Like wealthy men who care not how they give.
But thy strong Hours indignant worked their wills,
And beat me down and marr'd and wasted me,
And tho' they could not end me, left me maim'd 20
To dwell in presence of immortal youth,
Immortal age beside immortal youth,
And all I was, in ashes. Can thy love,
Thy beauty, make amends, tho' even now,
Close over us, the silver star, thy guide, 25
Shines in those tremulous eyes that fill with tears
To hear me? Let me go: take back thy gift:
Why should a man desire in any way
To vary from the kindly race of men,
Or pass beyond the goal of ordinance 30
Where all should pause, as is most meet for all?
  A soft air fans the cloud apart; there comes
A glimpse of that dark world where I was born.
Once more the old mysterious glimmer steals
From thy pure brows, and from thy shoulders pure, 35
And bosom beating with a heart renew'd.
Thy cheek begins to redden thro' the gloom,
Thy sweet eyes brighten slowly close to mine,
Ere yet they blind the stars, and the wild team
Which love thee, yearning for thy yoke, arise, 40
And shake the darkness from their loosen'd manes,
And beat the twilight into flakes of fire.
  Lo! ever thus thou growest beautiful
In silence, then before thine answer given
Departest, and thy tears are on my cheek. 45
  Why wilt thou ever scare me with thy tears,
And make me tremble lest a saying learnt,
In days far-off, on that dark earth, be true?
The Gods themselves cannot recall their gifts.
  Ay me! ay me! with what another heart 50
In days far-off, and with what other eyes

I used to watch—if I be he that watch'd—
The lucid outline forming round thee; saw
The dim curls kindle into sunny rings;
Changed with thy mystic change, and felt my blood 55
Glow with the glow that slowly crimson'd all
Thy presence and thy portals, while I lay,
Mouth, forehead, eyelids, growing dewy-warm
With kisses balmier than half-opening buds
Of April, and could hear the lips that kiss'd 60
Whispering I knew not what of wild and sweet,
Like that strange song I heard Apollo sing,
While Ilion like a mist rose into towers.
Yet hold me not forever in thine East;
How can my nature longer mix with thine? 65
Coldly thy rosy shadows bathe me, cold
Are all thy lights, and cold my wrinkled feet
Upon thy glimmering thresholds, when the steam
Floats up from those dim fields about the homes
Of happy men that have the power to die, 70
And grassy barrows of the happier dead.
Release me, and restore me to the ground.
Thou seëst all things, thou wilt see my grave:
Thou wilt renew thy beauty morn by morn;
I earth in earth forget these empty courts, 75
And thee returning on thy silver wheels.

ALFRED, LORD TENNYSON

1. Who is speaking? To whom does he speak? What is the predominant emotion or tone? Is the reason for his feeling made evident in the course of the poem? If so, how?
2. What evidence points to the fact that the person addressed is a goddess? the speaker a human?
3. Is some "general truth of human nature" embodied in this poem? Explain.

RABBI BEN EZRA

Grow old along with me!
The best is yet to be,
The last of life, for which the first was made:
Our times are in His hand
Who saith, "A whole I planned,
Youth shows but half; trust God: see all nor be afraid!"

Not that, amassing flowers,
Youth sighed, "Which rose make ours,
Which lily leave and then as best recall?"
Not that, admiring stars, 10
It yearned, "Nor Jove, nor Mars;
Mine be some figured flame which blends, transcends them all!"

Not for such hopes and fears
Annulling youth's brief years,
Do I remonstrate: folly wide the mark! 15
Rather I prize the doubt
Low kinds exist without,
Finished and finite clods, untroubled by a spark.

Poor vaunt of life indeed,
Were man but formed to feed 20
On joy, to solely seek and find and feast:
Such feasting ended, then
As sure an end to men;
Irks care the crop-full bird? Frets doubt the maw-crammed beast?

Rejoice we are allied 25
To That which doth provide
And not partake, effect and not receive!
A spark disturbs our clod;
Nearer we hold of God
Who gives, than of His tribes that take, I must believe. 30

Then, welcome each rebuff
That turns earth's smoothness rough,
Each sting that bids nor sit nor stand but go!
Be our joys three-parts pain!
Strive, and hold cheap the strain; 35
Learn, nor account the pang; dare, never grudge the throe!

For thence,—a paradox
Which comforts while it mocks,—
Shall life succeed in that it seems to fail:
What I aspired to be, 40
And was not, comforts me:
A brute I might have been, but would not sink i' the scale.

What is he but a brute
Whose flesh has soul to suit,
Whose spirit works lest arms and legs want play? 45
To man, propose this test—
Thy body at its best,
How far can that project thy soul on its lone way?

Yet gifts should prove their use.
I own the Past profuse 50
Of power each side, perfection every turn:
Eyes, ears took in their dole,
Brain treasured up the whole;
Should not the heart beat once, "How good to live and learn?"

Not once beat, "Praise be Thine! 55
I see the whole design,
I, who saw power, see now love perfect too:
Perfect I call Thy plan:
Thanks that I was a man!
Maker, remake, complete,—I trust what Thou shalt do!" 60

For pleasant is this flesh;
Our soul, in its rose-mesh
Pulled ever to the earth, still yearns for rest;
Would we some prize might hold
To match those manifold 65
Possessions of the brute,—gain most, as we did best!

Let us not always say,
"Spite of this flesh to-day
I strove, made head, gained ground upon the whole!"
As the bird wings and sings, 70
Let us cry, "All good things
Are ours, nor soul helps flesh more, now, than flesh helps soul!"

Therefore I summon age
To grant youth's heritage,
Life's struggle having so far reached its term: 75
Thence shall I pass, approved
A man, for aye removed
From the developed brute, a god though in the germ.

And I shall thereupon
Take rest, ere I be gone 80

Once more on my adventure brave and new:
Fearless and unperplexed,
When I wage battle next,
What weapons to select, what armor to indue.

Youth ended, I shall try 85
My gain or loss thereby;
Leave the fire ashes, what survives is gold:
And I shall weigh the same,
Give life its praise or blame.
Young, all lay in dispute; I shall know, being old. 90

For note, when evening shuts,
A certain moment cuts
The deed off, calls the glory from the gray:
A whisper from the west
Shoots—"Add this to the rest, 95
Take it and try its worth: here dies another day."

So, still within this life,
Though lifted o'er its strife,
Let me discern, compare, pronounce at last,
"This rage was right i' the main, 100
That acquiescence vain:
The Future I may face now I have proved the Past."

For more is not reserved
To man, with soul just nerved
To act tomorrow what he learns today: 105
Here, work enough to watch
The Master work, and catch
Hints of the proper craft, tricks of the tool's true play.

As it was better, youth
Should strive, through acts uncouth, 110
Toward making, than repose on aught found made:
So, better, age, exempt
From strife, should know, than tempt
Further. Thou waitedest age: wait death nor be afraid!

Enough now, if the Right 115
And Good and Infinite
Be named here, as thou callest thy hand thine own,

With knowledge absolute,
Subject to no dispute
From fools that crowded youth, nor let thee feel alone. 120

Be there, for once and all,
Severed great minds from small,
Announced to each his station in the Past!
Was I, the world arraigned,
Were they, my soul disdained, 125
Right? Let age speak the truth and give us peace at last!

Now, who shall arbitrate?
Ten men love what I hate,
Shun what I follow, slight what I receive;
Ten, who in ears and eyes 130
Match me: we all surmise,
They this thing, and I that: whom shall my soul believe?

Not on the vulgar mass
Called "work," must sentence pass,
Things done, that took the eye and had the price; 135
O'er which, from level stand,
The low world laid its hand,
Found straightway to its mind, could value in a trice:

But all the world's coarse thumb
And finger failed to plumb, 140
So passed in making up the main account;
All instincts immature,
All purposes unsure,
That weighed not as his work, yet swelled the man's amount:

Thoughts hardly to be packed 145
Into a narrow act,
Fancies that broke through language and escaped;
All I could never be,
All, men ignored in me,
This, I was worth to God, whose wheel the pitcher shaped. 150

Ay, note that Potter's wheel,
That metaphor! and feel
Why time spins fast, why passive lies our clay,—
Thou, to whom fools propound,

When the wine makes its round, 155
"Since life fleets, all is change; the Past gone, seize to-day!"

Fool! All that is, at all,
Lasts ever, past recall;
Earth changes, but thy soul and God stand sure:
What entered into thee, 160
That was, is, and shall be:
Time's wheel runs back or stops: Potter and clay endure.

He fixed thee 'mid this dance
Of plastic circumstance,
This Present, thou, forsooth, wouldst fain arrest: 165
Machinery just meant
To give thy soul its bent,
Try thee and turn thee forth, sufficiently impressed.

What though the earlier grooves
Which ran the laughing loves 170
Around thy base, no longer pause and press?
What though, about thy rim,
Skull-things in order grim
Grow out, in graver mood, obey the sterner stress?

Look not thou down but up! 175
To uses of a cup,
The festal board, lamp's flash and trumpet's peal,
The new-wine's foaming flow,
The Master's lips aglow!
Thou, heaven's consummate cup, what need'st thou with earth's
wheel? 180

But I need, now as then,
Thee, God, who mouldest men;
And since, not even while the whirl was worst,
Did I,—to the wheel of life
With shapes and colours rife, 185
Bound dizzily,—mistake my end, to slake Thy thirst:

So, take and use Thy work:
Amend what flaws may lurk,
What strain o' the stuff, what warpings past the aim!
My times be in Thy hand! 190

Perfect the cup as planned!
Let age approve of youth, and death complete the same!

ROBERT BROWNING

1. Who is speaking? Is there a unifying theme or structure to the discourse? Explain.
2. Is this poem concerned with the truths of ordinary discourse? of poetic discourse? If it contains both, are they in harmony? Explain.
3. Are the thoughts uttered by the speaker also Browning's thoughts? How can you tell?

✤ CHAPTER VII ✤

Imagination in Poetry: Literal Expression and Figurative Expression

In discussing the several elements of emotion, thought and imagination, we cannot stress too often that in poetry these elements are inseparable. Emotion is the mind's response to knowledge, itself the awareness of a situation. We cannot respond to what we do not in some way know. Knowledge in turn is based on the perceptions of the several senses and on a retentive memory of the impressions made upon the senses. Hence, in treating the imaginative aspect of poetry, we must remember that we are focussing our attention on a function that is intimately associated with other operations of the mind.

The term imagination has many different meanings. Psychologists define it as the ability to form mental representations of sensible objects that are not immediately present to the senses. Understood in this way, imagination is a power, common to all men, by which they mentally picture a mountain or a seashore or a person, even when they are by themselves far away from those objects. Critics and literary historians, however, regard imagination not as a passive, reproductive power that records actual impressions registered on the senses. Rather, they consider it as a power of apprehending reality in a concrete way, a faculty that combines sense perception and intelligence, and thus achieves an intuitive understanding of an object or action. Moreover, in poetry, imagination is not only the capacity to see or realize; it is also the capacity to create. The poet's imagination, cooperating with his other faculties, enables him to express his vision in the complete structure of the poem as well as in the details. John Keats hints at this creative power when he writes in "The Fall of Hyperion":

CANTO I

For Poesy alone can tell her dreams,—
With the fine spell of words alone can save
Imagination from the sable chain 10
And dumb enchantment. Who alive can say,
"Thou art no Poet—may'st not tell thy dreams?"
Since every man whose soul is not a clod
Hath visions and would speak, if he had loved,
And been well nurtured in his mother tongue. 15

The poet, unlike the average man, has been well nurtured in his mother tongue. He can express his dreams. His imagination is an inventive faculty that represents vividly the details of an object or event, employs figurative language to render its meaning even more vividly, and envisions a meaningful structure of incidents or situations or symbols. In this chapter we will be concerned with the vivid representation of details and with figurative language in general.

A. *Vividness of Sensory Details*

In ordinary experience we know and enjoy life first by using our senses. The eye delights in color and movement, the ear in harmonious sound, the nostrils in the scent of perfume, the tongue in sweet and sour, the touch in smooth and rough textures, the muscles in movement and rest. This activity of the senses, directed to some purpose, accounts for the pleasures of a walk in the country, where the soft earth, the blue sky, the song of birds, the odor of pine and the pelting of wind and rain arouse, invigorate, and delight.

As in nature, so in the poetic imitation of nature. The poet arouses, invigorates, and delights by compelling us to use our senses imaginatively. His words represent the sensory details of a scene, by explicit or suggestive reference to objects or actions. Notice, for example, the way Shakespeare compels us to use our senses in his "Winter."

When icicles hang by the wall
  And Dick the shepherd blows his nail,

And Tom bears logs into the hall,
  And milk comes frozen home in pail,
When blood is nipp'd, and ways be foul, 5
Then nightly sings the staring owl,
  Tu-who;
Tu-whit! tu-who—a merry note,
While greasy Joan doth keel the pot.

When all aloud the wind doth blow, 10
  And coughing drowns the parson's saw,
And birds sit brooding in the snow,
  And Marian's nose looks red and raw,
When roasted crabs hiss in the bowl,
Then nightly sings the staring owl, 15
  Tu-who;
Tu-whit, tu-who—a merry note,
While greasy Joan doth keel the pot.

This scene is meaningful only in terms of the impression formed by a series of details. Its sights—of icicles hanging by the wall, of log-bearing and frozen milk, of brooding birds and Marian's red raw nose; its sounds—of the owl's cry, the loud winds, the coughing congregation, the hissing crabs; its suggestions of touch—Dick's frostbitten fingers, greasy Joan's ladling; its sense of motion—the fetching of wood, the bearing of milk-pails, the stirring of the pot—all these details linked together form a single impression of a rural winter scene.

In a similar manner, William Blake's "The Echoing Green" compels us to recreate the sensitive experience of a rural fete on a village green. As you read the poem below, notice the many concrete words that summon up images of objects that you can see and hear. The sun shines, bells ring, birds sing, children shout, old folks sit under a tree. Indeed, the clarity of these individual images and their harmonious blending, the animation of the verse, and the narrative movement—from the energetic play of morning to the happy exhaustion of evening—all justify calling this poem a picture in motion.

THE ECHOING GREEN

The Sun does arise,
And make happy the skies;

The merry bells ring
To welcome the Spring;
The skylark and thrush, 5
The birds of the bush,
Sing louder around
To the bells' cheerful sound,
While our sports shall be seen
On the Echoing Green. 10

Old John, with white hair,
Does laugh away care,
Sitting under the oak,
Among the old folk.
They laugh at our play, 15
And soon they all say:
"Such, such were the joys
When we all, girls and boys,
In our youth time were seen
On the Echoing Green." 20

Till the little ones, weary,
No more can be merry;
The sun does descend,
And our sports have an end.
Round the laps of their mothers 25
Many sisters and brothers,
Like birds in their nest,
Are ready for rest,
And sport no more seen
On the darkening Green. 30

WILLIAM BLAKE

In both "Winter" and "The Echoing Green," the vividness of the details expressed in concrete language provides us not only with something to look *at*, an objective situation, but also with a point of view, an emotional attitude to the situation. In "Winter" Shakespeare communicates the bleakness of the season. It is a time "When blood is nipp'd and ways be *foul*," when birds *brood* and the owl's merry note is an ironic jeer. Winter is a time of cheerless domestic tasks refined in part by the comforts of the kitchen where Dick and Tom will eat their stew and afterwards, perhaps, drink a steaming cup of cider with greasy Joan and red-nosed Marian. So, too, in "The Echoing Green" Blake presents details that are objective, indeed almost literal in their descriptive quality, but that also suggest his own subjective response to the scene.

In the first two stanzas the images echo the song and play, reflect the joyous quality of sunlight on green earth. In the last stanza silence falls, the sun descends, not on the *echoing*, but on the *darkening* green. A hint of sadness creeps in, as if to suggest that, as with the day, so with life, all merriment must end, and the little ones now resting in the laps of their mothers will soon grow old. The poet's images point, then, to objects, but also to the thinking subject, to things, to the meanings behind the things, to a single scene, and to the human drama in which the scene is but a part. Imagination, we may say, supplies both an object or image and a voice, an external picture and an interior cry.

Hilaire Belloc's "Tarantella" is perhaps a more dramatic example of the many functions of imagery—its power to present concrete objects, to suggest emotional attitudes, and to provide the grounds for understanding the significance of human experience.

TARANTELLA

Do you remember an Inn,
Miranda?
Do you remember an Inn?
And the tedding and the spreading
Of the straw for a bedding, 5
And the fleas that tease in the High Pyrenees,
And the wine that tasted of the tar?
And the cheers and the jeers of the young muleteers
(Under the dark of the vine verandah)?
Do you remember an Inn, Miranda, 10
Do you remember an Inn?
And the cheers and the jeers of the young muleteers
Who hadn't got a penny,
And who weren't paying any,
And the hammer at the doors and the Din? 15
And the Hip! Hop! Hap!
Of the clap
Of the hands to the twirl and the swirl

Of the girl gone chancing,
Glancing, 20
Dancing,
Backing and advancing,
Snapping of the clapper to the spin
Out and in—
And the Ting, Tong, Tang of the Guitar! 25
Do you remember an Inn,
Miranda?
Do you remember an Inn!

Never more;
Miranda, 30
Never more.
Only the high peaks hoar:
And Aragon a torrent at the door.
No sound
In the walls of the Halls where falls 35
The tread
Of the feet of the dead to the ground.
No sound:
Only the boom
Of the far Waterfall like Doom. 40

HILAIRE BELLOC

The sensory appeal of this poem is as emphatic as the stamping in the rapid-whirling dance named in the title, or as the cracking triplets and abrupt transitions of the musical compositions that accompany such dances. Miranda is asked to remember the *sights* of the inn; the straw bedding, the dark veranda, the vivid movements of the dance within and the snow-covered peaks without; the *sounds* of the inn, the din of the muleteers mingling with the "ting, tong, tang" of guitars, the "hip, hop, hap" of the handclapping and footstamping, the boom of the waterfall outside; the *feel* of the straw bed and the bite of fleas; the *taste* of wine drawn from tarred wineskins.

But "Tarantella" is no mere virtuoso performance designed to exploit the resources of language or to represent color, shape, sound and movement for their own sake. The images serve also to express the poet's feelings about the scene. He is remembering a particularly vivid experience in the past, in which the dancing, singing, drinking, shouting in an inn perched among the wild mountains of Aragon evoke feelings of tumultuous joy. This joy, however, is nostalgic, for it has passed away. "Never more," he repeats, as if to say that youth has passed. Now all is silence, in which one hears the footsteps of the dead and the dirge-like fall of a cataract. Thus, without explicit statement, the images suggest remembered joy and present sorrow. The poet presents a scene, expresses a feeling, and indirectly comments on a truth of human experience.

B. Figurative Expression

The imagery in the three poems we have examined is for the most part literal. The concrete words mean just what they say: Icicles refer to icicles, skylarks to skylarks, and muleteers to muleteers. At times, however, the poets use *figurative* language; that is, they describe objects or events in language that is not literally applicable to that object or event.

In "The Echoing Green" Blake compares the children in their mothers' laps to birds in their nests, and he says that the sun makes "happy the skies." In "Tarantella" Belloc speaks of the footfalls of the dead. Obviously these writers do not mean that the children are exactly like birds or that the skies are happy in the sense that a human being is happy, or that the dead actually do walk. The transfer of an epithet proper to one object to another is an intellectual and imaginative leap, an abandonment of the literal in an effort to make one thing known in terms of another thing to which it is somehow related.

Is this description of one thing in terms of another illogical? If it is, then language itself is illogical, for many words that are now considered literal descriptions of things were once figurative expressions. *Daisy,* for instance, was originally the day's eye (the sun). So, too, customary usage permits sober, factual-minded reporters to say *the stage* when they mean theatrical productions in general, or *property,* a general term, when they mean a particular *parcel of real estate.* In everyday speech, too, we spice our literal communications with homely figures: "A difficult assignment this, it gives me a headache"; "This room is as hot as a fire ball"; "Hurry up; get the lead out of your feet."

This figurative habit, instinctive in human nature, is simply more highly developed in the poet. Gifted with a more active and creative imagination, and with a more expert skill in the use of language, he exploits the possibilities of imaginative association to make his meaning more vivid, emphatic, varied. He will take a thought, man's mortality for instance, and by associating that thought with other brief and passing realities, produce a statement far more meaningful than "brief is the life of man." Rather, he will say something like this:

MAN'S LIFE

Like to the falling of a star,
Or as the flights of eagles are,
Or like the fresh spring's gaudy hue,
Or silver drops of morning dew,
Or like the wind that chafes the flood, 5
Or bubbles which on water stood:
Even such is man, whose borrowed light
Is straight called in and paid to night:
The wind blows out, the bubble dies,
The spring intombed in Autumn lies: 10
The dew's dried up, the star is shot,
The flight is past, and man forgot.

HENRY KING

Few will deny that this figurative statement is more intense than purely literal statement. The comparisons of man's brief life to a falling star, the flight of an eagle, the passage of spring, the evaporation of dew, the fugitive wind, the dying bubbles, and to a loan that must quickly be paid—all are *vivid*. Each image, in its sensory appeal, directs us to something we can see or to something all men have experienced.

The accumulation of these images—all of them signifying falling, emptiness, death—repeat and thereby *emphasize* the central thought. But this repetition is not stale or wearisome, because each comparison is different, a slight variation, as in the movements of a fugue, on the main theme. Finally, the figurative imagery in this poem conveys more meaningful suggestions than would be possible in a literal statement however vivid. By describing man's fate in terms of other realities, the poet widens our span of vision so that we see man not as an isolated creature but as an integral part of a created universe.

Moreover, this development of the analogy between man and the star, the eagle, the spring, and so on, increases our range of feeling. It is as if the poet borrows the emotional value inherent in the other experiences. This sum of many remembered feelings results in a new concentration of feeling and a new awareness of the complexity of experience. Thus he compels us to see anew what our egotism prompts us so readily to forget—that our lives, like all created things, are brief.

Figurative expression then achieves the results of literal expression—vividness, feeling and suggested meaning, but often to a greater degree. Moreover, figurative imagery often succeeds in areas where literal imagery fails altogether. Abstractions, such as Philosophy, Passion, Virtue, are difficult to express in images without some loss of their essential meaning. Yet these subjects, and the relations between them, often provide the reflective poet with some of his most rewarding insights. But if he cannot express these insights literally, he can do so figuratively.

Note, for example, how George Meredith gives abstract thought a concrete body in "Kinship with the Stars." By personifying Philosophy as a climber in the high mountains, and Passion as a prisoner in a cell below, he makes the conflict between them visible. Moreover, he expresses the ambiguity of man's attitude to the contrary dictates of the head and the heart.

KINSHIP WITH THE STARS

Cold as a mountain in its star-pitched tent,
Stood high Philosophy, less friend than foe:
Whom self-caged Passion, from its prison-bars,
Is always watching with a wondering hate.
Not till the fire is dying in the grate,
Look we for any kinship with the stars.

GEORGE MEREDITH

Figurative expression is perhaps the poet's only means of dramatizing an idea that, like the one above, tends toward the generalized statement of informative or rational discourse. Small wonder, then, that poets endow abstract ideas with human traits, or identify Passion as a fire and Philosophy as a wanderer in the stars. It is for this reason, too, that a Wordsworth, despite his professed addiction to ordinary language, clothes his Platonic notion of the soul's pre-existence in figurative language. In his "Ode: Intimations of Immortality" (p. 208), how else could Wordsworth express a dim celestial memory—"a visionary gleam . . . a glory and a dream," a bodiless intuition, save in the correlative terms of a figure? The ineffable vision is thus translated into the metaphor of a star trailing clouds of glory.

Our birth is but a sleep and a forgetting:
The soul that rises with us, our life's Star,
    Hath had elsewhere its setting,
    And cometh from afar:
    Not in entire forgetfulness,
    And not in utter nakedness,
But trailing clouds of glory do we come
        From God, who is our home:
Heaven lies about us in our infancy!

WILLIAM WORDSWORTH

We may say then that while in general figurative expression is a means of greater vividness and intensity, it is in some cases a necessary means of communicating what is otherwise incommunicable, a way of expressing by indirection that which the poet cannot or does not wish to state directly.

Note: another kind of figure—that of syntax—is a departure from the normal order of speech, the inversion of the subject and predicate, for instance. Thus, when Meredith writes, "Look we for any kinship with the stars" instead of "We look for kinship . . ." he inverts the normal order of the English sentence for the sake of emphasis. Figuration of this kind varies the normal order of expression to underscore the important idea or to emphasize the predominant feeling. Like forceful repetition (iteration or anaphora), antithesis, hyperbole (overstatement or exaggeration for the sake of emphasis), litotes (or understatement), these devices do not exist for their own sake. Rather, they are directly related to the writer's thought. Figures of speech, whether of imagery or syntax, never are successful when they are merely ornamental, ingenious, or self-conscious. Indeed, they must appear to be the normal way of expressing the passionate perception and thought that is the life of poetry.

POEMS FOR DISCUSSION

HOME-THOUGHTS, FROM ABROAD

Oh, to be in England
Now that April's there,
And whoever wakes in England
Sees, some morning, unaware,
That the lowest boughs and the brushwood sheaf 5
Round the elm-tree bole are in tiny leaf,
While the chaffinch sings on the orchard bough
In England—now!

And after April, when May follows,
And the whitethroat builds, and all the swallows! 10
Hark, where my blossomed pear-tree in the hedge
Leans to the field and scatters on the clover
Blossoms and dewdrops—at the bent spray's edge—
That's the wise thrush; he sings each song twice over,
Lest you should think he never could recapture 15
The first fine careless rapture!
And though the fields look rough with hoary dew,
All will be gay when noontide wakes anew
The buttercups, the little children's dower
—Far brighter than this gaudy melon-flower! 20

ROBERT BROWNING

1. What is the predominant impression in this poem? Show how the details of spring support that impression.
2. What lines in the poem clearly convey the speaker's attitude or point of view? Is his point of view more or less discernible than that of the speaker in "Winter," p. 124? Explain.

BUGLE SONG

The splendor falls on castle walls
And snowy summits old in story:
The long light shakes across the lakes,
And the wild cataract leaps in glory.

Blow, bugle, blow, set the wild echoes flying, 5
Blow, bugle; answer, echoes, dying, dying, dying.

O hark, O hear! how thin and clear,
And thinner, clearer, farther going!
O sweet and far from cliff and scar
The horns of Elfland faintly blowing! 10
Blow, let us hear the purple glens replying:
Blow, bugle; answer, echoes, dying, dying, dying.

O love, they die in yon rich sky,
They faint on hill or field or river:
Our echoes roll from soul to soul, 15
And grow for ever and for ever.
Blow, bugle, blow, set the wild echoes flying,
And answer, echoes, answer, dying, dying, dying.

ALFRED, LORD TENNYSON
(From *The Princess*)

1. What sensory details are particularly vivid? Why?
2. What expressions are figurative rather than literal? Explain.

I WANDERED LONELY AS A CLOUD

I wandered lonely as a cloud
That floats on high o'er vales and hills,
When all at once I saw a crowd,
A host of golden daffodils;
Beside the lake, beneath the trees 5
Fluttering and dancing in the breeze.

Continuous as the stars that shine
And twinkle on the milky way,
They stretched in never-ending line
Along the margin of a bay: 10
Ten thousand saw I at a glance
Tossing their heads in sprightly dance.

The waves beside them danced; but they
Out-did the sparkling waves in glee:
A poet could not but be gay 15
In such a jocund company:

I gazed—and gazed—but little thought
What wealth the show to me had brought:

For oft, when on my couch I lie
In vacant or in pensive mood, 20
They flash upon that inward eye
Which is the bliss of solitude;
And then my heart with pleasure fills,
And dances with the daffodils.

WILLIAM WORDSWORTH

1. Show how the speaker's point of view is primarily objective in the first two stanzas and more personal in the last two.

THE HOUND OF HEAVEN

I fled Him, down the nights and down the days;
I fled Him, down the arches of the years;
I fled Him, down the labyrinthine ways
Of my own mind; and in the midst of tears
I hid from Him, and under running laughter. 5
Up vistaed hopes I sped;
And shot, precipitated,
Adown Titanic glooms of chasméd fears,
From those strong Feet that followed, followed after.

But with unhurrying chase, 10
And unperturbéd pace,
Deliberate speed, majestic instancy,
They beat—and a Voice beat
More instant than the Feet—
"All things betray thee, who betrayest Me." 15

I pleaded, outlaw-wise,
By many a hearted casement, curtained red,
Trellised with intertwining charities;
(For, though I knew His love Who followéd,
Yet was I sore adread 20
Lest, having Him, I must have naught beside);
But, if one little casement parted wide,
The gust of His approach would clash it to.
Fear wist not to evade as Love wist to pursue.

Across the margent of the world I fled, 25
And troubled the gold gateways of the stars,
Smiting for shelter on their clangéd bars;
Fretted to dulcet jars
And silvern chatter the pale ports o' the moon.
I said to Dawn, Be sudden; to Eve, Be soon; 30
With thy young skiey blossoms heap me over
From this tremendous Lover!
Float thy vague veil about me, lest He see!
I tempted all His servitors, but to find
My own betrayal in their constancy, 35
In faith to Him their fickleness to me,
Their traitorous trueness, and their loyal deceit.
To all swift things for swiftness did I sue;
Clung to the whistling mane of every wind.
But whether they swept, smoothly fleet, 40
The long savannahs of the blue;
Or whether, Thunder-driven,
They clanged His chariot 'thwart a heaven
Plashy with flying lightnings round the spurn o' their feet:—
Fear wist not to evade as Love wist to pursue. 45

Still with unhurrying chase,
And unperturbéd pace,
Deliberate speed, majestic instancy,
Came on the following Feet,
And a Voice above their beat— 50
"Naught shelters thee, who wilt not shelter Me."

I sought no more that after which I strayed
In face of man or maid;
But still within the little children's eyes
Seems something, something that replies; 55
They at least are for me, surely for me!
I turned me to them very wistfully;
But, just as their young eyes grew sudden fair
With dawning answers there,
Their angel plucked them from me by the hair. 60
"Come then, ye other children, Nature's—share
With me" (said I) "your delicate fellowship;
Let me greet you lip to lip,
Let me twine with you caresses,
Wantoning 65

With our Lady-Mother's vagrant tresses,
Banqueting
With her in her wind-walled palace,
Underneath her azured daïs,
Quaffing, as your taintless way is, 70
From a chalice
Lucent-weeping out of the dayspring."
So it was done:
I in their delicate fellowship was one—
Drew the bolt of Nature's secrecies. 75
I knew all the swift importings
On the willful face of skies;
I knew how the clouds arise
Spumèd of the wild sea-snortings;
All that's born or dies 80
Rose and drooped with—made them shapers
Of mine own moods, or wailful or divine—
With them joyed and was bereaven.
I was heavy with the even,
When she lit her glimmering tapers 85
Round the day's dead sanctities.
I laughed in the morning's eyes.
I triumphed and I saddened with all weather,
Heaven and I wept together,
And its sweet tears were salt with mortal mine; 90
Against the red throb of its sunset-heart
I laid my own to beat,
And share commingling heat;
But not by that, by that, was eased my human smart.
In vain my tears were wet on Heaven's grey cheek. 95
For ah! we know not what each other says,
These things and I; in sound *I* speak—
Their sound is but their stir, they speak by silences.
Nature, poor stepdame, cannot slake my drouth;
Let her, if she would owe me, 100
Drop yon blue bosom-veil of sky, and show me
The breasts o' her tenderness:
Never did any milk of hers once bless
My thirsting mouth.
Nigh and nigh draws the chase, 105
With unperturbèd pace,
Deliberate speed, majestic instancy;
And past those noisèd Feet

A Voice comes yet more fleet—
"Lo! naught contents thee, who content'st not Me." 110
Naked I wait Thy love's uplifted stroke!
My harness piece by piece Thou hast hewn from me,
And smitten me to my knee;
I am defenseless utterly.
I slept, methinks, and woke, 115
And, slowly gazing, find me stripped in sleep.
In the rash lustihead of my young powers,
I shook the pillaring hours
And pulled my life upon me; grimmed with smears,
I stand amid the dust o' the mounded years— 120
My mangled youth lies dead beneath the heap.
My days have crackled and gone up in smoke,
Have puffed and burst as sun-starts on a stream.
Yea, faileth now even dream
The dreamer, and the lute the lutanist; 125
Even the linked fantasies, in whose blossomy twist
I swung the earth a trinket at my wrist,
Are yielding; cords of all too weak account
For earth with heavy griefs so overplussed.
Ah! is Thy love indeed 130
A weed, albeit an amaranthine weed,
Suffering no flowers except its own to mount?
Ah! must—
Designer infinite!—
Ah! must Thou char the wood ere Thou canst limn with it? 135
My freshness spent its wavering shower i' the dust;
And now my heart is as a broken fount,
Wherein tear-drippings stagnate, spilt down ever
From the dank thoughts that shiver
Upon the sighful branches of my mind. 140
Such is; what is to be?
The pulp so bitter, how shall taste the rind?
I dimly guess what Time in mists confounds;
Yet ever and anon a trumpet sounds
From the hid battlements of Eternity; 145
Those shaken mists a space unsettle, then
Round the half-glimpséd turrets slowly wash again.
But not ere him who summoneth
I first have seen, enwound
With glooming robes purpureal, cypress-crowned; 150
His name I know, and what his trumpet saith.

Whether man's heart or life it be which yields
The harvest, must Thy harvest fields
Be dunged with rotten death?

Now of that long pursuit 155
Comes on at hand the bruit;
That Voice is round me like a bursting sea:
"And is thy earth so marred,
Shattered in shard on shard?
Lo, all things fly thee, for thou fliest Me! 160
Strange, piteous, futile thing!
Wherefore should any set thee love apart?
Seeing none but I makes much of naught" (He said),
"And human love needs human meriting:
How hast thou merited— 165
Of all man's clotted clay the dingiest clot?
Alack, thou knowest not
How little worthy of any love thou art!
Whom wilt thou find to love ignoble thee
Save Me, save only Me? 170
All which I took from thee I did but take,
Not for thy harms,
But just that thou might'st seek it in My arms.
All which thy child's mistake
Fancies as lost, I have stored for thee at home; 175
Rise, clasp My hand, and come!"

Halts by me that footfall:
Is my gloom, after all,
Shade of His Hand, outstretched caressingly?
"Ah, fondest, blindest, weakest, 180
I am He whom thou seekest!
Thou dravest love from thee, who dravest Me."

FRANCIS THOMPSON

1. The central idea of this poem is God's pursuit of man. While the thought is clear—the pursued cannot evade God—the imagery is often obscure. The main figures, that of God, as the Hound of Heaven, and man, as his prey, are explicit at the beginning but change before the end. God is pictured as a warrior, an artist, a harvester, a living father, but, at the end, He is identified in literal images (lines 157-183). Can you justify the shift in the imagery? Why or why not?

2. This poem is rich in incidental imagery. What do the images listed below suggest? Pay close attention to the context in which they appear.

labyrinthine ways	line 3	Lucent-weeping	line 72
chasméd fears	line 8	day's dead sanctities	line 86
hearted casement	line 17	Nature, poor stepdame	line 99
silvern chatter	line 29	pillaring hours	line 118
skiey blossoms	line 31	char the wood	line 135
traitorous trueness	line 37	hid battlements	line 145
long savannahs	line 41	cypress-crowned	line 150
Plashy with flying lightnings	line 44	dunged with rotten death	line 154
Wantoning	line 65	Shade of His Hand	line 179

3. Do the theme and tone of the poem justify the use of archaic language? Why or why not?

✣ CHAPTER VIII ✣

Imagination in Poetry: Simile, Metaphor, Personification, Allegory

GENERALLY SPEAKING most figurative expression is, we have suggested, a transfer of epithet, the description of one thing in terms of another. Upon closer view we discover that there are, broadly speaking, two kinds of figure: one kind stresses resemblances, the other, contrasts. The first kind, figures of similarity, contains four closely related species: simile, metaphor, personification, and allegory.

Both simile and metaphor are based on the perception of a likeness (C) between two objects or acts (A and B). They identify a beloved (A) with a red rose (B), man's life (A) with the flight of an eagle (B). Burn's beloved (A) is like the red rose (B) in that both are incomparably fresh (C); man's life (A) is like the flight of an eagle (B) in that both are quickly over (C); Death (A) is like a bragging soldier (B) in that both are less powerful than they pretend (C).

Simile and metaphor should not be confused with simple comparison which states resemblances between things in the same class. Moreover, simple comparisons, such as those between Mary's eyes and Phyllis's eyes, between the Alps and the Apennines, the Atlantic and the Pacific are not especially vivid or intense. They create no original effect, provoke little imaginative tension. Simile and metaphor also compare two objects or acts but, unlike simple comparison, these objects are not in the same class. The basis of this figurative comparison is not abstract logic, but imagination. A beautiful woman and a rose are fused into one image in the light and heat of intense thought and feeling.

SIMILE

A *simile* expresses the identity between the two terms of a comparison by the connectives *like, as, such, thus,* or by verbs like *seems, appears, resembles, compares,* and similar expressions.

Thus in "The River of Life," Thomas Campbell identifies the passage of time with the flow of a river.

> The more we live, more brief appear
>   Our life's succeeding stages:
> A day to childhood seems a year,
>   And years like passing ages.
>
> The gladsome current of our youth, 5
>   Ere passion yet disorders,
> Steals lingering like a river smooth
>   Along its grassy borders.
>
> But as the careworn cheek grows wan,
>   And sorrow's shafts fly thicker, 10
> Ye stars, that measure life to man,
>   Why seem your courses quicker?
>
> When joys have lost their bloom and breath,
>   And life itself is vapid,
> Why, as we reach the Falls of death, 15
>   Feel we its tide more rapid?
>
> It may be strange—yet who would change
>   Time's course to slower speeding,
> When one by one our friends have gone
>   And left our bosoms bleeding? 20
>
> Heaven gives our years of fading strength
>   Indemnifying fleetness;
> And those of youth, a seeming length,
>   Proportion'd to their sweetness.

The simile between life and the river is developed throughout the poem. The river, like youth, is "gladsome" at its source; when smooth, its current is slow. At its close, as in old age, the river runs rapidly. Note, too, how the simile is aided by the thought of the poem expressed in general statements in stanzas 1, 5, 6.

METAPHOR

Metaphor is an implied comparison. Instead of saying that life flows on *like* a river, it says that life *is* a river. The omission of the conjunctives or verbs indicating explicit comparison tends to make the metaphor more compressed, more vivid, more rapid than the simile.

> My prime of years is but a frost of cares,
> My feast of joy is but a dish of pain

writes Chidiock Tichbourne in his "Written on the Eve of Execution."

> I am a parcel of vain striving tied
> By a chance bond together

writes Thoreau in "I Am a Parcel." In these lines there are no interpositions of *like* and *as* to suggest, however briefly, that imagination has linked two terms together. Explicit comparison tends to disappear under the pressure of unusual emotion. Hence, metaphor is more impetuous than simile, impatient to express urgent feelings, less interested in establishing a precise point-for-point comparison between two objects than in fusing the two objects and actions in the heat of feeling. Notice, for instance, how Shakespeare employs both figures in *Romeo and Juliet:* similes to express Romeo's first impression of Juliet's appearance as she is dancing and metaphors to express his greater excitement as he holds her hand and talks to her.

Masked as a pilgrim, Romeo first spies Juliet at the ball in the Capulet house (Act I, Scene V). He is astonished by her beauty and utters his feelings thus:

> It seems she hangs upon the cheek of night
> As a rich jewel in an Ethiop's ear;
> Beauty too rich for use, for earth too dear!
> So shows a snowy dove trooping with crows,
> As yonder lady o'er her fellows shows.

The two similes in this passage express vivid personal impressions. But they do not suggest overwhelming feeling. However, when Romeo intercepts Juliet a moment later, and seizes her hand, his language leaps over the fences of formal comparison. Here he speaks more passionately, in metaphors:

> If I profane with my unworthiest hand
> This holy shrine, the holy fine is this:
> My lips, two blushing pilgrims, ready stand
> To smooth that rough touch with a tender kiss.

In this passage the metaphor interprets the action. Romeo identifies Juliet's hand with a shrine. In touching Juliet's hand he has profaned a holy place. In a succeeding metaphor, his lips become "blushing pilgrims" ready to pay the penalty for his profanation of the shrine. The metaphors glow with feeling. Needless to say, some literal statement of this thought, such as, "If you object to my holding your hand, I'm ready to kiss that hand," would be not only banal, but unjust to Romeo's character and to the dramatic situation.

PERSONIFICATION

In *personification* the poet endows an inhuman object or an abstraction with human traits. Like the metaphor, personification implies a comparison between an object or a thought and a human being. Most poems about nature contain incidental personifications. Wordsworth describes a field of daffodils, "Tossing their heads in sprightly dance," and a daisy as "A nun demure, of lowly port. . . . A queen in crown of rubies drest." As we have seen, Keats personifies autumn as a drowsy reaper. The smiling sun, the wise stars, the angry sea, fugitive time, stern duty, relentless winter—these and a thousand other conventional expressions imputing human qualities to natural objects or abstract ideas—all testify to the extent of poets' reliance on personification to animate their portrayal of nature.

Moreover, some poems are, in effect, extended personifications. In "The Brook" (p. 150), Tennyson's brook tells of its rise in the "haunts of coot and hern," its passage by "many a field and fallow," its joining the river. The brook too philosophizes: "For men may come and men may go,/But I go on for ever." In Shelley's "The Cloud" (p. 152), the cloud speaks of its activities as if it were a highly conscious Shelley, so that the extended personification exemplifies what is now sometimes called empathy, that is, the power of projecting oneself into, or feeling with, the object of contemplation. (Closely related to personification is the device of the fable, wherein animals are given human qualities. In Chaucer's "The Nun's Priest's Tale," for instance, Chanticleer and Pertelote are counterparts of human types.)

Because personification so closely resembles simile and metaphor, it is often used in conjunction with these figures. Thus, in "To a Skylark," Shelley first addresses the bird as a blithe spirit—a being with some human traits. Later the poet develops these human characteristics by comparing the bird to a poet.

> Like a Poet hidden
>   In the light of thought,
> Singing hymns unbidden,
>   Till the world is wrought
> To sympathy with hopes and fears it heeded not:

Again, in Emily Dickinson's "The Chariot" the abstraction, Death, is personified as a kindly gentleman who calls on a lady with his coachman, Immortality, and takes her for a drive. But in the course of the drive we are less conscious of the personification than we are that the chariot is a hearse and the drive is itself a metaphor for the approach to death.

THE CHARIOT

Because I could not stop for Death,
He kindly stopped for me;
The carriage held but just ourselves
And Immortality.

We slowly drove, he knew no haste, 5
And I had put away
My labour, and my leisure too,
For his civility.

We passed the school where children played,
Their lessons scarcely done; 10
We passed the fields of grazing grain,
We passed the setting sun.

We paused before a house that seemed
A swelling on the ground;

The roof was scarcely visible, 15
The cornice but a mound.

Since then 'tis centuries; but each
Feels shorter than the day
I first surmised the horses' heads
Were toward eternity. 20

EMILY DICKINSON

ALLEGORY

A sustained metaphor such as "The Chariot" is sometimes called an *allegory*. Emily Dickinson's brief descriptive narrative has a surface meaning; the carriage passes a school, fields of grain, pauses before a house. But beneath this surface meaning is a second meaning. The drive is meant to suggest or stand for the experience of death. Although we are concurrently aware of both meanings, it is the second or allegorical meaning that is the principal one.

Here, as in *Everyman, The Faerie Queene, Pilgrim's Progress,* and *The Idylls of the King,* the literal story symbolizes or shadows a secondary story. The term allegory usually is reserved to poems that establish more precise correspondences than those in "The Chariot"; that is, the correspondences between the surface story and the implied story are more methodically developed. This is especially true when the poet attempts to draw an analogy between nature and human life, or between the divine and the human. As an instance of the first, note how evenly Keats distributes his points of resemblance in his allegory of the human seasons:

THE HUMAN SEASONS

Four seasons fill the measure of the year;
There are four seasons in the mind of man:
He has his lusty Spring, when fancy clear
Takes in all beauty with an easy span:

He has his Summer, when luxuriously 5
Spring's honey'd cud of youthful thought he loves

To ruminate, and by such dreaming high
  Is nearest unto heaven: quiet coves

His soul has in its Autumn, when his wings
  He furleth close; contented so to look 10
On mists in idleness—to let fair things
  Pass by unheeded as a threshold brook:

He has his Winter too of pale misfeature,
Or else he would forgo his mortal nature.

JOHN KEATS

In George Herbert's "Redemption" there is a point-for-point resemblance between a story on a human level and a story on a divine level. The imaginary tenant stands for the soul, the rich lord for the Savior, the lease for the soul's debts to God. Notice how closely the surface story of a tenant seeking a new lease parallels the story of a Savior who redeems, that is, remits the debts of the sinner.

Having been tenant long to a rich lord, 1
  Not thriving, I resolved to be bold,
  And made a suit unto him to afford
A new small-rented lease and cancel th' old.

The speaker, a tenant, wishes to cancel his old lease and the debts it involves and to subsitute a new lease with a smaller rent. It is a commonplace human difficulty, impersonally stated, save for a vague suggestion that, since the lord is rich, he may be either the generous man or the avaricious man. In the next four lines, however, we become aware of a second theme. The speaker seeks his lord in heaven. Note how the identification of the lord and Christ is emphasized in the inverted order of the first sentence below:

In heaven at his manor I him sought. 5
  They told me there that he was lately gone
  About some land which he had dearly bought
Long since on earth, to take possession.

The speaker's search for his lord then is a search for God. The meaning of the title, "Redemption," is suggested in the phrase "land which he had dearly bought." Land, we begin to realize, refers both to a physical property and to man's spiritual indebtedness. The rich lord has come to earth, then, to take physical possession of his land, but also to claim his spiritual dominion over man. This second interpretation of the lines grows as the parallel between the rich lord and Christ becomes unequivocal. The speaker tells how he failed to find his lord among the great, but among thieves and murderers.

> I straight returned, and knowing his great birth,
> Sought him accordingly in great resorts, 10
> In cities, theatres, gardens, parks, and courts.
> At length I heard a ragged noise and mirth
> Of thieves and murderers; there I him espied,
> Who straight, Your suit is granted, said, and died.

The last three lines allude to Christ's death on the cross—an action that redeems mankind, or, in terms of the poem, one that grants mankind's suit for quittance of the debt for sin. In the light of this reading the highly condensed and dramatic story of the speaker's successful suit for release is principally an allegory of the way a man saves his soul. The speaker is aware of his sinfulness, since he is "not thriving." He resolves to seek mercy. After searching for God in heaven, he finds Him, in the person of the Savior, on earth, on the cross.

If "Redemption" illustrates the rich suggestiveness of allegory, its simultaneous activity on two levels of meaning and its power to relate two different worlds, it also betrays its tendency toward ambiguity. At best the extended metaphor that we call an allegory sacrifices a degree of clarity to achieve greater vividness, variety and dramatic appeal. In "Redemption," for instance, while the main points of similarity are clear, certain details are cloudy. Thus the old lease may refer to the covenant between God and Man in the Old Testament, or to the speaker's state of soul before he resolved to seek forgiveness. Contrariwise, the new "small-rented lease" may mean the new contract between God and Man revealed in the New Testament, or the regenerative action of divine grace obtained through Christ. There may, indeed, be other meanings latent in these parallels.

In longer poems allegory frequently achieves a momentary

clarity, then dissolves into the mist of plural meanings. Thus, in *The Faerie Queene*, Gloriana is a figure of Queen Elizabeth I and then a symbol of indefinite glory. In *The Idylls of the King*, King Arthur is partly a symbol of virtue and partly a figure of the Victorian gentleman.

Ambiguity of some kind, then, is inherent in figures of similarity. The objects compared will be alike in some respects, unlike in others. In the case of metaphor the likeness will only be by analogy or by proportion, and these proportions are not easily determined. Thus in "A Noiseless Patient Spider," Walt Whitman compares the activity of a spider and the activity of his soul.

A noiseless patient spider,
I mark'd where on a little promontory it stood isolated,
Mark'd how to explore the vacant vast surrounding,
It launch'd forth filament, filament, filament, out of itself,
Ever unreeling them, ever tirelessly speeding them. 5

And you O my soul where you stand,
Surrounded, detached, in measureless oceans of space,
Ceaselessly musing, venturing, throwing, seeking the spheres to con-
nect them,
Till the bridge you will need be form'd, till the ductile anchor hold,
Till the gossamer thread you fling catch somewhere, O my soul. 10

Just as the spider tirelessly unrolls filament after filament in its attempt to secure its web, so the soul ceaselessly ventures to bridge the gap between its own isolation and reality outside. The activities are parallel, but not identical. To what extent they are parallel can only be suggested. But the suggestion is one that extends our knowledge, or our appreciation, of the mysterious connections between all things in the universe.

POEMS FOR DISCUSSION

THE SILKEN TENT

She is as in a field a silken tent
At midday when a sunny summer breeze
Has dried the dew and all its ropes relent,
So that in guys it gently sways at ease,

And its supporting central cedar pole, 5
That is its pinnacle to heavenward
And signifies the sureness of the soul,
Seems to owe naught to any single cord,
But strictly held by none, is loosely bound
By countless silken ties of love and thought 10
To everything on earth the compass round,
And only by one's going slightly taut
In the capriciousness of summer air
Is of the slightest bondage made aware.

ROBERT FROST

1. Trace the various points of resemblance that are developed between the woman and the tent. Is the simile apt? Why or why not?
2. Does the simile in this poem contribute to an emotional effect? If it does, what is that effect? How does the simile contribute to it?
3. Decide whether this simile is too extended for a short poem. Give reasons for your answer.

THE BROOK

I come from haunts of coot and hern,
  I make a sudden sally
And sparkle out among the fern,
  To bicker down a valley.

By thirty hills I hurry down, 5
  Or slip between the ridges,
By twenty thorps, a little town,
  And half a hundred bridges.

Till last by Philip's farm I flow
  To join the brimming river, 10
For men may come and men may go,
  But I go on for ever.

I chatter over stony ways,
  In little sharps and trebles,
I bubble into eddying bays, 15
  I babble on the pebbles.

With many a curve my banks I fret
  By many a field and fallow,

And many a fairy foreland set
  With willow-weed and mallow. 20

I chatter, chatter, as I flow
  To join the brimming river,
For men may come and men may go,
  But I go on for ever.

I wind about, and in and out, 25
  With here a blossom sailing,
And here and there a lusty trout,
  And here and there a grayling,

And here and there a foamy flake
  Upon me, as I travel 30
With many a silvery waterbreak
  Above the golden gravel,

And draw them all along, and flow
  To join the brimming river,
For men may come and men may go, 35
  But I go on for ever.

I steal by lawns and grassy plots,
  I slide by hazel covers;
I move the sweet forget-me-nots
  That grow for happy lovers. 40

I slip, I slide, I gloom, I glance,
  Among my skimming swallows;
I make the netted sunbeam dance
  Against my sandy shallows.

I murmur under moon and stars 45
  In brambly wildernesses;
I linger by my shingly bars;
  I loiter round my cresses;

And out again I curve and flow
  To join the brimming river, 50
For men may come and men may go,
  But I go on for ever.

ALFRED, LORD TENNYSON

1. Is Tennyson's personification of the brook plausible? Before framing your answer consider the age, temperament, and attitude of the fictitious person.
2. Show how the incidents described and narrated are consistent with the imagined personality.
3. Show how the images in the poem and the metrical devices unite to create an harmonious emotional effect.
4. Show how the poem successfully employs onomatopoeia, assonance, alliteration.
5. May this poem be considered allegorical? Why or why not?

THE CLOUD

I bring fresh showers for the thirsting flowers,
  From the seas and the streams;
I bear light shade for the leaves when laid
  In their noonday dreams.
From my wings are shaken the dews that waken 5
  The sweet buds every one,
When rocked to rest on their mother's breast,
  As she dances about the sun.
I wield the flail of the lashing hail,
  And whiten the green plains under, 10
And then again I dissolve it in rain,
  And laugh as I pass in thunder.

I sift the snow on the mountains below,
  And their great pines groan aghast;
And all the night 'tis my pillow white, 15
  While I sleep in the arms of the blast.
Sublime on the towers of my skiey bowers,
  Lightning my pilot sits;
In a cavern under is fettered the thunder,
  It struggles and howls at fits; 20
Over earth and ocean, with gentle motion,
  This pilot is guiding me,
Lured by the love of the genii that move
  In the depths of the purple sea;
Over the rills, and the crags, and the hills, 25
  Over the lakes and the plains,
Wherever he dream, under mountain or stream,
  The Spirit he loves remains;

And I all the while bask in Heaven's blue smile,
  Whilst he is dissolving in rains. 30

The sanguine Sunrise, with his meteor eyes,
  And his burning plumes outspread,
Leaps on the back of my sailing rack,
  When the morning star shines dead;
As on the jag of a mountain crag, 35
  Which an earthquake rocks and swings,
An eagle alit one moment may sit
  In the light of its golden wings.
And when Sunset may breathe, from the lit sea beneath,
  Its ardors of rest and of love, 40
And the crimson pall of eve may fall
  From the depth of Heaven above,
With wings folded I rest, on mine aëry nest,
  As still as a brooding dove.

That orbéd maiden with white fire laden, 45
  Whom mortals call the Moon,
Glides glimmering o'er my fleece-like floor,
  By the midnight breezes strewn;
And wherever the beat of her unseen feet,
  Which only the angels hear, 50
May have broken the woof of my tent's thin roof,
  The stars peep behind her and peer;
And I laugh to see them whirl and flee,
  Like a swarm of golden bees,
When I widen the rent in my wind-built tent, 55
  Till the calm rivers, lakes, and seas,
Like strips of the sky fallen through me on high,
  Are each paved with the moon and these.

I bind the Sun's throne with a burning zone,
  And the Moon's with a girdle of pearl; 60
The volcanoes are dim, and the stars reel and swim,
  When the whirlwinds my banner unfurl.
From cape to cape, with a bridge-like shape,
  Over a torrent sea,
Sunbeam-proof, I hang like a roof,— 65
  The mountains its columns be.
The triumphal arch, through which I march
  With hurricane, fire, and snow,

When the Powers of the air are chained to my chair,
Is the million-coloured bow; 70
The sphere-fire above its soft colours wove,
While the moist Earth was laughing below.

I am the daughter of Earth and Water,
And the nursling of the Sky;
I pass through the pores of the ocean and shores;
I change, but I cannot die.
For after the rain when with never a stain
The pavilion of Heaven is bare,
And the winds and sunbeams with their convex gleams
Build up the blue dome of air, 80
I silently laugh at my own cenotaph,
And out of the caverns of rain,
Like a child from the womb, like a ghost from the tomb,
I arise and unbuild it again.

PERCY BYSSHE SHELLEY

1. How does the fictitious person in this poem differ in age, temperament, and attitude from Tennyson's personified brook in the poem above?
2. What principle of structure (see Chapter IV) is employed in this poem? Explain.
3. In addition to the predominant figure of personification, show how the poem contains incidental metaphors and similes. Are these incidental figures consistent with the predominant one? Why or why not?
4. Show how the melody and rhythm of the lines help establish the tone of this poem.

THE SEVEN AGES OF MAN

All the world's a stage,
And all the men and women merely players: 140
They have their exits and their entrances,
And one man in his time plays many parts,
His acts being seven ages. At first the infant,
Mewling and puking in the nurse's arms.
And then the whining school-boy, with his satchel 145
And shining morning face, creeping like snail
Unwillingly to school. And then the lover,
Sighing like furnace, with a woeful ballad
Made to his mistress' eyebrow. Then a soldier,

Full of strange oaths, and bearded like the pard, 150
Jealous in honour, sudden, and quick in quarrel,
Seeking the bubble reputation
Even in the cannon's mouth. And then the justice,
In fair round belly with good capon lin'd,
With eyes severe and beard of formal cut, 155
Full of wise saws and modern instances;
And so he plays his part. The sixth age shifts
Into the lean and slipper'd pantaloon,
With spectacles on nose and pouch on side,
His youthful hose well sav'd, a world too wide 160
For his shrunk shank; and his big manly voice,
Turning again toward childish treble, pipes
And whistles in his sound. Last scene of all,
That ends this strange eventful history,
Is second childishness and mere oblivion, 165
Sans teeth, sans eyes, sans taste, sans everything.

WILLIAM SHAKESPEARE

(Act II, Scene VII, *As You Like It*)

1. Is this passage an allegory? Why or why not?
2. Compare this passage with "The Human Seasons," p. 146. Point out several similarities and differences.

TO SLEEP

O soft embalmer of the still midnight,
  Shutting, with careful fingers and benign,
Our gloom-pleas'd eyes, embower'd from the light,
  Enshaded in forgetfulness divine:
O soothest Sleep! if so it please thee, close 5
  In midst of this thine hymn, my willing eyes,
Or wait the 'Amen,' ere thy poppy throws
  Around my bed its lulling charities.
  Then save me, or the passed day will shine
Upon my pillow, breeding many woes,— 10
  Save me from curious Conscience, that still lords
Its strength for darkness, burrowing like a mole;
  Turn the key deftly in the oiled wards,
And seal the hushed Casket of my Soul.

JOHN KEATS

1. What is the predominant metaphor in this poem? Is it appropriate? Why or why not?
2. Comment on the relevance of the following metaphorical expressions in the context of the poem. Show how they are interrelated: "soft embalmer"; "thine hymn"; "lulling charities"; "oiled wards"; "hushed Casket."

SNOW

The room was suddenly rich and the great bay-window was
Spawning snow and pink roses against it
Soundlessly collateral and incompatible:
World is suddener than we fancy it.

World is crazier and more of it than we think, 5
Incorrigibly plural. I peel and portion
A tangerine and spit the pips and feel
The drunkenness of things being various.

And the fire flames with a bubbling sound for world
Is more spiteful and gay than one supposes— 10
On the tongue on the eyes on the ears in the palms of your hands—
There is more than glass between the snow and the huge roses.

LOUIS MACNEICE

1. Identify as many figurative expressions as you can.
2. Show how these figures, within the context of the poem, help to make a common experience vivid.

ALL LOVELY THINGS

All lovely things will have an ending,
All lovely things will fade and die,
And youth, that's now so bravely spending,
Will beg a penny by and by.

Fine ladies all are soon forgotten, 5
And goldenrod is dust when dead,
The sweetest flesh and flowers are rotten
And cobwebs tent the brightest head.

Come back, true love! Sweet youth, return!—
But time goes on, and will, unheeding, 10

Though hands will reach, and eyes will yearn,
And the wild days set true hearts bleeding.

Come back, true love! Sweet youth, remain!—
But goldenrod and daisies wither,
And over them blows autumn rain, 15
They pass, they pass, and know not whither.

CONRAD AIKEN

1. Point out some resemblances between the theme of this poem and that of "The River of Life" (p. 142).
2. Show how, despite the similarity of theme, the two poems differ in tone.
3. Show how the difference in tone can be explained in terms of the selection and handling of similes and metaphors.
4. Which poem do you consider more successful? Why?

❈ CHAPTER IX ❈

Imagination in Poetry: The Symbol

In previous discussions (pp. 88-100) we showed how a symbol was an object or action that, in addition to its surface meaning, implies or evokes deeper or wider meanings. We showed how Matthew Arnold's "The Scholar-Gipsy" on one level was a character in an idyll; on another, a symbol of the free and spontaneous man in contrast to the man fettered by doubt and self-contempt. In that discussion, however, we were principally concerned with the structure of thought in a particular poem. Here we will examine the symbol in more detail and see how it differs from the simple image, simile, and metaphor. We shall see, too, how a symbol is not simply an incidental detail in a poem, but the imaginative conception that endows a poem with many meanings.

A simple image is a word that refers directly to some object perceptible through the senses. Thus, in the sentence, "The tiger stalks his prey," the term *tiger* must be presumed to refer to the animal named. But, in a different context, the same word may be used figuratively, to signify the ferocity of a warrior. Thus we may use a simile such as, "Ulysses sprang like a tiger upon his foes." Or, once Ulysses' tigerlike character has been established in the context of a poem, we may use the term *tiger* as a metaphor: "The tiger [referring to Ulysses] sprang upon his foes." Thus a simple image refers to one thing, in this case, the animal named. The figures, whether simile or metaphor, refer to two dissimilar things —the tiger and Ulysses—uniting them imaginatively by virtue of a quality they possess in common (p. 141).

But we may also use the term *tiger* as a symbol. A symbol, like the metaphor, is an image that suggests or implies a relation between objects. Unlike the metaphor, however, the symbol is not simply an unexpressed comparison between two objects. The *tiger*, taken as a symbol, may refer to several objects. In short, a symbol may have multiple meanings.

Thus in William Blake's poem, "The Tiger," the tiger is not just the animal named. It is not limited to a comparison with one other object. Rather, it is an image that is meant to suggest all the forces that underlie creation. Let us examine the poem.

THE TIGER

Tiger! Tiger! burning bright
In the forests of the night,
What immortal hand or eye
Could frame thy fearful symmetry?

In what distant deeps or skies 5
Burnt the fire of thine eyes?
On what wings dare he aspire?
What the hand dare seize the fire?

And what shoulder, and what art,
Could twist the sinews of thy heart? 10
And when thy heart began to beat,
What dread hand? and what dread feet?

What the hammer? what the chain?
In what furnace was thy brain?
What the anvil? what dread grasp 15
Dare its deadly terrors clasp?

When the stars threw down their spears,
And water'd heaven with their tears,
Did he smile his work to see?
Did he who made the Lamb make thee? 20

Tiger! Tiger! burning bright
In the forests of the night,
What immortal hand or eye
Dare frame thy fearful symmetry?

WILLIAM BLAKE

At first reading we are aware of a vivid image, as of a particularly dynamic impressionistic painting. The series of rhetorical questions, hammered out on the anvils of *whats* and *ands*, clanging with strong monosyllabic rhymes, glowing with imagery of fire and light, suggest the violence in the tiger. The impact of the questions builds up to an overwhelming astonishment. Who could have framed such cruel but magnificent strength? How could he have framed it? And when he did, what did he think of his work? In one sense the questions do not require an answer, because they simply represent the poet's emotional attitude, his gasp of wonder. We may accept the poem, then, as a vivid impassioned recognition of a mysterious force.

As we reread the poem, however, we notice that there are more mysterious suggestions. Who are the stars that "threw down their spears?" Why did they weep at the creation of the destructive tiger? Who is the *he*? Why did he dare? Why was his daring associated with weeping by the stars? These questions are pointless, unless Blake intends them as speculations on the mystery of creation. Beneath the surface imagery of the poem there lurks Blake's view that creation is a struggle between two sets of mighty opposites. On one side stands the force symbolized by the tiger; on the other the force symbolized by the Lamb and the stars. The tiger stands for the presence of evil, or in Blake's language, experience; the Lamb for the presence of good, or innocence. The tiger is a symbol of violence, the Lamb a symbol of peace. The tiger stands for the dark underworld of instinct and passion; the stars for the overworld of abstract reason. Hence the stars weep and cast down their weapons, not in defiance but in acknowledgment of defeat. They have witnessed the emergence of their necessary opposite, the dark forces, symbolized by the tiger, from "the forests of the night."

The tiger then is a fearful force. But could it be he was created not to destroy, but rather to perform his appointed task according to the Divine Will? He may be, moreover, a symbol of the wrath of God, just as the Lamb is more clearly a symbol of God's mercy. Perhaps he stands for the obscure mysteries of being, whereas the stars represent the radiant clarities of thought.

Hence it is possible to read the lines,

Did he smile his work to see?
Did he who made the Lamb make thee?

not as blasphemous insinuations against the justice of God, but as expressions of awe at the wisdom of a creation that reconciles opposites and turns all things to good.

A recent interpreter of this poem declares that "we can be confident that the fifth stanza shows the dread tiger to be not only a divine creation but also, despite its dreadfulness, an aspect of the Divine Will, at whatever level we read the poem. . . ."* The poem as a whole "emerges quite clearly as a complex but essentially positive statement affirming the dread tiger's divinity."** These statements may well be true. Nevertheless, the general reader need not hesitate to regard the poem as obscure. For, despite the vividness and the clarity with which Blake expresses his astonishment, the total meaning of the poem cannot be reduced to one unambiguous meaning. If, as has been shown, Blake struggled to embody many meanings in his poem, we need not be surprised if his readers, recreating his complex poetic experience according to their own sensibilities, will discover additional meanings. A reader of Milton, for instance, may associate the tiger with Lucifer. Or, again, a reader of Dante may discover a resemblance between the tiger and the lion that stood in Dante's path (Inferno I). But the presence of many meanings is not necessarily a defect in a poem. Rather, it witnesses to an encounter with reality, and reality is a mystery truly inexhaustible.

CONVENTIONAL SYMBOLS AND PERSONAL SYMBOLS

In one sense the tiger is a conventional symbol; everyone recognizes that the tiger stands for violence. But the tiger is also a personal symbol, that is, one derived from Blake's own experience made partly understandable by the context of the poem, and partly by the context of Blake's thought in general. A personal symbol is more difficult to understand fully than a conventional symbol. Thus we understand conventional symbols readily; for example, a river represents the flow of life, sleep suggests death, the ocean signifies infinity, a withered tree conveys the idea of

* Martin K. Nurmi, "Blake's Revisions of *The Tyger*," *PMLA,* LXXI, Part 1 (September 1951), p. 674.

** *Ibid.,* p. 670.

sterility, an up-hill climb portrays struggle. Christina Rossetti's "Uphill," for instance, presents few difficulties.

> Does the road wind up-hill all the way?
> Yes, to the very end.
> Will the day's journey take the whole long day?
> From morn to night, my friend.
>
> But is there for the night a resting-place? 5
> A roof for when the slow dark hours begin.
> May not the darkness hide it from my face?
> You cannot miss that inn.
>
> Shall I meet other wayfarers at night?
> Those who have gone before. 10
> Then must I knock, or call when just in sight?
> They will not keep you standing at that door.
>
> Shall I find comfort, travel-sore and weak?
> Of labour you shall find the sum.
> Will there be beds for me and all who seek? 15
> Yea, beds for all who come.

We are unable, however, to grasp immediately, or completely, the meaning of highly personal symbols. Thus, for example, in T. S. Eliot's "Burnt Norton," a rose garden, which many readers take to be a *natural* or conventional symbol for secluded beauty, is a *personal* symbol for a time, a place, an experience of pleasure or pain. It is the fundamental intuition of the meaning of life grasped in childhood, but pondered and more vividly understood in maturity.

A persistent symbol employed through Eliot's poetry, the rose garden does not display the same surface clarity as the uphill climb in Christina Rossetti's poem.

> Footfalls echo in the memory
> Down the passage which we did not take
> Towards the door we never opened
> Into the rose-garden. My words echo

Thus, in your mind. 15
But to what purpose
Disturbing the dust on a bowl of rose-leaves
I do not know.
Other echoes
Inhabit the garden. Shall we follow? 20
Quick, said the bird, find them, find them,
Round the corner. Through the first gate,
Into our first world, shall we follow
The deception of the thrush? . . . .

T. S. ELIOT
(From "Burnt Norton")

Yet, persistent study of Eliot's use of the rose garden symbol suggests that it means for Eliot a memorable instant in which the world of sense emerges into moral and spiritual significance. It evokes an aura of intense feeling, a struggle to recover a lost memory.

Symbols like the rose garden, bubbling from the wells of the subconscious—"But to what purpose . . . I do not know"—often resemble the elliptical movements of a dream. They are alternately blurred and distinct, and always portentous. Sometimes the blurred symbol is felt with more immediacy and greater excitement than the clearer conventional image that, revealing its meaning more exactly, also empties itself of mystery. To the sophisticated reader of poetry there is sometimes more challenge in discovering what a personal symbol means. Thus, in Wallace Steven's "Anecdote of the Jar," the significance of the jar is not immediately evident. At first glance it appears merely to stand in some opposition to a slovenly wilderness.

I placed a jar in Tennessee
And round it was, upon a hill.
It made the slovenly wilderness
Surround that hill.

In the next stanza the jar seems to have conquered the wilderness. We may be tempted to take it as a symbol of art's superiority to nature, for it has a position, symmetry, and dignity that rebuffs the sprawling wilderness.

The wilderness rose up to it,
And sprawled around, no longer wild.
The jar was round upon the ground
And tall and of a port in air.

But in the third stanza the jar takes on another meaning. It is gray, bare, sterile. It now stands for the dominion of the machine over nature.

It took dominion everywhere,
The jar was gray and bare.
It did not give a bird or bush,
Like nothing else in Tennessee.

The jar thus becomes a symbol of man's interference with nature.

In short, some personal symbols, however much they express meaning for the poet himself, do not always communicate clear impressions to the reader.* We must always allow for the congenital ambiguity of symbolism, and for the poet's privilege of addressing only those readers who are willing, by extended effort if necessary, to re-create his experience. Profound poetry is necessarily difficult; but difficult poetry is not necessarily profound. Some difficult poetry may well be described as the work of lazy or self-indulgent writers. G. K. Chesterton was thinking of the difficult but not profound poetry when he wrote his celebrated parody, "To a Modern Poet."

Well,
What
about it?

I am sorry
if you have 5
a green pain
gnawing your brain away
I suppose
quite a lot of it is
gnawed away 10
by this time.

* For a further discussion of obscurity in modern poetry, see p. 332.

I did not give you
a green pain
or even
a grey powder. 15
It is rather you, so winged, so vortical,
who give me a pain.

When I have a pain
I never notice
the colour. 20

But I am very unobservant.
I cannot say
I ever noticed that the pillar-box
was like a baby
skinned alive and screaming. 25
I have not
a Poet's
Eye
which can see Beauty
everywhere. 30

Now you mention it,
of course, the sky
is like a large mouth
shown to a dentist,
and I never noticed 35
a little thing
like that.

But I can't help wishing
you got more fun out of it;
you seem to have taken 40
quite a dislike
to things
They seem to make you jump
And double up unexpectedly—

And when you write 45
like other poets,
on subjects
not entirely
novel

such as, for instance, 50
the Sea,
it is mostly about
Sea-sickness.
As you say—
It is the New Movement, 55
the Emetic Ecstasy.

POEMS FOR DISCUSSION

PRELUDES

(I)

The winter evening settles down
With smell of steaks in passageways.
Six o'clock.
The burnt-out ends of smoky days.
And now a gusty shower wraps 5
The grimy scraps
Of withered leaves about your feet
And newspapers from vacant lots;
The showers beat
On broken blinds and chimney-pots, 10
And at the corner of the street
A lonely cab-horse steams and stamps.
And then the lighting of the lamps.

(II)

The morning comes to consciousness
Of faint stale smells of beer 15
From the sawdust-trampled street
With all its muddy feet that press
To early coffee-stands.
With the other masquerades
That time resumes, 20
One thinks of all the hands
That are raising dingy shades
In a thousand furnished rooms.

(III)

You tossed a blanket from the bed,
You lay upon your back, and waited; 25

You dozed, and watched the night revealing
The thousand sordid images
Of which your soul was constituted;
They flickered against the ceiling.
And when all the world came back 30
And the light crept up between the shutters,
And you heard the sparrows in the gutters,
You had such a vision of the street
As the street hardly understands;
Sitting along the bed's edge, where 35
You curled the papers from your hair,
Or clasped the yellow soles of feet
In the palms of both soiled hands.

(IV)

His soul stretched tight across the skies
That fade behind a city block, 40
Or trampled by insistent feet
At four and five and six o'clock;
And short square fingers stuffing pipes,
And evening newspapers, and eyes
Assured of certain certainties, 45
The conscience of a blackened street
Impatient to assume the world.

I am moved by fancies that are curled
Around these images, and cling:
The notion of some infinitely gentle 50
Infinitely suffering thing.

Wipe your hand across your mouth, and laugh;
The worlds revolve like ancient women
Gathering fuel in vacant lots.

T. S. ELIOT

1. What is the significance of the title? Show how this poem moves from objective description (Stanzas I, II) to symbolic reference (Stanzas III, IV).
2. Can you account for the shift in point of view: first from that of a speaker addressing no one in particular, to that of a speaker directly addressing you, line 24, then to that of another person, line 39, and finally to that of the poet, line 48? What additional insight does each point of view afford?

3. Decide whether the last three lines sum up the main impression of the poem.

TO HELEN

Helen, thy beauty is to me
  Like those Nicéan barks of yore,
That gently, o'er a perfumed sea,
  The weary, way-worn wanderer bore
  To his own native shore. 5

On desperate seas long wont to roam,
  Thy hyacinth hair, thy classic face,
Thy Naiad airs have brought me home
  To the glory that was Greece,
  And the grandeur that was Rome. 10

Lo! in yon brilliant window-niche
  How statue-like I see thee stand,
The agate lamp within thy hand!
  Ah, Psyche, from the regions which
  Are Holy-Land! 15

EDGAR ALLAN POE

1. In the first stanza, is the comparison between Helen's beauty and a Nicean bark appropriate? Why or why not?
2. How is the imagery in the second stanza connected with that in the first? Explain.
3. How is the imagery of the third stanza connected with that of the second stanza? Explain.
4. What elements in the concluding stanza suggest that Helen is a symbol of ideal love? Explain.
5. Show how this poem moves from simple imagery and simile to symbolic statement.

TEARS, IDLE TEARS

Tears, idle tears, I know not what they mean,
Tears from the depth of some divine despair
Rise in the heart, and gather to the eyes,
In looking on the happy Autumn-fields,
And thinking of the days that are no more. 5

Fresh as the first beam glittering on a sail,
That brings our friends up from the underworld,
Sad as the last which reddens over one
That sinks with all we love below the verge;
So sad, so fresh, the days that are no more. 10

Ah, sad and strange as in dark summer dawns
The earliest pipe of half-awakened birds
To dying ears, when unto dying eyes
The casement slowly grows a glimmering square;
So sad, so strange, the days that are no more. 15

Dear as remembered kisses after death,
And sweet as those by hopeless fancy feigned
On lips that are for others; deep as love,
Deep as first love, and wild with all regret;
O Death in Life, the days that are no more. 20

ALFRED, LORD TENNYSON

(From *The Princess*)

1. Are the tears really idle or do they spring from experience felt and understood? Explain.
2. Point out a paradox in stanzas 1, 2, and 4. Are these paradoxes closely linked with irony? If so, show how.
3. Do you detect any personal symbols in this poem? Explain.

THE ALBATROSS

Sometimes, for sport, the men of the crew
Will snare a bird, the vast albatross,
That indolent companion of voyage, who
Follows their glide through bitter gulfs.

Scarcely is their victim decoyed to deck 5
When that king of azure, shameful and gauche,
Piteously lets his great wings wreck
Like oars that trail an unmanned boat.

The winged voyager grows clumsy and weak.
The beautiful swimmer now seems a clown. 10
One, to torment, props a pipe in his beak,
Another limps him high and down.

The Poet is like that prince of the clouds
Who frequents the storm, the archer mocks;
Exiled aground in sporting crowds, 15
His giant wings will not let him walk.

CHARLES BAUDELAIRE

(Translated by Warren Carrier)

1. What does the albatross symbolize?
2. At what point does the symbol become clear?
3. Does the simile in the fourth stanza make the symbol too clear? Why or why not?

THE PANTHER

From bending always over bars, his glance
Holds nothing more, grown tired, as if there curled
Against him but a thousand bars expanse,
Behind a thousand bars no other world.

The wary walking of that strong stride, dark 5
Around the littlest circle of his land
Is like a dance of power around an arc
Where, stupefied, a mighty Will may stand.

Only sometimes the live lid of the eye
Lifts, and an image enters quietly, 10
Travels the taut, still limbs without a cry—
And ceases in the heart to be.

RAINER MARIA RILKE

(Translated by Paul Engle)

1. What expressions in this poem suggest that the poet is attempting to convey something more than a vivid picture of the panther? What is that something more? Explain.
2. Have Rilke's "The Panther" and Blake's "The Tiger" anything in common? How do they differ? Explain.
3. In what sense may this poem be considered more successful than "The Albatross"? Explain.

⁜ CHAPTER X ⁜

Imagination in Poetry: Contrast, Paradox and Irony

THE IMAGINATION delights in discovering the likenesses between objects and actions and in expressing these likenesses in similes, metaphors, symbols, allegories and parables; it delights no less in discovering the real and seeming contradictions between like objects and like activities and in expressing those contradictions by way of witty contrast, paradox, irony, understatement and overstatement. For contrast, no less than comparison, is a natural habit of imaginative thinking combined with strong feeling. In moments of stress Hamlet contrasts the virtues of his father with the vices of his uncle, the outward beauty of the world with its inner decay. In Dante's "Inferno" the suffering of the damned, rendered immensely vivid by comparisons and figures of similarity, is yet further intensified by contrast with the joys of the blessed. Indeed, most poems—excepting the briefest lyrics—imply some kind of contrast, for contrast is basically a witness to the complex realities the poet is talking about, and to the necessity of sometimes stating those realities in terms of their opposites.

CONTRAST

In *contrast* we contemplate an object or event in its relation to its opposite or contrary. To view London in terms of its opposite, the unspoiled Lake country, as in Wordsworth's "September, 1802," or the unheroic milieu of the 1920's in contrast to the heroic past, as in T. S. Eliot's "The Wasteland," or the modern worship of the dynamo as opposed to the medieval worship of the Virgin as in Henry Adam's "The Virgin and the Dynamo," is to bring together, within a single focus, an enormous range of human experience. Just as the musician enriches his melody by counterpoint, or as a painter deepens his perceptions by figures in perspective, so the poet makes us see the present in terms of the past, change in terms of permanence, summer in terms of winter, darkness in terms of light. Thus, in Robert Burns's "John Anderson My Jo" (p. 114), the speaker, a woman brimming with affection for the husband she still calls sweetheart, sees him simultaneously as a balding, white-haired old man, tottering toward the grave, and as the smooth-browed, raven-haired young man with whom she spent many a merry day.

The contrast in "John Anderson My Jo," set off in the expressions "But now," and "Now we maun," suggests a complete experience. The telescopic view of past, present and future, the memory of commingled joy and sorrow, the sense of the tragic passage of time and the triumphant permanence of love and constancy, are all connoted by the contrasts. In longer poems, *The Divine Comedy*, for instance, where each figure evokes its opposite figure, as a shadow does its substance, the sense of complete understanding is more fully gratified.

PARADOX

Stemming from contrast is the figurative device of *paradox*. Paradox, as the word implies, is an apparent contradiction that is superficially false but in a deeper sense true. Thus, when we say, "silence is eloquent," we are in a literal sense contradicting ourselves. Silence is an absence of speech; eloquence is full and persuasive speech. Yet, in a figurative sense, silence is eloquent because, in certain contexts, as in Jesus's silence before Caiphas, failure to speak testifies to the malice of the accusers. Or again, when we say that "one must lose one's life in order to save it" we are in a literal sense speaking absurdly, but in a figurative sense we are uttering a truth. In that statement we imply that there is a contrast between one kind of life (physical life) and another kind of life (spiritual life). Moreover, we imply that, in some instances, physical life—the reckless enjoyment of senses and appetites—may destroy the life of the spirit, as in the case of those whose god is their belly. Similarly, when we speak of a wise fool, or the ignorance of science, or a happy fault, or the foolish wisdom of love, or the absurdity of logic, or the irregularity of rules, we imply in each case a contrast between a superficial, literal meaning and a deeper, figurative meaning. The fool thinks he is wise, but isn't; science, one kind of knowledge, may attempt to contradict other kinds of knowledge; a fault, even a serious crime, can be called happy if it results in the reformation of the criminal; love's wisdom is foolish in terms of selfishness but not in terms of its own desire for sacrifice; logic is absurd when it attempts to reduce irreducibly complex human problems to purely abstract terms; rules (regularity) are irregular because they must be applied differently in each case.

Paradoxical statements abound in the works of most poets: "Our birth is but a sleep and a forgetting" (Wordsworth); "O world invisible we view thee" (Thompson); "Others by going ahead advance, I by going back" (Vaughan); "So shalt thou feed on Death, that feeds on men" (Shakespeare); "Strength stoops unto the grave" (Nash); "They also serve who only stand and wait" (Milton); "Two paradises t'were in one,/ To live in paradise alone" (Marvel); "Heard melodies are sweet, but those unheard/ Are sweeter" (Keats); "All his vows be such,/ As what he loves may never like too much" (Ben Jonson); "And Death shall be no more: Death, thou shall die" (Donne). To these we might add Dante Rossetti's lines on the sonnet:

> A sonnet is a moment's monument—
> Memorial from the soul's eternity
> To one dead, deathless hour.

Apart from their context in the poems, these paradoxical statements are short, pithy, vivid and, above all, challenging. Like Wordsworth's ideal woman, they haunt, startle and waylay. They compel us to question their seeming errors and by thinking deeply and seeing more sharply to penetrate to the real truth that they contain. In the context of the poems, however, these paradoxes are more than verbal statements. They point, rather, to the contrasts inherent in life itself. Reality is itself paradoxical, embracing as it does a host of contraries—some humorous, some pathetic, some tragic. In serious poetry, the verbal paradox is the manifestation of the paradox that exists in being itself. Thus, in John Donne's well-known Holy Sonnets, or in the less familiar "A Song of Divine Love" by Richard Crashaw, the play upon the words life in death and death in life is not merely a startling verbal gesture, nor yet an unconscious display of the baroque love of intricate craftsmanship. Rather, it is the external manifestation of the Christian's awareness of the coexistence of supernatural and natural life. This coexistence breeds the kind of tension whose proper expression is paradox.

A SONG OF DIVINE LOVE

Lord, when the sense of thy sweet grace
Sends up my soul to seek thy face,
Thy blessèd eyes breed such desire
I die in love's delicious fire.
O love, I am thy sacrifice. 5
Be still triumphant, blessèd eyes.
Still shine on me, fair suns, that I
Still may behold though still I die.

Though still I die, I live again,
Still longing so to be still slain; 10
So gainful is such loss of breath,
I die even in desire of death.
Still live in me this loving strife
Of living death and dying life:
For while thou sweetly slayest me, 15
Dead to myself, I live in Thee.

RICHARD CRASHAW

In Crashaw's poem the verbal paradoxes about life in death and death in life are readily identified, particularly in the second stanza. But these paradoxes are not meant merely to gain attention by their apparent absurdity. They are meant to dramatize the belief that, for a Christian, he loses his life in order to gain it.

That paradox is in things—in a situation and not simply in words—may be determined, too, from the very large body of poetry that dramatizes the contrary feelings that spring up in virtually all serious searching of experience. In Thomas Hardy's "The Darkling Thrush," for instance, the speaker, steeped in despair, is yet aware of the presence of some blessed hope.

I leant upon a coppice gate
    When Frost was spectre-gray,
And Winter's dregs made desolate
    The weakening eye of day.
The tangled bine-stems scored the sky 5
    Like strings of broken lyres,
And all mankind that haunted nigh
    Had sought their household fires.

The land's sharp features seemed to be
    The Century's corpse outleant, 10
His crypt the cloudy canopy,
    The wind his death-lament.
The ancient pulse of germ and birth
    Was shrunken hard and dry,
And every spirit upon earth 15
    Seemed fervourless as I.

At once a voice arose among
    The bleak twigs overhead
In a full-hearted evensong
    Of joy illimited; 20
An aged thrush, frail, gaunt, and small,
    In blast-beruffled plume,
Had chosen thus to fling his soul
    Upon the growing gloom.

So little cause for carolings 25
    Of such ecstatic sound
Was written on terrestrial things
    Afar or nigh around,
That I could think there trembled through
    His happy good-night air 30
Some blessed Hope, whereof he knew
    And I was unaware.

In the first two stanzas images of death ("spectre-gray," "the Century's corpse," "cloudy canopy," "death lament"), of inanition and decay ("dregs," "weakening eye," "shrunken hard and dry," "broken lyres"), establish a mood of unrelieved despair. The fervorless mood of the speaker, the tone of the time and place, all conspire to create a feeling of gloom. But this experience is too one-sided. Note how it is at once relieved and completed in the concluding stanzas.

Here the presence of joy modifies, but does not cancel, the previous impression of sadness. It is still a bleak world, with little apparent cause for ecstasy. The thrush is aged, gaunt, small and blast-beruffled. But the joy coexists somehow with sadness. This coexistence is part of the paradox of life. Without the aged thrush we would have a unified composition, but an incomplete human experience.

IRONY

Irony is closely related to paradox in that it, too, is a figure of contrast. As a figure of speech, irony (literally, dissembled speech) refers to a statement that indicates a meaning opposite or contrary to what is actually said. In short, an ironical statement, or verbal irony, says one thing and means another.

Verbal irony is a commonplace of ordinary speech, where it has many employments. It is used humorously, as in calling a baby Goliath to emphasize the infant's tininess. Or, contrariwise, we sometimes describe a giant as a Tiny Tim, meaning by this understatement to emphasize his immense size. Verbal irony is used, too, in satire or ridicule. A book reviewer, commenting on a writer's omission of Napoleon's name in an account of the rise of the French Empire, might say: "Napoleon has not been mentioned, although it is commonly believed that he is an important person in the history of the period." Or, in a more sardonic way, we may hear a well-known swindler described as "the model of the good, simon-pure business man."

But these examples of verbal irony are, on the whole, obvious. In poetry and literature irony is used more subtly to attract the attention of the reader and then to compel him to explore the imaginative implications of the writer's statement. In the lines below, the words *fame* and *unknown* are ironically contrasted.

> Mark how my fame rings out from zone to zone:
> A thousand critics shouting: "He's unknown."
>
> AMBROSE BIERCE

Needless to say, verbal irony is a difficult, and sometimes a dangerous device. In oral discourse, the ironical intention may be conveyed by the tone of voice, gestures, and facial expressions.

The poet, on the other hand, must depend upon the reader to be alert to the verbal counterparts of voice, gesture, and expression. He invites the reader to read between the lines. In "The Latest Decalogue" (p. 181), Arthur Hugh Clough begins with a statement that seems to convey a literal religious meaning. But then he shifts immediately to a mocking tone. He wants the reader to realize that the speaker in the poem is not to be understood literally.

Conceivably, a literal-minded reader might regard this poem as a manifesto, so to speak, of a hard-headed, cynical businessman. But to understand the poem in this way would be to mistake its ironical intention—an intention clearly implied by the selfish, worldly interpretation of each commandment, and by the cynical tone of these interpretations. The total effect of the poem is to underline the contrast between the true and false interpretation of the commandments.

Verbal irony is especially effective when it comes suddenly, with the shock of revelation. When this happens, the reader sees, often in one explosive word, the essential meaning of human experience. Such is the case in W. H. Auden's poem "In Schrafft's", where the verbal irony of the word *tabernacled* suddenly charges the poem with new meaning.

IN SCHRAFFT'S

Having finished the Blue-plate Special
And reached the coffee stage,
Stirring her cup she sat,
A somewhat shapeless figure
Of indeterminate age 5
In an undistinguished hat.

When she lifted her eyes it was plain
That our globular furore,
Our international rout
Of sin and apparatus 10
And dying men galore,
Was not being bothered about.

Which of the seven heavens
Was responsible her smile

Wouldn't be sure but attested
That, whoever it was, a god
Worth kneeling-to for a while
Had tabernacled and rested. 15

W. H. AUDEN

The first stanza contains a literal description of an undistinguished, middle-aged woman just finishing an ordinary dinner at an ordinary restaurant. In the second stanza her character is explained. Her eyes give no sign that she is aware of the world she lives in. Spiritually unconscious of crisis and confusion, she is a type, perhaps even a caricature, of the self-centered, bourgeois, "ordinary" person who avoids being bothered by anything that does not directly concern herself.

The language of the speaker is literal from the beginning up until the first few lines of the third stanza. Then, suddenly, the word *tabernacled* makes the reader reconsider. What does tabernacled mean in the context of this poem? Literally, it means, in its verb form, "to dwell for a time, to sojourn."* But, figuratively, it usually means "the sojourning of Christ on earth, or 'in the flesh,' and the indwelling of the Spirit of Christ."** In this poem, then, the word compels the attentive reader to imagine that some unknown god, possibly the god of alimentary gratification who is responsible for her smile, is dwelling and resting in the woman's body. Inevitably, too, the attentive reader will perceive an implied contrast between this sensuous "communion" and the way a devout communicant receives Christ into his own body and soul. Hence, the word tabernacled expresses a daring, indeed, an appalling irony. By indirection it suggests that the woman is unaware, for the moment at least, of the deeper meanings of the human spirit, just as she is unaware of war, sin, and death.

Irony of Situation

In verbal irony a speaker says one thing and means another. Sometimes, however, a situation or an event may involve an irony, even though the language is literal. Irony of situation may be defined as "a contradictory outcome of events as if in mockery of

* *Shorter Oxford English Dictionary.*
** *Ibid.*

the promise and fitness of things."* Hence, in ordinary speech, we call a situation ironic when our normal expectations of success or failure, or of reward or punishment, are upset. We expect the honor student in a class to achieve high grades on his examination. If he fails that examination, we call the failure ironic. On the other hand we expect some one who neglects to study to fail his examination. If he succeeds in passing we call that success ironic.

The poet, however, is usually concerned with those ironies that touch the deeper springs of thought and feeling. The great dramatic poets, particularly the Greeks, frequently explore the ironic situation involving an essentially good man, worthy of success and honor, who falls into disgrace and misfortune because of a forgivable fault, or perhaps even because of an excess of virtue. A classic instance is the case of Oedipus in Sophocles' play of the same name, where, Oedipus unknowingly brings about his own downfall.

Other instances of irony have already been seen. "The Man He Killed" (p. 18) involves the ironic situation of a soldier who would have treated his enemy had he met him in an inn, but, through the irony of war, had been forced to shoot him down. "Is My Team Ploughing?" (p. 84) develops another ironic situation, that of the dead man who finds himself soon forgotten. Still another ironic situation, that of the rich man who is seemingly successful but really miserably unhappy, is the theme of E. A. Robinson's "Richard Cory" (p. 53).

Closely related to irony of situation is *dramatic irony,* a term that is frequently employed in the criticism of tragic drama. This kind of irony presupposes superior knowledge on the part of the reader who can thus recognize that a speaker's thoughts or actions will not develop as the speaker plans or hopes. In *Othello,* when Desdemona intercedes with Othello on behalf of Cassio, the reader recognizes that her hopes of success are foolish, since Othello is already unjustly suspicious.

To sum up, both paradox and irony refer to the figurative use of language and to events or situations. Their purpose is to stimulate the reader to a greater awareness of the complexity of human experience.

* *Ibid.*

POEMS FOR DISCUSSION

IN WASTE PLACES

As a naked man I go
Through the desert, sore afraid;
Holding high my head, although
I'm as frightened as a maid.

The lion crouches there! I saw 5
In barren rocks his amber eye!
He parts the cactus with his paw!
He stares at me as I go by!

He would pad upon my trace
If he thought I was afraid! 10
If he knew my hardy face
Veils the terrors of a maid.

He rises in the night-time, and
He stretches forth! He snuffs the air!
He roars! He leaps along the sand! 15
He creeps! He watches everywhere!

His burning eyes, his eyes of bale
Through the darkness I can see!
He lashes fiercely with his tail!
He makes again to spring at me! 20

I am the lion, and his lair!
I am the fear that frightens me!
I am the desert of despair!
And the night of agony!

Night or day, whate'er befall, 25
I must walk that desert land,
Until I dare my fear and call
The lion out to lick my hand.

JAMES STEPHENS

1. Decide whether this poem contains paradox, or irony, or both. Explain. Does it contain other figures of speech? Point them out.

2. Show how the figurative expressions contribute to the total effect of the poem.
3. Point out some resemblance between this poem and "The Tiger" (p. 159).

THE LATEST DECALOGUE

Thou shalt have one God only; who
Would be at the expense of two?
No graven images may be
Worshiped, except the currency!
Swear not at all; for, for thy curse 5
Thine enemy is none the worse:
At church on Sunday to attend
Will serve to keep the world thy friend:
Honor thy parents; that is, all
From whom advancement may befall: 10
Thou shalt not kill; but need'st not strive
Officiously to keep alive:
Do not adultery commit;
Advantage rarely comes of it:
Thou shalt not steal; an empty feat, 15
When it's so lucrative to cheat:
Bear not false witness; let the lie
Have time on its own wings to fly:
Thou shalt not covet, but tradition
Approves all forms of competition. 20

The sum of all is, thou shalt love,
If any body, God above:
At any rate shall never labour
More than thyself to love thy neighbour.

ARTHUR HUGH CLOUGH

1. Compare the use of irony in this poem with the use of irony in "In Schrafft's."

THE SCHOLARS

Bald heads forgetful of their sins,
Old, learned, respectable bald heads
Edit and annotate the lines
That young men, tossing on their beds,

Rhymed out in love's despair 5
To flatter beauty's ignorant ear.

All shuffle there; all cough in ink;
All wear the carpet with their shoes;
All think what other people think;
All know the man their neighbour knows. 10
Lord, what would they say
Did their Catullus walk that way?

WILLIAM BUTLER YEATS

1. Is the last line the climactic irony of this poem? Why or why not?
2. Comment on the aptness of the expressions below in the context of this poem:
"beauty's ignorant ear"; "all cough in ink"; "what other people think."

THE DUNCE

And "Science" said,
"Attention, Child, to me!
Have I not taught you all
You touch; taste; hear; and see?

"Naught that's true knowledge now 5
In print is pent
Which my sole method
Did not circumvent.

"Think you, the amoeba
In its primal slime 10
Wasted on dreams
Its destiny sublime?

"Yet, when I bid
Your eyes survey the board
Whereon life's How, When, Where 15
I now record,

"I find them fixed
In daydream; and you sigh;
Or, like a silly sheep,
You bleat me, *Why?* 20

"'Why is the grass so cool, and fresh, and green?
The sky so deep, and blue?'
Get to your Chemistry,
You dullard, you!

"'Why must I sit at books, and learn, and learn,
Yet long to play?'
Where's your Psychology,
You popinjay?

"'Why stay I here,
Not where my heart would be?' 30
Wait, dunce, and ask that
Of Philosophy!

"Reason is yours
Wherewith to con your task;
Not that unanswerable 35
Questions you should ask.

"Stretch out your hands, then—
Grubby, shallow bowl—
And be refreshed, Child—
Mind, and, maybe, soul! 40

"Then—when you grow into
A man—like me;
You will as learnèd, wise,
And—happy be!"

WALTER DE LA MARE

1. Who is the dunce? What makes you sure?
2. Is the irony in this poem more or less effective than that of "The Scholars"? Why or why not?

❈ CHAPTER XI ❈

Types of Poetry: The Lyric, Sonnet, Elegy, Ode

THE PRECEDING chapters have dealt principally with the essentials of poetry, that is, with those elements that are common to all kinds of poetry. Thus, the song as well as the epic, the sonnet no less than the poetic drama, will embody in a meaningful structure of language the elements of emotion, thought, and imagination, and all the concomitant delights that derive from their harmonious development. But each poem contains these essentials in decidedly different ways. In the next two chapters we shall explore the different ways these elements are present in lyric, narrative, and dramatic poetry.

This threefold division is as ancient as poetry itself. True, these terms have acquired new meanings since they were first established. The ancient lyric, once a brief song by a single person, is now considered to be almost any kind of personal expression in verse. True also, the lyric has mingled with the narrative and the drama, just as those two types of poetry have increasingly absorbed lyrical elements. As a result, many writers on poetry refuse to distinguish among the various types. But, though each original type has fused with the others, the division of poetry into lyric, narrative, and dramatic forms is as necessary as it is useful.

This division is necessary because each type describes a different kind of poetic experience, and a different attitude to that experience. Thus, the lyric is normally concerned with a highly intense moment of experience, one that requires direct, brief utterance. In "When First We Met" by Robert Bridges, the poet's attitude towards his experience is highly subjective and personal.

He tells us few details of a lover's quarrel, but in a concentrated way he expresses his personal attitude of sore distress.

WHEN FIRST WE MET

When first we met we did not guess
That Love would prove so hard a master;
Of more than common friendliness
When first we met we did not guess.
Who could foretell this sore distress
This irretrievable disaster
When first we met?—We did not guess
That Love would prove so hard a master.

ROBERT BRIDGES

This lyric, we notice also, is concerned with a *present* attitude —how the speaker feels at the moment of writing, even though the events of the poem are set in the past.

The narrative poem, on the other hand, is primarily concerned with an action or event that happened in the *past*. Moreover, the attitude of a narrator is necessarily more objective even when, as in "Richard Cory" (p. 53), the poet's personal feelings are clearly suggested by the irony of the story.

The dramatic poem resembles the narrative in that it, too, tells a story about some event that happened in the past. But, unlike the narrative poem, the dramatic poem presents the action by way of a character. Thus, Browning does not directly tell the story of "My Last Duchess."

That's my last Duchess painted on the wall,
Looking as if she were alive. I call
That piece a wonder, now: Frà Pandolf's hands
Worked busily a day, and there she stands.
Will't please you sit and look at her? I said 5
"Frà Pandolf" by design, for never read
Strangers like you that pictured countenance,
The depth and passion of its earnest glance,
But to myself they turned (since none puts by
The curtain I have drawn for you, but I) 10
And seemed as they would ask me, if they durst,
How such a glance came there; so, not the first

Are you to turn and ask thus. Sir, 'twas not
Her husband's presence only, called that spot
Of joy into the Duchess' cheek: perhaps 15
Frà Pandolf chanced to say, "Her mantle laps
Over my lady's wrist too much," or "Paint
Must never hope to reproduce the faint
Half-flush that dies along her throat"; such stuff
Was courtesy, she thought, and cause enough 20
For calling up that spot of joy. She had
A heart—how shall I say?—too soon made glad,
Too easily impressed: she liked whate'er
She looked on, and her looks went everywhere.
Sir, 'twas all one! My favour at her breast, 25
The dropping of the daylight in the West,
The bough of cherries some officious fool
Broke in the orchard for her, the white mule
She rode with round the terrace—all and each
Would draw from her alike the approving speech, 30
Or blush, at least. She thanked men,—good! but thanked
Somehow—I know not how—as if she ranked
My gift of a nine-hundred-years-old name
With anybody's gift. Who'd stoop to blame
This sort of trifling? Even had you skill 35
In speech—(which I have not)—to make your will
Quite clear to such an one, and say, "Just this
Or that in you disgusts me; here you miss,
Or there exceed the mark"—and if she let
Herself be lessoned so, nor plainly set 40
Her wits to yours, forsooth, and made excuse,
—E'en then would be some stooping; and I choose
Never to stoop. Oh sir, she smiled, no doubt,
Whene'er I passed her; but who passed without
Much the same smile? This grew; I gave commands; 45
Then all smiles stopped together. There she stands
As if alive. Will't please you rise? We'll meet
The company below, then. I repeat,
The Count your master's known munificence
Is ample warrant that no just pretence 50
Of mine for dowry will be disallowed;
Though his fair daughter's self, as I avowed
At starting, is my object. Nay, we'll go
Together down, sir. Notice Neptune, though,
Taming a sea-horse, thought a rarity, 55
Which Claus of Innsbruck cast in bronze for me!

Note, too, that, while the action of this dramatic poem is in the past, it is presented as if it were happening now. Thus, the dramatic poem deals with an experience that is both past and present. The attitude towards that experience is both impersonal or objective—Browning's feelings—and personal or subjective—the Duke's feelings. Browning cloaks his own attitude the better to present those of the Duke.

This brief inspection of the poems by Bridges, Robinson, and Browning suggests that the three different types of poetry are necessary to express different kinds of experience and different attitudes toward experience. If we were restricted to the lyric alone, we could not tell a story; if we were restricted to telling stories, we could not present a host of imaginary characters in a dramatic way; if we were restricted to drama, we could not express our purely personal feelings.

The usefulness, as well as the necessity, of respecting the differences among the several types of poetry becomes clear when we consider the absurdity of the opposite position. Suppose, disrespecting the specific aims of Shakespeare's sonnets, we compare them unfavorably with *Hamlet,* because they lack that play's vigorous action. Suppose, too, we reject Tennyson's "The Brook," a descriptive lyric, because it lacks the caustic bite of "My Last Duchess" or the pathos of "When First We Met." We may be saved from these and other absurdities by realizing that each different kind of experience requires its own typical mode of expression. This is to say, too, that a close study of the various types of poetry can help us see more clearly the rich variety of poetic experience and the varied means of expressing that variety.

THE LYRIC: GENERAL CHARACTERISTICS

Because the lyric expresses an intense moment of experience it is necessarily direct, brief, and unified. Perhaps the one quality that sums up these characteristics is *concentration.* In general, the lyric poem aims at one unified emotional impression. Sometimes it focuses on a single experience, as in "The Eagle" by Alfred Lord Tennyson.

> He clasps the crag with crooked hands;
> Close to the sun in lonely lands,
> Ringed with the azure world, he stands.

The wrinkled sea beneath him crawls;
He watches from his mountain walls,
And like a thunderbolt he falls.

Here the poet gives a single, intense impression of majestic power.

More often the poet concentrates from the very beginning of the poem not on the experience itself, but on his attitude towards it. Robert Herrick displays this typical lyrical concentration by announcing his grief in the first lines, and then by extending the emotion with each successive step in the comparison between the daffodils and human life.

TO DAFFODILS

Faire daffodills, we weep to see
You haste away so soone;
As yet the early-rising sun
Has not attain'd his noone.
Stay, stay, 5
Until the hasting day
Has run
But to the even-song;
And, having pray'd together, we
Will go with you along. 10

We have short time to stay, as you,
We have as short a spring;
As quick a growth to meet decay,
As you, or anything.
We die, 15
As your hours doe, and drie
Away,
Like to the summer's raine;
Or as the pearls of mornings dew,
Ne'r to be found againe. 20

ROBERT HERRICK

Here the poet has avoided a particular description of the daffodil or the cycle of human life. Rather, he concentrates on the one emotion of regret. So, too, in "The Solitary Reaper" Wordsworth does not describe the highland lass, nor does he give us snatches of her song. Instead, he speaks of the impression the singing made upon him.

THE SOLITARY REAPER

Behold her, single in the field,
Yon solitary Highland Lass!
Reaping and singing by herself;
Stop here, or gently pass!
Alone she cuts and binds the grain, 5
And sings a melancholy strain;
O listen! for the Vale profound
Is overflowing with the sound.

No Nightingale did ever chaunt
More welcome notes to weary bands 10
Of travellers in some shady haunt,
Among Arabian sands:
A voice so thrilling ne'er was heard
In springtime from the Cuckoo-bird,
Breaking the silence of the seas 15
Among the farthest Hebrides.

Will no one tell me what she sings?—
Perhaps the plaintive numbers flow
For old, unhappy, far-off things,
And battles long ago: 20
Or is it some more humble lay,
Familiar matter of to-day?
Some natural sorrow, loss, or pain,
That has been, and may be again?

Whate'er the theme, the Maiden sang 25
As if her song could have no ending;
I saw her singing at her work,
And o'er the sickle bending,—
I listened, motionless and still;
And, as I mounted up the hill, 30
The music in my heart I bore,
Long after it was heard no more.

WILLIAM WORDSWORTH

Lyrical concentration on a single, intense personal feeling could hardly be successful without *sincerity*. A poem reveals its sincerity by its spontaneity, that is, its own native energy and freedom of expression. A spontaneous poem is not dictated by custom, is not whipped into being by a premeditated purpose to say something about love, for instance. Rather it leaps to the mind in a series of natural associations and ends when its impulse is exhausted, as in Wordsworth's "My Heart Leaps Up."

My heart leaps up when I behold
    A rainbow in the sky:
So was it when my life began;
So is it now I am a man;
So be it when I shall grow old,   5
    Or let me die!
The Child is father of the Man;
And I could wish my days to be
Bound each to each by natural piety.

In "My Heart Leaps Up" and in the other lyric poems cited in this book the personal vision is predominant. The poet is, in one sense of the word, haunted by an image, a song, a glimpse of truth, a longing, a sudden realization that love and life are fleeting. Hence, lyrical poetry is frequently stark, or strange. The lightning of poetry reveals not only the poet's soul but the dark and brooding mystery beyond the lightning's reach. Often the lyric writer makes us more aware of mystery than of meaning.

O THAT 'TWERE POSSIBLE

O that 'twere possible
After long grief and pain
To find the arms of my true love
Round me once again! . . .

A shadow flits before me,   5
Not thou, but like to thee:
Ah, Christ! that it were possible
For one short hour to see
The souls we loved, that they might tell us
What and where they be!   10

ALFRED, LORD TENNYSON

Although a successful lyric is always personal and often mysterious, it is also *universal.* It appeals to all men because, as the examples have shown, it does not stress the local, peculiar, or exceptional situation that gave rise to the feeling, but the feeling itself. Thus, one need not have lost a loved one to appreciate Tennyson's sigh nor be an Irishman to share in an exile's love of his native land as seen in the following translation by Sir Samuel Ferguson.

And I will make my journey, if life and health but stand,
Unto that pleasant country, that fresh and fragrant strand,
And leave your boasted braveries, your wealth and high command, 15
For the fair hills of holy Ireland.
Large and profitable are the stacks upon the ground,

. . .

The bitter and the cream do wondrously abound;

. . .

The cresses on the water and the sorrels are at hand, 21
And the cuckoo's calling daily his note of music bland,
And the bold thrush sings so bravely his song i' the forest grand
On the fair hills of holy Ireland.

(From "The Fair Hills of Ireland")

Concentration, sincerity, universality—all these qualities make special demands on the poet's ability to express his vision. Concentration connotes unity; sincerity, the absence of irrelevant comment; universality, a concern for the essential. Whereas the narrative writer may occasionally digress without destroying the main threads of his story, the lyric writer is especially committed to perfect structure. That structure in its ideal sense consists of a perfect adjustment of means to end. This often involves the elaborate development of thought, as in certain formal odes; the sophisticated use of a literary tradition, as in pastoral elegies; and a rich use of allusion, as in much modern poetry that attempts to evoke the literature of the past. But in the great body of lyrics the structure is as simple as that of the song from which the lyric sprang, and to which it always tends to return. A perfect short lyric, like Ariel's song from Shakespeare's *The Tempest,* justifies

Blake's comment that "Every word and every letter is studied and put into its fit place."

FULL FATHOM FIVE

Full fathom five thy father lies;
  Of his bones are coral made;
Those are pearls that were his eyes:
  Nothing of him that doth fade
But doth suffer a sea-change
Into something rich and strange.
Sea-nymphs hourly ring his knell:
Ding-dong. Hark! now I hear them,—ding-dong, bell.

WILLIAM SHAKESPEARE
(Act I, Scene II, *The Tempest*)

Here the vocabulary is neither learned, ornate, or recondite; the sentence structure is uncommonly lucid; the sound structure not only suits the sense, but provides a combination of vowels and consonants that harmonizes with the feeling. (Note particularly the repetition of *f*, *l*, and *th* sounds in line 1, the *s* and *th* sounds in lines 3-5, the onomatopoeic words in the concluding lines.)

The main characteristic of lyrical structure, however, is its coherence or fluidity. Each line flows into the other not only by logical progression, but by a natural rhythmic movement. An excellent example of this is Edmund Waller's "Go, Lovely Rose" (p. 31). Like Herrick's "To Daffodils" (p. 188), it is based on the common fate of a flower and a human being—the imminence of death.

But it differs from "To Daffodils," in that the speaker does not merely extend and intensify his introductory impression. Rather, he establishes a natural climactic order that begins with graceful compliments and then with artful suddenness he bids the rose

Then die, that she,
The common fate of all things rare,
May read in thee;
How small a part of time they share,
That are so wondrous sweet and fair.

SPECIAL FORMS OF THE LYRIC: THE SONNET

The characteristics we have just examined apply to lyrics in general. But certain special forms of the lyric display features of their own. Of these the sonnet (literally, a little song) is by far the most important. For about six centuries some of the greatest poets have chosen this form, chiefly, we must suppose, because they find it a challenge to their skill. In meeting the challenge they have demonstrated that the sonnet form helps them to contain, compress, and perfect lyrical expression. Some commentators even say that the sonnet is the perfect length for expressing lyric emotion.

The Petrarchan or Italian sonnet consists of fourteen lines, each of five iambic feet (see p. 268). It is divided into two distinct parts, an octave whose rhyme scheme is *a b b a a b b a*, and a sestet, consisting of two tercets whose rhyme scheme is variable. More frequently, however, the rhyme scheme is *c d c c d c* or *c d c d c d*. In addition to this rhyme scheme, the Italian sonnet developed definite procedures in considering a single thought. The octave states a problem, or asks a question, or offers a speculation, or advances a premise; to this the sestet provides a solution, or an answer, or a practical application, or a conclusion. Often the octave develops one term of a comparison and the sestet another, or the octave sets forth a cause, the sestet an effect, or the octave describes a particular scene or situation from which the sestet derives a general truth.

In "The Sound of the Sea" Longfellow describes the sound of the sea in the octave and then its analogy, the voice of inspiration, in the sestet.

The sea awoke at midnight from its sleep,
 And round the pebbly beaches far and wide
 I heard the first wave of the rising tide
 Rush onward with uninterrupted sweep;
A voice out of the silence of the deep, 5
 A sound mysteriously multiplied
 As of a cataract from the mountain's side,
 Or roar of winds upon a wooded steep.
So comes to us at times, from the unknown
 And inaccessible solitudes of being, 10
 The rushing of the sea-tides of the soul;
And inspirations, that we deem our own,
 Are some divine foreshadowing and foreseeing
 Of things beyond our reason or control.

In the Shakespearean sonnet the distinction between the octave and sestet tends to disappear. Instead, there are three quatrains of iambic pentameters alternately rhymed, in which a thought or impression is stated in various ways, followed by a rhyming couplet which is a conclusion, a climax, and frequently an epigram. Since we have already examined several of Shakespeare's sonnets (pp. 42, 44) let us take a fresh example from John Keats.

WHEN I HAVE FEARS THAT I MAY CEASE TO BE

When I have fears that I may cease to be
Before my pen has glean'd my teeming brain,
Before high-piled books, in charactry,
Hold like rich garners the full ripen'd grain;
When I behold, upon the night's starr'd face, 5
Huge cloudy symbols of a high romance,
And think that I may never live to trace
Their shadows, with the magic hand of chance;
And when I feel, fair creature of an hour,
That I shall never look upon thee more, 10
Never have relish in the faery power
Of unreflecting love;—then on the shore
Of the wide world I stand alone, and think
Till love and fame to nothingness do sink.

JOHN KEATS

Like Robert Frost's "The Silken Tent" (p. 149), this sonnet consists of one sentence. Each quatrain develops an adverbial clause introduced by "when." The main clause, beginning with "then" in the twelfth line, glides into the concluding couplet. Note how this couplet not only completes the sentence grammatically but also completes the thought and the feeling of the poem.

Both the Petrarchan and the Shakespearean forms of the sonnet have their special virtues and defects. The Petrarchan sonnet* is more tightly organized. The close relationship between octave and sestet encourages neat, logically balanced and proportioned treatment of the thought. By repeating only two rhymes in the

* Other Petrarchan sonnets are treated on pp. 7, 10, 304; other Shakespearean sonnets are found on pp. 76, 146.

octave and two, or at most three, in the sestet, the Petrarchan sonnet achieves more gravity, emphasis, and resonance. On the other hand, the rigidity of the Petrarchan sonnet may hinder originality of thought and expression. Moreover, its rhyme scheme seems better adapted to Romance languages with their plethora of rhyming words.

It was partly for these reasons that the Elizabethans first departed from the Italian form. They found in the so-called Shakespearean sonnet more fluidity, a more pleasant variation in rhyme scheme, a special value in the concluding couplet—in short, greater liberty. But, as rigidity is the defect of the Petrarchan sonnet, so is formlessness that of the Shakespearean. Too often it ceased to be, in Theodore Watts-Dunton's language,

> a wave of melody
> From heaving waters of the impassioned soul
> A billow of tidal music one and whole.

In careless hands, the Shakespearean sonnet tends to become a loose confederacy of quatrains illegitimately united in a clashing couplet.

Most poets have respected the conventions of the sonnet. Yet the sonnet, seemingly forever fixed, is forever extending its channels and chafing at its banks. Many poets—Shakespeare, Sidney and Spenser among the Elizabethans, Elizabeth Barrett Browning, Dante Rossetti and George Meredith among the Victorians, Edna St. Vincent Millay and W. H. Auden among the moderns—have written sonnet sequences, that is, a series of sonnets on a related theme. Some of these sequences resemble autobiographies and thus introduce a narrative element. Other poets have altered the rhyme scheme. Shelley's "Ozymandias" (p. 27), for instance, consists of fourteen lines of iambic pentameters with the following rhyme scheme: *a b a b a c d c e d e f e f*. Milton adapted most of the features of the Petrarchan sonnet but omitted the full pause before the start of the sestet, the better to achieve a steady flow. Milton also composed so-called tailed sonnets employing six added lines. Later, G. M. Hopkins in the octave of "The Windhover" employed a single rhyme. That adventurous poet also experimented with a "curtal sonnet," in which the octave is reduced to six lines (*a b c a b c*) and the sestet to five (*d b c d c*), as in "Pied Beauty."

PIED BEAUTY

Glory be to God for dappled things—
For skies of couple-colour as a brinded cow;
For rose-moles all in stipple upon trout that swim;
Fresh-firecoal chestnut-falls; finches' wings;
Landscape plotted and pieced—fold, fallow, and plough; 5
And áll trádes, their gear and tackle and trim.

All things counter, original, spare, strange;
Whatever is fickle, freckled (who knows how?)
With swift, slow; sweet, sour; adazzle, dim;
He fathers-forth whose beauty is past change: 10
Praise him.

GERARD MANLEY HOPKINS

THE ELEGY

An elegy is a lyric poem that expresses the poet's serious reflections on some phase of death. Frequently it is a lamentation for a dead friend, as in Milton's "Lycidas" in memory of Edward King, Shelley's "Adonais" in memory of John Keats, Matthew Arnold's "Thyrsis" in memory of Arthur Hugh Clough. The form of most elegies differs little, if at all, from other types of lyric poetry. It has no special metrical pattern, rhyme scheme, or method of developing the body of the poem.

The pastoral elegy, however, is linked with a long tradition that began with the Sicilian Greek poet Theocritus. In the pastoral elegy there are numerous artificial conventions, many of them illustrated in John Milton's "Lycidas" (p. 55). The poet assumes the identity of a shepherd lamenting the death of his friend. The pattern of "Lycidas" may be described in terms of five phases. First, Milton states the cause of his grief,

For Lycidas is dead, dead ere his prime,
Young Lycidas, and hath not left his peer.

In the second phase he invokes the muses, in the manner of the ancient classics, to help him to sing his lament.

Begin then, Sisters of the sacred well,
That from beneath the seat of Jove doth spring;
Begin, and somewhat loudly sweep the string.

The third phase of the poem recalls the happy days he had spent with his dead friend who is presented in the traditional guise of a shepherd. (See lines 25-84.) The fourth phase (lines 132-164) is an expression of intense grief in which Milton bids the muses to gather all the flowers of earth and

> To strew the laureat hearse where Lycid lies.

The final section of the poem searches out reasons for consolation.

> Weep no more, woful Shepherds, weep no more,
> For Lycidas, your sorrow, is not dead,

Here Milton proposes a Christian meditation on the immortality of the soul. Confident that his friend is in heaven, he rises refreshed to face life with courage:

> Tomorrow to fresh woods, and pastures new.

Rich, ornate, formal, the pastoral elegy nevertheless tolerates frequent digressions. Thus, in "Lycidas" (lines 103-131) Milton discusses ecclesiastical politics which are only remotely connected with the theme of the poem. Similarly in "Adonais," Shelley's grief for Keats permits him to attack various attitudes which he felt were hostile to the spirit of his dead friend.

THE ODE

The ode is a lyric poem that is formal in manner, lofty in tone, and dignified in its subject or theme. Just as the simple lyric or the sonnet is an ideal form to express a single and simple thought and feeling, so the ode is the design that permits the poet to elaborate and refine a complex body of thoughts and feelings. Originally the ode derived from the choral sections of ancient Greek tragedy. There the chorus sang a song as it moved up one side of the stage (the strophe). As it returned the chorus sang another song (the antistrophe) identical in structure. As it stood it sang a third song (the epode) which was different from the first two. Eventually the ode was developed as a lyric poem outside a dramatic context by the Greek poet Pindar.

Some few poets, notably Ben Jonson and Thomas Gray, wrote in the Pindaric tradition. A good example of the Pindaric ode is

Gray's "The Progress of Poesy," which consists of three triads. In the third triad, Gray summarizes the development of English poetry.

THE PROGRESS OF POESY

III

The Strophe

Far from the sun and summer-gale,
In thy green lap was Nature's Darling laid,
What time, where lucid Avon stray'd, 85
To Him the mighty Mother did unveil
Her awful face: the dauntless Child
Stretch'd forth his little arms, and smiled.
This pencil take (she said) whose colours clear
Richly paint the vernal year: 90
Thine too these golden keys, immortal Boy!
This can unlock the gates of Joy;
Of Horrour that, and thrilling Fears,
Or ope the sacred source of sympathetic Tears.

The Antistrophe

Nor second He, that rode sublime 95
Upon the seraph-wings of Ecstasy,
The secrets of th' Abyss to spy.
He passed the flaming bounds of Place and Time:
The living Throne, the sapphire-blaze,
Where angels tremble, while they gaze, 100
He saw; but blasted with excess of light,
Closed his eyes in endless night.
Behold, where Dryden's less presumptuous car,
Wide o'er the fields of Glory bear
Two coursers of ethereal race, 105
With necks in thunder cloath'd, and long-resounding pace.

The Epode

Hark, his hands the lyre explore!
Bright-eyed Fancy hovering o'er
Scatters from her pictured urn
Thoughts that breathe, and words that burn. 110

But ah! 'tis heard no more—
Oh! Lyre divine, what daring Spirit
Wakes thee now? Tho' he inherit
Nor the pride nor ample pinion,
That the Theban Eagle bear 115
Sailing with supreme dominion
Thro' the azure deep of air:
Yet oft before his infant eyes would run
Such forms, as glitter in the Muse's ray
With orient hues, unborrow'd of the Sun: 120
Yet shall he mount, and keep his distant way
Beyond the limits of a vulgar fate,
Beneath the Good how far—but far above the Great.

THOMAS GRAY

Perhaps because of its extreme formality, evident in the passage above, the Pindaric ode was rarely attempted by English poets. They much preferred the regular homostrophic ode, that is, one whose stanzas are alike in structure and rhyme scheme. The advantage of this form, probably derived from the Roman poet, Horace, is its fluidity. The poet is not compelled to alter his pattern in the epode, often at the risk of changing tone and point of view, and therefore destroying the unity of the work. Moreover, the homostrophic ode permits that special coherence or fluidity that is a characteristic of lyric poetry. Shelley's "Ode to the West Wind" shows us how a uniform stanzaic and metrical pattern helps to secure rhythmic unity and coherence. (See p. 213.)

A third type of ode, the so-called irregular Cowleyan ode, is extremely free in stanzaic pattern, length of line, and rhyme scheme. Used to perfection by Dryden in "A Song for St. Cecilia's Day" (p. 299), and by Wordsworth in "Ode: Intimations of Immortality" (p. 208), this type of ode allows the poet the greatest opportunities for spontaneous feeling and expression. It also helps him avoid the procrustean bed of fixed metrical forms, wherein thoughts and feelings are chopped off to accommodate the tyranny of custom.

We must not assume, however, that the irregular ode is anarchic. Wordsworth's "Intimations," for instance, is as carefully developed as any Pindaric or homostrophic ode. In the first four stanzas it proposes a question based on Wordsworth's personal experiences but framed in the light of the Platonic theory of pre-existent forms. In childhood and in early youth he enjoyed a direct, immediate vision of the glory of life. He came "trailing clouds of glory" from God. He asks now

> Whither is fled the visionary gleam?
> Where is it now, the glory and the dream?

Wordsworth's answer to that question is partly sorrowful. In stanzas 5-8 he shows how the splendid vision of childhood eventually grows dull, and custom lies upon man

> . . . with a weight,
> Heavy as frost, and deep almost as life!

A second answer in stanzas 9-11 shows that there are compensations for the loss of the splendid vision of childhood. We still have shadowy recollections of the earlier vision and a distant sight of an immortal sea. The two concluding stanzas speak of the wisdom, derived from suffering, that results

> In the faith that looks through death,
> In years that bring the philosophic mind.

Thus, the irregularity of the ode is not the result of random thinking or of an undisciplined poetic impulse. Rather it is a painstaking effort to accommodate rhythm and rhyme to the many different tones, colors, and thoughts of a complex poetic experience.

POEMS FOR DISCUSSION

SWEET AND LOW

Sweet and low, sweet and low,
 Wind of the western sea,
Low, low, breathe and blow,
 Wind of the western sea!
 Over the rolling waters go, 5
Come from the dying moon, and blow,
 Blow him again to me;
While my little one, while my pretty one, sleeps.

Sleep and rest, sleep and rest,
  Father will come to thee soon; 10
Rest, rest, on mother's breast,
  Father will come to thee soon;
Father will come to his babe in the nest,
Silver sails all out of the west
  Under the silver moon: 15
Sleep, my little one, sleep, my pretty one, sleep.

ALFRED, LORD TENNYSON
(From *The Princess*)

1. Show how this poem does or does not reveal the essential characteristics of the lyric, namely, concentration, sincerity and universality.

ROMANCE

Romance, who loves to nod and sing,
With drowsy head and folded wing,
Among the green leaves as they shake
Far down within some shadowy lake,
To me a painted paroquet 5
Hath been—a most familiar bird—
Taught me my alphabet to say—
To lisp my very earliest word
While in the wild wood I did lie,
A child—with a most knowing eye. 10

Of late, eternal condor years
So shake the very Heaven on high
With tumult as they thunder by,
I have no time for idle cares
Through gazing on the unquiet sky. 15
And when an hour with calmer wings
Its down upon my spirit flings—
That little time with lyre and rhyme
To while away—forbidden things!
My heart would feel to be a crime 20
Unless it trembled with the strings.

EDGAR ALLAN POE

1. Discuss this poem from the point of view of coherence of structure.
2. Is its structure as successful as that of Edmund Waller's "Go, Lovely Rose" p. 31 and Robert Herrick's "To Daffodils" p. 188? Why or why not?

A POISON TREE

I was angry with my friend:
I told my wrath, my wrath did end.
I was angry with my foe:
I told it not, my wrath did grow.

And I water'd it in fears, 5
Night and morning with my tears;
And I sunnéd it with smiles,
And with soft deceitful wiles.

And it grew both day and night,
Till it bore an apple bright; 10
And my foe beheld it shine,
And he knew that it was mine,

And into my garden stole
When the night had veil'd the pole:
In the morning glad I see 15
My foe outstretch'd beneath the tree.

WILLIAM BLAKE

1. Decide whether this poem is lyrical, or narrative, or both. Explain your answer.

INTO MY HEART AN AIR THAT KILLS

Into my heart an air that kills
From yon far country blows:
What are those blue remembered hills,
What spires, what farms are those?

That is the land of lost content, 5
I see it shining plain,
The happy highways where I went
And cannot come again.

A. E. HOUSMAN

1. Is this poem lyrical in the sense of the following description? A lyric is concerned with a highly intense moment of experience, direct, brief, and reflecting the speaker's feeling at the moment of utterance. Explain.

THE WINDHOVER

To Christ Our Lord

I caught this morning morning's minion, king-
 dom of daylight's dauphin, dapple-dawn-drawn Falcon,
  in his riding
 Of the rolling level underneath him steady air, and striding
High there, how he rung upon the rein of a wimpling wing
In his ecstasy! then off, off forth on swing, 5
 As a skate's heel sweeps smooth on a bow-bend: the hurl
  and gliding
 Rebuffed the big wing. My heart in hiding
Stirred for a bird,—the achieve of, the mastery of the thing!

Brute beauty and valour and act, oh, air, pride, plume, here
 Buckle! AND the fire that breaks from thee then, a billion 10
Times told lovelier, more dangerous, O my chevalier!

 No wonder of it: shéer plód makes plough down sillion
Shine, and blue-bleak embers, ah my dear,
 Fall, gall themselves, and gash gold-vermilion.

GERARD MANLEY HOPKINS

1. Show how the octave of this sonnet describes both the activity of the windhover or falcon and the speaker's attitude toward the scene.
2. Show how the sestet develops the contrast between the falcon's beauty and the beauty that is a billion times lovelier. What is the nature of the lovelier beauty? Before answering be sure to discover (a) What is the meaning of "Buckle" in line 10; (b) Why is "AND" capitalized in line 10? (c) Who is the "chevalier" addressed in line 11? (d) To whom does "my dear" refer in line 12?
3. Point out the relation of the subtitle of this poem to the terms "minion," "kingdom," "dauphin," "chevalier."
4. Show how the "achieve of" of the falcon is displayed in its flight. What is the "achieve of" of the lovelier kind of beauty—a plow shining from use, embers glowing from fire? Or is something else suggested by "gash gold-vermilion"?

ODE TO EVENING

If aught of oaten stop, or pastoral song,
May hope, chaste Eve, to soothe thy modest ear,

Like thy own solemn springs,
Thy springs, and dying gales,
O Nymph reserv'd, while now the bright-hair'd sun 5
Sits in yon western tent, whose cloudy skirts,
With brede ethereal wove,
O'erhang his wavy bed:
Now air is hush'd, save where the weak-ey'd bat,
With short shrill shriek flits by on leathern wing, 10
Or where the beetle winds
His small but sullen horn,
As oft he rises 'midst the twilight path,
Against the Pilgrim born in heedless hum:
Now teach me, maid compos'd, 15
To breathe some soften'd strain,
Whose numbers stealing thro' thy darkning vale,
May not unseemly with its stillness suit,
As, musing slow, I hail
Thy genial lov'd return! 20
For when thy folding-star arising shews
His paly circlet, at his warning lamp
The fragrant Hours, and elves
Who slept in flowers the day,
And many a nymph who wreaths her brows with sedge, 25
And sheds the fresh'ning dew, and lovelier still,
The pensive Pleasures sweet
Prepare thy shadowy car.
Then, lead, calm vot'ress, where some sheety lake
Cheers the lone heath, or some time-hallow'd pile, 30
Or upland fallows grey
Reflect its last cold gleam.
But when chill blust'ring winds, or driving rain,
Forbid my willing feet, be mine the hut
That from the mountain's side, 35
Views wilds, and swelling floods,
And hamlets brown, and dim-discover'd spires,
And hears their simple bell, and marks o'er all
Thy dewy fingers draw
The gradual dusky veil. 40
While Spring shall pour his show'rs, as oft he wont,
And bathe thy breathing tresses, meekest Eve!
While Summer loves to sport,
Beneath thy ling'ring light;
While sallow Autumn fills thy lap with leaves, 45

Or Winter yelling thro' the troublous air,
Affrights thy shrinking train,
And rudely rends thy robes:
So long, sure-found beneath the sylvan shed,
Shall Fancy, Friendship, Science, rose-lipp'd Health, 50
Thy gentlest influence own,
And hymn thy fav'rite name!

WILLIAM COLLINS

1. In terms of the description of the ode on pp. 197-200 explain (a) what kind of ode this is; (b) whether it develops its thought in formal order; (c) whether the concluding stanza sums up the meaning of the poem or gratuitously associates Fancy, Friendship, Science, and Health with evening.

SCORN NOT THE SONNET

Scorn not the Sonnet; Critic, you have frowned,
Mindless of its just honours; with this key
Shakespeare unlocked his heart; the melody
Of this small lute gave ease to Petrarch's wound;
A thousand times this pipe did Tasso sound; 5
With it Camöens soothed an exile's grief;
The Sonnet glittered a gay myrtle leaf
Amid the cypress with which Dante crowned
His visionary brow: a glow-worm lamp,
It cheered mild Spenser, called from Faery-land 10
To struggle through dark ways; and when a damp
Fell round the path of Milton, in his hand
The Thing became a trumpet; whence he blew
Soul-animating strains—alas, too few!

WILLIAM WORDSWORTH

1. What kind of sonnet is this one?
2. Are the octave and sestet logically related? How?

ODE ON LYRIC POETRY

I.1

Inmate of smoaking cots, whose rustic shed,
Within its humble bed,
Her twittering progeny contains,
The swallow sweeps the plains,

Or lightly skims from level lakes the dew. 5
The ringdove ever true
In plaintive accents tells of unrelenting fate,
Far from the raven's croak, and bird of night,
That shrieking wings her flight
When, at his mutter'd rite, 10
Hid in the dusky desart vale,
With starting eye, and visage pale,
The grimly wizard sees the spectres rise unholy;
But haunts the woods that held her beauteous mate,
And wooes the Echo soft with murmurs melancholy. 15

I.2

Sublime alone the feather'd monarch flies,
His nest dark mists upon the mountains shrowd;
In vain the howling storms arise,
When borne on outstretch'd plume aloft he springs,
Dashing with many a stroke the parting cloud, 20
Or to the buoyant air commits his wings
Floating with even sail adown the liquid skies;
Then darting upward, swift his wings aspire,
Where thunders keep their gloomy seat,
And light'nings arm'd with heaven's avenging ire. 25
None can the dread artillery meet,
Or through the airy region rove,
But he who guards the throne of Jove,
And grasps the flaming bolt of sacred fire.

I.3

Know, with young Ambition bold, 30
In vain, my Muse, thy dazzled eyes explore
Distant aims, where wont to soar,
Their burning way the kindling spirits hold.
Heights too arduous wisely shun;
Humbler flights thy wings attend; 35
For heaven-taught Genius can alone ascend
Back to her native sky,
And with directed eagle eye
Pervade the lofty spheres, and view the blazing sun.

II.1

But hark! o'er all the flower-enamell'd ground 40
What music breathes around!

I see, I see the virgin train
Unlock their streams again,
Rolling to many a vale their liquid lapse along,
While at the warbled song 45
Which holds entranc'd Attention's wakeful ear,
Broke are the magic bands of iron sleep.
Love, wayward child, oft want to weep,
In tears his robe to steep
Forgets; and Care that counts his store, 50
Now thinks each mighty business o'er;
While sits on ruin'd cities, war's wide-wasting glory,
Ambition, ceasing the proud pile to rear,
And sighs; unfinish'd leaving half her ample story.

II.2

Then once more, sweet enthusiast, happy lyre, 55
Thy soothing solace deign awhile to bring.
I strive to catch the sacred fire,
And wake thee emulous on Granta's plain,
Where all the Muses haunt his hallow'd spring,
And where the Graces shun the sordid train 60
Scornful of heav'n-born arts which thee and peace inspire;
On life's sequester'd scenes they silent wait,
Nor heed the baseless pomp of power,
Nor shining dreams that crowd at Fortune's gate;
But smooth th' inevitable hour 65
Of pain, which man is doom'd to know,
And teach the mortal mind to glow
With pleasures plac'd beyond the shaft of Fate.

II.3

But, alas! th' amusive reed
Ill suits the lyre that asks a master's hand, 70
And fond fancies vainly feed
A breast that life's more active scenes demand.
Sloth ignoble to disclaim
'Tis enough: the lyre unstring.
At other feet the victor palm I fling 75
In Granta's glorious shrine;
Where crown'd with radiance divine
Her smiles shall nurse the Muse; the Muse shall lift her fame.

SIR JAMES MARRIOT

1. What kind of ode is this one?
2. What characteristics of lyrical poetry are set forth figuratively in this passage?
3. Is the expression in this passage too formal and conventional? Why or why not?

ODE: INTIMATIONS OF IMMORTALITY FROM RECOLLECTIONS OF EARLY CHILDHOOD

The Child is father of the Man;
And I could wish my days to be
Bound each to each by natural piety.

1

There was a time when meadow, grove, and stream,
The earth, and every common sight,
To me did seem
Apparelled in celestial light,
The glory and the freshness of a dream. 5
It is not now as it hath been of yore;—
Turn wheresoe'er I may,
By night or day,
The things which I have seen I now can see no more.

2

The Rainbow comes and goes, 10
And lovely is the Rose,
The Moon doth with delight
Look round her when the heavens are bare,
Waters on a starry night
Are beautiful and fair; 15
The sunshine is a glorious birth;
But yet I know, where'er I go,
That there hath passed away a glory from the earth.

3

Now, while the birds thus sing a joyous song,
And while the young lambs bound 20
As to the tabor's sound,
To me alone there came a thought of grief:
A timely utterance gave that thought relief,
And I again am strong:

The cataracts blow their trumpets from the steep; 25
No more shall grief of mine the season wrong;
I hear the Echoes through the mountains throng,
The Winds come to me from the fields of sleep,
And all the earth is gay;
Land and sea 30
Give themselves up to jollity,
And with the heart of May
Doth every Beast keep holiday;—
Thou Child of Joy,
Shout round me, let me hear thy shouts, thou happy Shepherd-boy! 35

4

Ye blesséd Creatures, I have heard the call
Ye to each other make; I see
The heavens laugh with you in your jubilee;
My heart is at your festival,
My head hath its coronal, 40
The fulness of your bliss, I feel—I feel it all.
Oh evil day! If I were sullen
While Earth herself is adorning,
This sweet May-morning,
And the Children are culling 45
On every side,
In a thousand valleys far and wide,
Fresh flowers; while the sun shines warm,
And the Babe leaps up on his Mother's arm:—
I hear, I hear, with joy I hear! 50
—But there's a Tree, of many, one,
A single Field which I have looked upon,
Both of them speak of something that is gone:
The Pansy at my feet
Doth the same tale repeat: 55
Whither is fled the visionary gleam?
Where is it now, the glory and the dream?

5

Our birth is but a sleep and a forgetting:
The Soul that rises with us, our life's Star,
Hath had elsewhere its setting, 60
And cometh from afar:
Not in entire forgetfulness,
And not in utter nakedness,

But trailing clouds of glory do we come
    From God, who is our home: 65
Heaven lies about us in our infancy!
Shades of the prison-house begin to close
    Upon the growing Boy,
But he beholds the light, and whence it flows,
    He sees it in his joy; 70
The Youth, who daily farther from the east
    Must travel, still is Nature's Priest,
    And by the vision splendid
    Is on his way attended;
At length the Man perceives it die away, 75
And fade into the light of common day.

6

Earth fills her lap with pleasures of her own;
Yearnings she hath in her own natural kind,
And, even with something of a Mother's mind,
    And no unworthy aim, 80
    The homely Nurse doth all she can
To make her Foster-child, her Inmate Man,
    Forget the glories he hath known,
And that imperial palace whence he came.

7

Behold the Child among his new-born blisses, 85
A six years' Darling of a pigmy size!
See, where 'mid work of his own hand he lies,
Fretted by sallies of his mother's kisses,
With light upon him from his father's eyes!
See, at his feet, some little plan or chart, 90
Some fragment from his dream of human life,
Shaped by himself with newly-learned art;
    A wedding or a festival,
    A mourning or a funeral;
    And this hath now his heart, 95
    And unto this he frames his song:
    Then will he fit his tongue
To dialogues of business, love, or strife;
    But it will not be long
    Ere this be thrown aside, 100
    And with new joy and pride
The little Actor cons another part;

Filling from time to time his "humorous stage"
With all the Persons, down to palsied Age,
That Life brings with her in her equipage; 105
    As if his whole vocation
    Were endless imitation.

8

Thou, whose exterior semblance doth belie
    Thy Soul's immensity;
Thou best Philosopher, who yet dost keep 110
Thy heritage, thou Eye among the blind,
That, deaf and silent, read'st the eternal deep,
Haunted for ever by the eternal mind,—
    Mighty Prophet! Seer blest!
    On whom those truths do rest, 115
Which we are toiling all our lives to find,
In darkness lost, the darkness of the grave;
Thou, over whom thy Immortality
Broods like the Day, a Master o'er a Slave,
A Presence which is not to be put by; 120
Thou little Child, yet glorious in the might
Of heaven-born freedom on thy being's height,
Why with such earnest pains dost thou provoke
The years to bring the inevitable yoke,
Thus blindly with thy blessedness at strife? 125
Full soon thy Soul shall have her earthly freight,
And custom lie upon thee with a weight,
Heavy as frost, and deep almost as life!

9

    O joy! that in our embers
    Is something that does live, 130
    That nature yet remembers
    What was so fugitive!
The thought of our past years in me doth breed
Perpetual benediction: not indeed
For that which is most worthy to be blest; 135
Delight and liberty, the simple creed
Of Childhood, whether busy or at rest,
With new-fledged hope still fluttering in his breast:—
    Not for these I raise
    The song of thanks and praise; 140
  But for those obstinate questionings

Of sense and outward things,
Fallings from us, vanishings;
Blank misgivings of a Creature
Moving about in worlds not realized, 145
High instincts before which our mortal Nature
Did tremble like a guilty Thing surprised:
But for those first affections,
Those shadowy recollections,
Which, be they what they may, 150
Are yet the fountain light of all our day,
Are yet a master light of all our seeing;
Uphold us, cherish, and have power to make
Our noisy years seem moments in the being
Of the eternal Silence: truths that wake, 155
To perish never:
Which neither listlessness, nor mad endeavor,
Nor Man nor Boy,
Nor all that is at enmity with joy,
Can utterly abolish or destroy! 160
Hence in a season of calm weather
Though inland far we be,
Our Souls have sight of that immortal sea
Which brought us hither,
Can in a moment travel thither, 165
And see the Children sport upon the shore,
And hear the mighty waters rolling evermore.

10

Then sing, ye Birds, sing, sing a joyous song!
And let the young Lambs bound
As to the tabor's sound! 170
We in thought will join your throng,
Ye that pipe and ye that play,
Ye that through your hearts today
Feel the gladness of the May!
What though the radiance which was once so bright 175
Be now for ever taken from my sight,
Though nothing can bring back the hour
Of splendor in the grass, of glory in the flower;
We will grieve not, rather find
Strength in what remains behind; 180
In the primal sympathy
Which having been must ever be;

In the soothing thoughts that spring
Out of human suffering;
In the faith that looks through death, 185
In years that bring the philosophic mind.

11

And O, ye Fountains, Meadows, Hills, and Groves,
Forebode not any severing of our loves!
Yet in my heart of hearts I feel your might;
I only have relinquished one delight 190
To live beneath your more habitual sway.
I love the Brooks which down their channels fret,
Even more than when I tripped lightly as they;
The innocent brightness of a new-born Day
Is lovely yet; 195
The Clouds that gather round the setting sun
Do take a sober coloring from an eye
That hath kept watch o'er man's mortality;
Another race hath been, and other palms are won.
Thanks to the human heart by which we live 200
Thanks to its tenderness, its joys, and fears,
To me the meanest flower that blows can give
Thoughts that do often lie too deep for tears.

WILLIAM WORDSWORTH

1. See p. 199 for comment on this poem. How do the irregular stanzaic patterns of this poem reflect the idea and mood of the several parts? **Explain.**
2. What effects are achieved in this poem that are not achieved by the "Ode on Lyric Poetry?" Show how these effects may be traced to the particular form of Wordsworth's ode.

ODE TO THE WEST WIND

1

O Wild West Wind, thou breath of Autumn's being,
Thou, from whose unseen presence the leaves dead
Are driven, like ghosts from an enchanter fleeing,

Yellow, and black, and pale, and hectic red,
Pestilence-stricken multitudes: O thou, 5
Who chariotest to their dark wintry bed

The wingéd seeds, where they lie cold and low,
Each like a corpse within its grave, until
Thine azure sister of the Spring shall blow

Her clarion o'er the dreaming earth, and fill 10
(Driving sweet buds like flocks to feed in air)
With living hues and odors plain and hill:

Wild Spirit, which art moving everywhere;
Destroyer and preserver; hear, oh, hear!

2

Thou on whose stream, mid the steep sky's commotion, 15
Loose clouds like earth's decaying leaves are shed,
Shook from the tangled boughs of Heaven and Ocean,

Angels of rain and lightning: there are spread
On the blue surface of thine aëry surge,
Like the bright hair uplifted from the head 20

Of some fierce Maenad, even from the dim verge
Of the horizon to the zenith's height,
The locks of the approaching storm. Thou dirge

Of the dying year, to which this closing night
Will be the dome of a vast sepulchre, 25
Vaulted with all thy congregated might

Of vapours, from whose solid atmosphere
Black rain, and fire, and hail will burst: oh, hear!

3

Thou who didst waken from his summer dreams
The blue Mediterranean, where he lay, 30
Lulled by the coil of his crystálline streams,

Beside a pumice isle in Baiae's bay,
And saw in sleep old palaces and towers
Quivering within the wave's intenser day,

All overgrown with azure moss and flowers 35
So sweet, the sense faints picturing them! Thou
For whose path the Atlantic's level powers

Cleave themselves into chasms, while far below
The sea-blooms and the oozy woods which wear
The sapless foliage of the ocean, know 40

Thy voice, and suddenly grow gray with fear,
And tremble and despoil themselves: oh, hear!

4

If I were a dead leaf thou mightest bear;
If I were a swift cloud to fly with thee;
A wave to pant beneath thy power, and share 45

The impulse of thy strength, only less free
Than thou, O uncontrollable! If even
I were as in my boyhood, and could be

The comrade of thy wanderings over Heaven,
As then, when to outstrip thy skiey speed 50
Scarce seemed a vision; I would n'er have striven

As thus with thee in prayer in my sore need.
Oh, lift me as a wave, a leaf, a cloud!
I fall upon the thorns of life! I bleed!

A heavy weight of hours has chained and bowed 55
One too like thee: tameless, and swift, and proud.

5

Make me thy lyre, even as the forest is:
What if my leaves are falling like its own!
The tumult of thy mighty harmonies

Will take from both a deep, autumnal tone, 60
Sweet though in sadness. Be thou, Spirit fierce,
My spirit! Be thou me, impetuous one!

Drive my dead thoughts over the universe
Like withered leaves to quicken a new birth!
And, by the incantation of this verse, 65

Scatter, as from an unextinguished hearth
Ashes and sparks, my words among mankind!
Be through my lips to unawakened earth

The trumpet of a prophecy! O, Wind,
If Winter comes, can Spring be far behind? 70

PERCY BYSSHE SHELLEY

1. Compare the structure of this ode with Wordsworth's "Intimations. . . ."
2. Show how this ode is built upon a paradox, namely, that the "West Wind" is both a destroyer and a preserver.
3. What are the principal divisions of this ode? What is the function of each part? How is coherence established within each part, and from part to part?
4. Show how personification and metaphor function within this poem.

THE OLD FAMILIAR FACES

Where are they gone, the old familiar faces?
I had a mother, but she died, and left me,
Died prematurely in a day of horrors—
All, all are gone, the old familiar faces.

I have had playmates, I have had companions, 5
In my days of childhood, in my joyful schooldays—
All, all are gone, the old familiar faces.

I have been laughing, I have been carousing,
Drinking late, sitting late, with my bosom cronies—
All, all are gone, the old familiar faces. 10

I loved a love once, fairest among women;
Closed are her doors on me, I must not see her—
All, all are gone, the old familiar faces.

I have a friend, a kinder friend has no man;
Like an ingrate, I left my friend abruptly; 15
Left him, to muse on the old familiar faces.

Ghost-like, I paced round the haunts of my childhood.
Earth seem'd a desert I was bound to traverse,
Seeking to find the old familiar faces.

Friend of my bosom, thou more than a brother, 20
Why wert not thou born in my father's dwelling?
So might we talk of the old familiar faces.

How some they have died, and some they have left me,
And some are taken from me; all are departed;
All, all are gone, the old familiar faces. 25

CHARLES LAMB

1. With what justice could you describe this poem as an elegiac lyric? Explain.
2. Compare and contrast this poem with the elegies by Gray p. 60 and Milton p. 55.

HERE LIES A LADY

Here lies a lady of beauty and high degree.
Of chills and fever she died, of fever and chills,
The delight of her husband, her aunts, and infant of three,
And of medicos marveling sweetly on her ills.

For either she burned, and her confident eyes would blaze, 5
And her fingers fly in a manner to puzzle their heads—
What was she making? Why, nothing; she sat in a maze
Of old scraps of laces, snipped into curious shreds—

Or this would pass, and the light of her fire decline
Till she lay discouraged and cold, like a stalk white and blown, 10
And would not open her eyes, to kisses, to wine;
The sixth of these states was her last; the cold settled down.

Sweet ladies, long may ye bloom, and toughly I hope ye may thole,
But was she not lucky? In flowers and lace and mourning,
In love and great honor we bade God rest her soul 15
After six little spaces of chill, and six of burning.

JOHN CROWE RANSOM

13. Thole: endure

1. Decide whether this poem is more appropriately called an elegy or a lyric.
2. What elements in the poem make it more or less successful than "The Old Familiar Faces"?
3. Compare this poem with "An Epitaph" by Walter de la Mare, p. 263.

✣ CHAPTER XII ✣

Narrative, Dramatic and Other Types of Poetry

NARRATIVE POETRY aims to tell a story. Hence it has many points in common with prose narrative, particularly the short story. Like the short story, a good narrative poem will swiftly attract the attention of the reader by presenting an initial situation that promises excitement, conflict, suspense, and delight. It shows character in a net of circumstances, facing the perils of battle, death at sea, the snares of enemies, the solace of love, the mirth of festival, the ghosts of conscience—any and all the possible dangers and delights that make pulses quicken, minds stretch, and hearts contract and expand. Narrative poetry has a definite order or unity, a coherent movement from one incident to another, suspense, climax and resolution—in short all the devices of story telling. Small wonder since narrative poetry is the mother of prose narrative.

But narrative poetry differs from prose narrative in several ways. It tells its story more concisely, more rhythmically, more effectively. Like the lyric the narrative poem sings, and it is this singing quality that distinguishes it from prose. The principal types of narrative poetry are the ballad, the romance, the story, the dramatic poem, and the epic.

THE BALLAD

The ballad is a short lyric tale that was originally meant to be sung, chanted, or recited. The English ballad sprang up in the Middle Ages and aimed to satisfy a popular and often primitive audience. Its first appeal was its subject matter. A representative group of early ballads might involve a shipwreck as in "Sir

Patrick Spens"; a wanton murder of a sister on her wedding day, as in "The Cruel Brother"; a patricide, as in "Edward"; death from a broken heart, as in "Bonnie Barbara Allan"; a marriage of a woman to a demon, as in "The Demon Lover"; or a humorous spat between man and wife, as in "Get Up and Bar the Door." These ballads appealed to elemental emotions as much by the manner of telling as by the substance of the tales.

Most ballads develop a single episode in a series of swift actions. Characterization is rarely complicated. Indeed, most of the characters are barely identified. The author does not express his own personal attitudes; rather, he is the reporter of some climactic event of a well-known story. Often the ballad is composed of dialogue, sometimes in the form of a series of questions and answers as in "Edward."

EDWARD

"Why dois your brand sae drap wi bluid,
Edward, Edward,
Why dois your brand sae drap wi bluid,
And why sae sad gang yee O?"
"O I hae killed my hauke sae guid, 5
Mither, mither,
O I hae killed my hauke sae guid,
And I had nae mair bot hee O."

"Your haukis bluid was nevir sae reid,
Edward, Edward, 10
Your haukis bluid was nevir sae reid,
My deir son I tell thee O."
"O I hae killed my reid-roan steid,
Mither, mither,
O I hae killed my reid-roan steid, 15
That erst was sae fair and frie O."

"Your steid was auld, and ye hae gat mair,
Edward, Edward,
Your steid was auld, and ye hae gat mair,
Sum other dule ye drie O." 20
"O I hae killed my fadir deir,
Mither, mither,

1. Brand: sword 20. Dule: grief 20. Dire: endure

O I hae killed my fadir deir,
  Alas, and wae is mee O!"

"And whatten penance wul ye drie for that, 25
          Edward, Edward?
And whatten penance wul ye drie for that?
  My deir son, now tell me O."
"Ile set my feit in yonder boat,
          Mither, mither, 30
Ile set my feit in yonder boat,
  And Ile fare ovir the sea O."

"And what wul ye doe wi your towirs and your ha,
          Edward, Edward?
And what wul ye doe wi your towirs and your ha, 35
  That were sae fair to see O?"
"Ile let thame stand tul they doun fa,
          Mither, mither,
Ile let thame stand tul they doun fa,
  For here nevir mair maun I bee O." 40

"And what wul ye leive to your bairns and your wife,
          Edward, Edward?
And what wul ye leive to your bairns and your wife,
  Whan ye gang ovir the sea O?"
"The warldis room, late them beg thrae life, 45
          Mither, mither,
The warldis room, late them beg thrae life,
  For thame nevir mair wul I see O."

"And what wul ye leive to your ain mither deir,
          Edward, Edward? 50
And what wul ye leive to your ain mither deir?
  My deir son, now tell me O."
"The curse of hell frae me sall ye beir,
          Mither, mither,
The curse of hell frae me sall ye beir, 55
  Sic counseils ye gave to me O."

The structure of this poem centers on seven questions and answers. Note how each successive question reveals additional information about the joint crime of Edward and his mother.

This poem illustrates another characteristic of the ballad—the use of repeated epithets and refrains. The diction is simple and the phrasing is adapted to the music of ballad singing. Like most ballads, it evokes a powerful emotion—in this instance horror at the unnatural deed of mother and son.

Not all ballads are as dismal as "Edward." A few of them are humorous, as in "Get Up and Bar the Door"—a joke cast in the more typical four-line stanza with alternating four stress and three stress lines.

GET UP AND BAR THE DOOR

It fell about the Martinmas time,
  And a gay time it was then,
When our goodwife got puddings to make,
  And she's boild them in the pan.

The wind sae cauld blew south and north, 5
  And blew into the floor;
Quoth our goodman to our goodwife,
  "Gae out and bar the door."

"My hand is in my hussfskap,
  Goodman, as ye may see; 10
An it should nae be barrd this hundred year,
  It's no be barrd for me."

They made a paction tween them twa,
  They made it firm and sure,
That the first word whaeer should speak, 15
  Shoud rise and bar the door.

Then by there came two gentlemen,
  At twelve o'clock at night,
And they could neither see house nor hall,
  Nor coal nor candlelight 20

"Now whether is this a rich man's house,
  Or whether is it a poor?"
But neer a word wad ane o' them speak,
  For barring of the door.

And first they ate the white puddings, 25
  And then they ate the black;

9. Hussfskap: housekeeping

Tho muckle thought the goodwife to hersel,
  Yet neer a word she spake.

Then said the one unto the other,
  "Here, man, tak ye my knife; 30
Do ye tak aff the auld man's beard,
  And I'll kiss the goodwife."

"But there's nae water in the house,
  And what shall we do than?"
"What ails ye at the pudding-broo, 35
  That boils into the pan?"

O up then started our goodman,
  An angry man was he:
"Will ye kiss my wife before my een,
  And scad me wi pudding-bree?" 40

Then up and started our goodwife,
  Gied three skips on the floor:
"Goodman, you've spoken the foremost word;
  Get up and bar the door."

The ballad was the achievement of a vigorous, but primitive society. It could hardly survive in a more sophisticated age, but its vitality, its charm, and its essentially poetic qualities attracted writers of subsequent generations. Sir Walter Scott edited, studied, and imitated the border balladry with such success that in the Romantic period the ballad achieved great literary importance. But in the so-called "literary" ballad, writers like John Keats and Samuel Taylor Coleridge did not really restore the older primitive form. Rather, they adapted the ballad both to their own conditions and their specific poetic aims. For one thing, they no longer centered on the story for its own sake. Instead, they used the story to create subtle literary effects as in "La Belle Dame Sans Merci."

LA BELLE DAME SANS MERCI

Oh what can ail thee, knight-at-arms,
  Alone and palely loitering?
The sedge has wither'd from the lake,
  And no birds sing.

Oh what can ail thee, knight-at-arms, 5
So haggard and so woe-begone?
The squirrel's granary is full,
And the harvest's done.

I see a lily on thy brow
With anguish moist and fever dew, 10
And on thy cheeks a fading rose
Fast withereth too.

"I met a lady in the meads,
Full beautiful—a faery's child,
Her hair was long, her foot was light, 15
And her eyes were wild.

"I made a garland for her head,
And bracelets too, and fragrant zone;
She looked at me as she did love,
And made sweet moan. 20

"I set her on my pacing steed,
And nothing else saw all day long.
For sidelong would she bend, and sing
A faery's song.

"She found me roots of relish sweet, 25
And honey wild and manna-dew;
And sure in language strange she said,
'I love thee true.'

"She took me to her elfin grot,
And there she wept and sighed full sore; 30
And there I shut her wild, wild eyes
With kisses four.

"And there she lulled me asleep,
And there I dreamed—ah! woe betide!—
The latest dream I ever dreamed 35
On the cold hill side.

"I saw pale kings, and princes too,
Pale warriors, death-pale were they all:
They cried—'La Belle Dame sans Merci
Hath thee in thrall!' 40

"I saw their starved lips in the gloam
  With horrid warning gapèd wide,
And I awoke, and found me here
  On the cold hill side.

"And this is why I sojourn here 45
  Alone and palely loitering,
Though the sedge is withered from the lake,
  And no birds sing."

JOHN KEATS

At first glance this literary ballad seems to resemble the primitive ballads about demon lovers. Its structure, too, imitates the question-and-answer technique characteristic of the old ballad.

O what can ail thee, knight-at-arms!
  Alone and palely loitering!

seems to be answered in the concluding stanza in the words

And this is why I sojourn here.

But a close reading of the poem reveals that the enthrallment of the knight-at-arms is not presented for literal acceptance. The poem evokes a state of mind, a concern with strangeness, rather than simple belief in the preternatural. Moreover, the diction is highly self-conscious, betraying in numerous instances a subtle use of figurative language and symbolism.

The literary ballad continued to enjoy a great vogue during the nineteenth century. Tennyson, Morris, D. G. Rossetti, Thomas Hardy, A. E. Housman, Rudyard Kipling, Oscar Wilde are among the masters of that form. In the twentieth century W. B. Yeats, Robert Frost, Stephen Vincent Benét, Dylan Thomas, and R. P. Warren are among the many writers who perpetuate the ballad tradition.

THE ROMANCE

Like the ballad, the verse romance tells a story. Unlike the ballad, it was originally addressed to courtly audiences, and, instead of treating popular subjects popularly, it traced the rise and fall of noble heroes in a highly sophisticated way. In medieval times the "matter" of the romance centered on the deeds of

Alexander the Great and other real and legendary heroes of Greece and Rome, the exploits of Charlemagne and other French heroes, and above all on the adventures of King Arthur and the Knights of the Round Table. The principal themes were courtly love, chivalry, quests and exotic adventures.

The medieval verse romance provided literary entertainment for the upper classes; but it also presented a picture of chivalric ideals, feudal customs, gallantry and a penetrating study of character. Chaucer's *Troilus and Criseyde,* for instance, although set against the background of the Trojan War, is nevertheless an elaborate scrutiny of the conflict between realistic human values and the illusory code of courtly love.

It was this serious phase of the metrical romance, rather than Merlin's magic, Lancelot's military supermanship, and puckish fantasy that attracted a host of later writers. The heroes of romance—Arthur, Lancelot, Tristram, Gawain, Percival—were selected as models by Spenser, Tennyson, Arnold, Longfellow, E. A. Robinson and others because their legendary lives gave them the opportunity of dramatizing the conflicts involved in moral choice; the choice of duty before ambition, honor before self-indulgence, commitment before compromise. Tennyson's "medieval" poems particularly demonstrate the vitality of the verse romance. Some of the perennial characteristics of the metrical romance are revealed in the concluding lines from "The Coming of Arthur."

THE COMING OF ARTHUR

Then Arthur charged his warrior whom he loved
And honor'd most, Sir Lancelot, to ride forth
And bring the Queen, and watch'd him from the gates;
And Lancelot past away among the flowers—
For then was latter April—and return'd 450
Among the flowers, in May, with Guinevere.
To whom arrived, by Dubric the high saint,
Chief of the church in Britain, and before
The stateliest of her altar-shrines, the King
That morn was married, while in stainless white, 455
The fair beginners of a nobler time,
And glorying in their vows and him, his knights

Stood round him, and rejoicing in his joy.
Far shone the fields of May thro' open door,
The sacred altar blossom'd white with May, 460
The sun of May descended on their King,
They gazed on all earth's beauty in their Queen,
Roll'd incense, and there past along the hymns
A voice as of the waters, while the two
Sware at the shrine of Christ a deathless love. 465
And Arthur said, "Behold, thy doom is mine.
Let chance what will, I love thee to the death!"
To whom the Queen replied with drooping eyes,
"King and my lord, I love thee to the death!"
And holy Dubric spread his hands and spake: 470
"Reign ye, and live and love, and make the world
Other, and may thy Queen be one with thee,
And all this Order of thy Table Round
Fulfil the boundless purpose of their King!"

So Dubric said; but when they left the shrine 475
Great lords from Rome before the portal stood,
In scornful stillness gazing as they past;
Then while they paced a city all on fire
With sun and cloth of gold, the trumpets blew,
And Arthur's knighthood sang before the King:— 480

"Blow trumpet, for the world is white with May!
Blow trumpet, the long night hath roll'd away!
Blow thro' the living world—'Let the King reign!'

"Shall Rome or Heathen rule in Arthur's realm?
Flash brand and lance, fall battle-axe upon helm, 485
Fall battle-axe, and flash brand; Let the King reign!

"Strike for the King and live! his knights have heard
That God hath told the King a secret word.
Fall battle-axe, and flash brand! Let the King reign!

"Blow trumpet! he will lift us from the dust. 490
Blow trumpet! live the strength, and die the lust!
Clang battle-axe, and clash brand! Let the King reign!

"Strike for the King and die! and if thou diest,
The King is king, and ever wills the highest.
Clang battle-axe, and clash brand! Let the King reign! 495

"Blow, for our Sun is mighty in his May!
Blow, for our Sun is mightier day by day!
Clang battle-axe, and clash brand! Let the King reign!

"The King will follow Christ, and we the King,
In whom high God hath breathed a secret thing. 500
Fall battle-axe, and clash brand! Let the King reign!"

So sang the knighthood, moving to their hall.
There at the banquet those great lords from Rome,
The slowly-fading mistress of the world,
Strode in and claim'd their tribute as of yore. 505
But Arthur spake: "Behold, for these have sworn
To wage my wars, and worship me their King;
The old order changeth, yielding place to new,
And we that fight for our fair father Christ,
Seeing that ye be grown too weak and old 510
To drive the heathen from your Roman wall,
No tribute will we pay." So those great lords
Drew back in wrath, and Arthur strove with Rome.

And Arthur and his knighthood for a space
Were all one will, and thro' that strength the King 515
Drew in the petty princedoms under him,
Fought, and in twelve great battles overcame
The heathen hordes, and made a realm and reign'd.

ALFRED, LORD TENNYSON
(From *The Idylls of the King*)

THE STORY AND THE DRAMATIC NARRATIVE

The term *story* embraces a great variety of narrative verse that cannot properly be called either a ballad or a romance. It ranges in length from brief verse-tales—Chaucer's "The Pardoner's Tale" and Robert Burns's "Tam o' Shanter," both short stories in verse—to elaborate "verse-novels"—Lord Byron's *Childe Harold,* Coventry Patmore's *The Angel in the House,* Robert Browning's *The Ring and the Book.* It ranges in tone from the pathos of Longfellow's *Evangeline* to the satirical bite of Byron's *Don Juan,* from the homely sentiment of Crabbe's *The Village* to the near epic sublimity of Keat's *Hyperion.* In some narratives, Matthew Arnold's *Sohrab and Rustum* for example, the action is suspended, indeed sometimes smothered, in the reflections of the two chief characters; in others, like Thomas Hood's "The Bridge of Sighs," it blends with the personal emotions of the narrator and thus takes on some characteristics of the lyric.

A strictly narrative poem, however, such as Robert Browning's "How They Brought the Good News from Ghent to Aix," concentrates on telling a story.

HOW THEY BOUGHT THE GOOD NEWS FROM GHENT TO AIX

I sprang to the stirrup, and Joris, and he;
I galloped, Dirck galloped, we galloped all three;
"Good speed!" cried the watch, as the gatebolts undrew;
"Speed!" echoed the wall to us galloping through;
Behind shut the postern, the lights sank to rest, 5
And into the midnight we galloped abreast.

Not a word to each other; we kept the great pace
Neck by neck, stride by stride, never changing our place;
I turned in my saddle and made its girths tight,
Then shortened each stirrup, and set the pique right, 10
Rebuckled the cheek-strap, chained slacker the bit,
Nor galloped less steadily Roland a whit.

'Twas moonset at starting; but while we drew near
Lokeren, the cocks crew and twilight dawned clear;
At Boom, a great yellow star came out to see; 15
At Duffeld, 'twas morning as plain as could be;
And from Mecheln church-steeple we heard the half-chime,
So Joris broke silence with, "Yet there is time!"

At Aershot, up leaped of a sudden the sun,
And against him the cattle stood black every one, 20
To stare through the mist at us galloping past,
And I saw my stout galloper Roland at last,
With resolute shoulders, each butting away
The haze, as some bluff river headland its spray;

And his low head and crest, just one sharp ear bent back 25
For my voice, and the other pricked out on his track;
And one eye's black intelligence—ever that glance

O'er its white edge at me, his own master, askance!
And the thick heavy spume-flakes which aye and anon
His fierce lips shook upwards in galloping on. 30

By Hasselt, Dirck groaned; and cried Joris, "Stay spur!
Your Roos galloped bravely, the fault's not in her,
We'll remember at Aix"—for one heard the quick wheeze
Of her chest, saw the stretched neck and staggering knees,
And sunk tail, and horrible heave of the flank, 35
As down on her haunches she shuddered and sank.

So we were left galloping, Joris and I,
Past Looz and past Tongres, no cloud in the sky;
The broad sun above laughed a pitiless laugh,
'Neath our feet broke the brittle bright stubble like chaff; 40
Till over by Dalhem a dome-spire sprang white,
And "Gallop," gasped Joris, "for Aix is in sight!"

"How they'll greet us!"—and all in a moment his roan
Rolled neck and croup over, lay dead as a stone;
And there was my Roland to bear the whole weight 45
Of the news which alone could save Aix from her fate,
With his nostrils like pits full of blood to the brim,
And with circles of red for his eye-sockets' rim.

Then I cast loose my buffcoat, each holster let fall,
Shook off both my jack-boots, let go belt and all, 50
Stood up in the stirrup, leaned, patted his ear,
Called my Roland his pet-name, my horse without peer;
Clapped my hands, laughed and sang, any noise, bad or good,
Till at length into Aix Roland galloped and stood.

And all I remember is—friends flocking round 55
As I sat with his head 'twixt my knees on the ground;
And no voice but was praising this Roland of mine,
As I poured down his throat our last measure of wine,
Which (the burgesses voted by common consent)
Was no more than his due who brought good news from Ghent. 60

ROBERT BROWNING

This poem tells its story not from the point of view of the poet, as in a lyrical narrative, but from the point of view of the narrator. The main question or theme is: "Will the rider reach Aix in time to save the city?" He starts off with his two companions at a breakneck speed. Suspense mounts as first one and then the other companion rides his horse to death. Marked by their rapid pace, the lines echo the gallop of the horses and their final exhausted heaves. The answer to the main question of the poem and its climax occur at the end of the action—a fact that underlines the unity of structure in this narrative.

In a dramatic narrative, on the other hand, the action is not told by the writer himself or the narrator, that is, the fictitious *I*, but consists rather of a character's own thoughts or statements. A comparison of "How They Brought the Good News from Ghent to Aix" with "My Last Duchess" (p. 185) helps to reveal the different emphasis of these two kinds of poetry. In the narrative poem the emphasis is on the action—what happened and how it happened. In the dramatic poem the emphasis is on the motives behind the action. In the narrative poem the story is told about a past event; in "My Last Duchess" the impression is created that the scene is being acted out before our eyes. The Duke speaks to an envoy from the Count and walks and gestures as if he were on stage.

Browning's longer dramatic poems, "Andrea del Sarto" for instance (p. 238), approximates even more closely the structure of the true drama, that is, an action suitable for actual presentation on a stage. In that poem he has a *starting point*—Andrea seeks to persuade his wife Lucrezia to spend the evening with him;—a *rising action*—his persuasive appeal based upon his total dedication to Lucrezia; a swift *turning point* and *resolution*—Lucrezia decides to go out, after all, with her "cousin." More important than this illusion of dramatic action, however, is the depth, range, and, above all, the plausibility of the characterization. Because Andrea del Sarto is himself speaking we take him at his own word. His testimony about himself has all the force of a private confession, whereas the narrative poem, even when written in the first person, is a public or less personal revelation.

For all its dramatic qualities, the so-called dramatic poem is not true poetic drama. A verse play of Sophocles, Shakespeare, or Racine possesses many advantages that the shorter dramatic poem lacks. First of all, the drama proper presents a whole action with its developed beginning, middle, and end, whereas the dramatic poem merely suggests the whole action and concentrates on a specific crucial incident, the moment that shapes a life. Moreover, drama proper tells its story through action as well as through monologue, soliloquy, and dialogue, whereas the dramatic poem merely hints at action in the course of a monologue or a soliloquy. Again, the true poetic drama exhibits several main characters and often a large number of minor ones, while the dramatic poem merely refers to the presence of one or two necessarily shadowy presences. Finally, the dramatic monologue is restricted to one predominant tone or point of view, whereas the drama proper can emphasize in successive scenes the attitudes of kings and queens, saints and sinners.

THE EPIC

The epic is a long narrative poem that is distinguished from other forms of narrative by its aim, action, central character, method of development, tone, and style. Its aim is exalted admiration for a hero who triumphs over many extraordinary difficulties. The hero himself is a leader, either of a race, a nation, or a religion. The action is a series of incidents and episodes unified around a central theme; in *The Iliad,* how Achilles' wrath affected the destiny of the Greeks and Trojans; in *The Odyssey,* how Odysseus's inspiring courage brought him home to Ithaca; in *The Aeneid,* how Aeneas's sense of duty founded the Roman state; in *Beowulf,* how that chieftain's courage saved the Geats from Grendel and other mythological monsters; in *Paradise Lost* and *Paradise Regained,* how Adam lost paradise and was redeemed by the mercy of Christ.

Primitive epics, *The Iliad* and *Beowulf* for instance, originated in folk tales or popular lays about folk heroes. These tales were transmitted orally from generation to generation, refined, amplified and fashioned to the public image of a hero who embodied the ideals and traditions of a race, a nation, or a religion. Then, an individual poet gathered these fragments into a continuous narrative poem. But the primitive epic, like the ballad, is often uneven in narrative technique. On the other hand the literary epic, or epic of art—chiefly the creation of the Roman poet Vergil—is the result of a careful study and modification of Homer's practice in *The Iliad* and *The Odyssey.* Subsequent poets imitated Vergil's practice in *The Aeneid;* from this body of poetry, critics and schoolmasters derived rules and conventions that eventually established an epic tradition.

The epic tradition demands a noble, even a godlike hero, one capable of expressing the aspirations of a whole people. Even the subordinate figures, like Hector in *The Iliad,* are heroic. The characters are partly historical, partly legendary, partly mythological. Pagan gods and goddesses, unseen and unknowable fates, or, in Christian poetry, God, the Virgin, and the saints, are all actors in the epic.

The structure or order of development is on the same grand scale as the hero and the action. Very frequently the poem begins with a solemn invocation to the Muse, the goddess of poetry, or to the Holy Spirit, the source of divine inspiration. This prayerful opening leads often to a formal statement of the theme, as in Milton's *Paradise Lost,*

> And chiefly Thou, O Spirit, . . .
> Instruct me, . . .
> what in me is dark
> Illumine, what is low raise and support;
> That to the height of this great argument
> I may assert Eternal Providence,
> And justify the ways of God to men.

The initial action is presented sometimes in chronological order, more often *in medias res,* in the middle of things, the better to bring the reader to a crucial moment of the story. Thus, *The Aeneid* begins in the sixth year of Aeneas's wandering. Then, in Books II-III, the parts that have been omitted are described or narrated. *Paradise Lost* begins long after Satan's original revolt; later, in Book VII, the Archangel Raphael tells Adam of this earlier history.

The subsequent action centers on the difficulties of the hero. He confronts a main obstacle or conflict, as well as minor ones that are related to it. Thus, in *The Aeneid* Aeneas's main obstacle is the goddess Juno's opposition to the founding of Rome. Minor obstacles are storms at sea, Aeneas's infatuation with Dido, who would deter him from his task, and the war with King Turnus. The literary epic tolerates digressions, that is, incidents that are only indirectly related to the main action, but are interesting for their own sake and contribute to the variety of the poem.

The tone of the literary epic is heroic, dignified, even exalted and in harmony with the emotions it attempts to evoke and the noble characters and ideals that are exhibited for our admiration. Only a great personality may attempt the literary epic. The epic writer must possess a deep sense of national history, a philosophic understanding of human destiny, the imaginative power to represent complicated action, and the gift of contemplation that has been defined as "the impassioned vision of the worth of things." Moreover, he must possess extraordinary technical skill. He must maintain a style that is dignified yet vigorous, uniform yet sufficiently varied to avoid monotony. Although the epic is predominantly narrative, the writer must be able to dramatize scenes effectively, to present speeches with appropriate rhetorical effects, to describe realistically without tilting his poem toward mere notation, and to introduce lyrical elements at appropriate moments in the story.

It is not surprising, therefore, that there are so few epics. English literature numbers one great primitive epic, *Beowulf*, and one great literary epic, *Paradise Lost.* Poems that derive from the epic abound. Alexander Pope's *The Rape of the Lock* employs the conventions of the epic and its methods and style for the purpose of satirizing the society of his day. But this "mock epic" is the anti-type of the parent form. Tennyson's *The Idylls of the King* has at least one epic figure, King Arthur, but the book is not a unified whole. King Arthur is central but not essential to an action that is discontinuous and unresolved. More recent attempts at the epic, Thomas Hardy's *The Dynasts,* Alfred Noyes's *Drake,* Stephen Vincent Benét's *John Brown's Body,* and Archibald MacLeish's *Conquistador,* all testify to the endurance of the epic impulse, even in times when disbelief in the noble hero undermined the very assumptions upon which the epic is based.

With the epic we conclude our discussion of the major types of poetry. The so-called minor types, the French forms (the ballade, rondeau, the triolet), the epigram and the epitaph, light verse of various kinds—all these varieties of poetry may usually be considered lyrics, or narratives, or combinations of these types. It is obvious, however, that many poems cannot be properly classified in any of these categories or even in any of the cross classifications described by terms like lyric narrative, dramatic lyric, elegiac epic, and so on. Dante's *The Divine Comedy,* for instance, is unique, even though it is frequently called an epic.

Other poems that are neither lyrics, narratives, or dramas may be conveniently described as verse essays. The verse essay, like its prose counterpart, may be either formal or informal. The formal variety attempts systematically and explicitly to instruct its readers in some philosophical system, as in Lucretius' *De Rerum Natura* (*On the Nature of Things*) or Pope's *Essay on Man* (p. 85). Poems of this type often come perilously close to prose statement. Many of them nevertheless do contain important poetic values, particularly in passages where the thought glows white hot and imagination comes to the aid of reason. The informal verse essay often consists in a series of reflective comments that have a generally didactic purpose, as in James Thomson's *The Seasons,* where the poet sees in nature not only the source of poetic enthusiasm, but also "of philosophical reflection and moral sentiment."

SATIRE

Another segment of poetry that defies classification is satire. Strictly speaking, there is no special form of satirical writing. For satire, the ridicule of vice or folly, may be found in a lyric poem like W. B. Yeats's "The Scholars" (p. 181), in a narrative poem like W. H. Auden's "In Schrafft's" (p. 177), in a dramatic narrative like Robert Browning's "Soliloquy of the Spanish Cloister" (p. 27), in a mock epic like Pope's *The Rape of the Lock,* in a verse essay like Lord Byron's "English Bards and Scotch Reviewers" (p. 257), indeed, in any form of poetry. Satire is really an attitude that a writer takes toward his material and conveys through the tone of his work. Hence, we divide satire according to its predominant tone. One tone is traditionally called Horatian; the other, Juvenalian.

Horatian satire (after the Roman poet, Horace) is genial, general and urbane—genial in the sense that the Horatian satirist is not bitter or violently angry; general in the sense that he is concerned with human nature rather than individuals; urbane in the sense that he expresses his views with elegance and restraint. On the other hand, Juvenalian satire (after the Roman poet, Juvenal) is often extremely angry and violent. The Juvenalian satirist is revolted at some moral laxity or culpable stupidity, directs his attacks at a person or at clearly recognizable groups and frequently carries invective to an excess. For him "'Tis an action of virtue to make an example of vicious men." Pope, England's greatest satirist, has given us perhaps the best examples of both kinds of satire, the Horatian kind in his humorous *The Rape of the Lock*, the Juvenalian kind in his angry epistle, *The Dunciad*.

Since the eighteenth century, a period especially favorable to satire because of its neo-classical emphasis on the teaching (and correcting) function of poetry, few major satires have been attempted. Among the nineteenth-century Romantics only Byron could be properly called an important satirist. The satirical temper is now expressed less directly, often in humorless irony and paradox, or in light verse. Frequently, modern satire appears in the form of ironic self-revelation, as in T. S. Eliot's "The Love Song of J. Alfred Prufrock." Perhaps one reason for the decline of satire is the gradual attrition of standards. For a true satirist is a man who has strong intellectual, moral, social, and esthetic convictions. Because he knows, or thinks he knows, what is right, he resents what he knows, or thinks he knows, is wrong. He is angry, "and sins not," at error, vice, unmannerliness, and poor taste. Once doubt creeps in, the poet no longer feels free to say what *is* right or wrong, true or false, beautiful or ugly, and thus one motive for satire weakens, if it does not entirely disappear.

POEMS FOR DISCUSSION

THE DEMON LOVER

"O where have you been, my long, long love,
  This long seven years and mair?"
"O I'm come to seek my former vows
  Ye granted me before."

"O hold your tongue of your former vows, 5
  For they will breed sad strife;
O hold your tongue of your former vows,
  For I am become a wife."

He turned him right and round about,
  And the tear blinded his ee: 10

"I wad never hae trodden on Irish ground,
  If it had not been for thee.

"I might hae had a king's daughter,
  Far, far beyond the sea;
I might have had a king's daughter, 15
  Had it not been for love o thee."

"If ye might have had a king's daughter,
  Yer sel ye had to blame;
Ye might have had taken the king's daughter,
  For ye kend that I was nane. 20

"If I was to leave my husband dear,
  And my two babes also,
O what have you to take me to,
  If with you I should go?"

"I hae seven ships upon the sea— 25
  The eighth brought me to land—
With four-and-twenty bold mariners,
  And music on every hand."

She has taken up her two little babes,
  Kissd them baith cheek and chin: 30
"O fair ye weel, my ain two babes,
  For I'll never see you again."

She set her foot upon the ship,
  No mariners could she behold;
But the sails were o the taffetie, 35
  And the masts o the beaten gold.

She had not sailed a league, a league,
  A league but barely three,
When dismal grew his countenance,
  And drumlie grew his ee. 40

They had not sailed a league, a league,
  A league but barely three,
Until she espied his cloven foot,
  And she wept right bitterlie.

40. Drumlie: dark

"O hold your tongue of your weeping," says he, 45
"Of your weeping now let me be;
I will shew you how the lilies grow
On the banks of Italy."

"O what hills are yon, yon pleasant hills,
That the sun shines sweetly on?" 50
"O yon are the hills of heaven," he said,
"Where you will never win."

"O whaten a mountain is yon," she said,
"All so dreary wi frost and snow?"
"O yon is the mountain of hell," he cried, 55
"Where you and I will go."

He strack the tap-mast wi his hand,
The fore-mast wi his knee,
And he brake the gallant ship in twain,
And sank her in the sea. 60

ANONYMOUS

1. What characteristics of the ballad (see pp. 218-21) are evident in this poem?
2. Both this poem and "La Belle Dame Sans Merci" (p. 222) tell stories. Compare and contrast their narrative methods.

THE LISTENERS

"Is there anybody there?" said the Traveler,
Knocking on the moonlit door;
And his horse in the silence champed the grasses
Of the forest's ferny floor:
And a bird flew up out of the turret, 5
Above the Traveler's head:
And he smote upon the door again a second time;
"Is there anybody there?" he said.
But no one descended to the Traveler;
No head from the leaf-fringed sill 10
Leaned over and looked into his grey eyes,
Where he stood perplexed and still.
But only a host of phantom listeners
That dwelt in the lone house then

Stood listening in the quiet of the moonlight 15
  To that voice from the world of men:
Stood thronging the faint moonbeams on the dark stair,
  That goes down to the empty hall,
Hearkening in an air stirred and shaken
  By the lonely Traveler's call. 20
And he felt in his heart their strangeness,
  Their stillness answering his cry,
While his horse moved, cropping the dark turf,
  'Neath the starred and leafy sky;
For he suddenly smote on the door, even 25
  Louder, and lifted his head—
"Tell them I came, and no one answered,
  That I kept my word," he said.
Never the least stir made the listeners,
  Though every word he spake 30
Fell echoing through the shadowiness of the still house
  From the one man left awake:
Ay, they heard his foot upon the stirrup,
  And the sound of iron on stone,
And how the silence surged softly backward, 35
  When the plunging hoofs were gone.

WALTER DE LA MARE

1. Who is the Traveler? Is he meant to have a real or symbolic existence? Explain.
2. Who are the listeners? Are they meant to have a real or symbolic existence? Explain.
3. Why is the house empty yet full of listeners?
4. What does the promise (line 28) suggest? Does the indefiniteness of the suggestion harmonize with the tone of the passage?
5. Point out some resemblances between this poem and the preceding poem. Point out some differences.

ANDREA DEL SARTO

(called "The Faultless Painter")

But do not let us quarrel any more,
No, my Lucrezia; bear with me for once:
Sit down and all shall happen as you wish.
You turn your face, but does it bring your heart?

I'll work then for your friend's friend, never fear, 5
Treat his own subject after his own way,
Fix his own time, accept too his own price,
And shut the money into this small hand
When next it takes mine. Will it? tenderly?
Oh, I'll content him,—but tomorrow, Love! 10
I often am much wearier than you think,
This evening more than usual, and it seems
As if—forgive now—should you let me sit
Here by the window with your hand in mine
And look a half-hour forth on Fiesole, 15
Both of one mind, as married people use,
Quietly, quietly, the evening through,
I might get up tomorrow to my work
Cheerful and fresh as ever. Let us try.
Tomorrow how you shall be glad for this! 20
Your soft hand is a woman of itself,
And mine the man's bared breast she curls inside.
Don't count the time lost, neither; you must serve
For each of the five pictures we require—
It saves a model. So! keep looking so— 25
My serpentining beauty, rounds on rounds!
—How could you ever prick those perfect ears,
Even to put the pearl there! oh, so sweet—
My face, my moon, my everybody's moon,
Which everybody looks on and calls his, 30
And, I suppose, is looked on by in turn,
While she looks—no one's: very dear, no less!
You smile? why, there's my picture ready made.
There's what we painters call our harmony!
A common greyness silvers everything,— 35
All in a twilight, you and I alike
—You, at the point of your first pride in me
(That's gone, you know),—but I, at every point;
My youth, my hope, my art, being all toned down
To yonder sober pleasant Fiesole. 40
There's the bell clinking from the chapel-top;
That length of convent-wall across the way
Holds the trees safer, huddled more inside;
The last monk leaves the garden; days decrease
And autumn grows, autumn is everything. 45
Eh? the whole seems to fall into a shape
As if I saw alike my work and self

And all that I was born to be and do,
A twilight-piece. Love, we are in God's hand.
How strange now, looks the life he makes us lead; 50
So free we seem, so fettered fast we are!
I feel he laid the fetter: let it lie!
This chamber for example—turn your head—
All that's behind us! You don't understand
Nor care to understand about my art, 55
But you can hear at least when people speak;
And that cartoon, the second from the door
—It is the thing, Love! So such things should be—
Behold Madonna! I am bold to say.
I can do with my pencil what I know, 60
What I see, what at bottom of my heart
I wish for, if I ever wish so deep—
Do easily, too—when I say perfectly
I do not boast, perhaps: yourself are judge
Who listened to the Legate's talk last week. 65
And just as much they used to say in France.
At any rate 'tis easy, all of it,
No sketches first, no studies, that's long past—
I do what many dream of all their lives
—Dream? strive to do, and agonize to do, 70
And fail in doing. I could count twenty such
On twice your fingers, and not leave this town,
Who strive—you don't know how the others strive
To paint a little thing like that you smeared
Carelessly passing with your robes afloat,— 75
Yet do much less, so much less, Someone says,
(I know his name, no matter)—so much less!
Well, less is more, Lucrezia: I am judged.
There burns a truer light of God in them,
In their vexed, beating, stuffed and stopped-up brain, 80
Heart, or whate'er else, than goes on to prompt
This low-pulsed forthright craftsman's hand of mine.
Their works drop groundward, but themselves, I know,
Reach many a time a heaven that's shut to me,
Enter and take their place there sure enough, 85
Though they come back and cannot tell the world.
My works are nearer heaven, but I sit here.
The sudden blood of these men! at a word—
Praise them, it boils, or blame them, it boils too.
I, painting from myself and to myself, 90

Know what I do, am unmoved by men's blame
Or their praise either. Somebody remarks
Morello's outline there is wrongly traced,
His hue mistaken; what of that? or else,
Rightly traced and well ordered; what of that? 95
Speak as they please, what does the mountain care?
Ah, but a man's reach should exceed his grasp,
Or what's a heaven for? All is silver-grey
Placid and perfect with my art: the worse!
I know both what I want and what might gain, 100
And yet how profitless to know, to sigh
"Had I been two, another and myself,
Our head would have o'erlooked the world!" No doubt.
Yonder's a work now, of that famous youth
The Urbinate who died five years ago. 105
('Tis copied, George Vasari sent it me.)
Well, I can fancy how he did it all,
Pouring his soul, with kings and popes to see,
Reaching, that heaven might so replenish him,
Above and through his art—for it gives way; 110
That arm is wrongly put—and there again—
A fault to pardon in the drawing's lines,
Its body, so to speak: its soul is right,
He means right—that, a child may understand.
Still, what an arm! and I could alter it: 115
But all the play, the insight and the stretch—
Out of me, out of me! And wherefore out?
Had you enjoined them on me, given me soul,
We might have risen to Rafael, I and you!
Nay, Love, you did give all I asked, I think— 120
More than I merit, yes, by many times.
But had you—oh, with the same perfect brow,
And perfect eyes, and more than perfect mouth,
And the low voice my soul hears, as a bird
The fowler's pipe, and follows to the snare— 125
Had you, with these the same, but brought a mind!
Some women do so. Had the mouth there urged
"God and the glory! never care for gain.
The present by the future, what is that?
Live for fame, side by side with Agnolo! 130
Rafael is waiting; up to God, all three!"

93. Morello: mountain peak near Florence
105. Urbinate: Raphael, born in Urbino

I might have done it for you. So it seems:
Perhaps not. All is as God over-rules.
Besides, incentives come from the soul's self;
The rest avail not. Why do I need you? 135
What wife had Rafael, or has Agnolo?
In this world, who can do a thing, will not;
And who would do it, cannot, I perceive:
Yet the will's somewhat—somewhat, too, the power—
And thus we half-men struggle. At the end, 140
God, I conclude, compensates, punishes.
'Tis safer for me, if the award be strict,
That I am something underrated here,
Poor this long while, despised, to speak the truth.
I dared not, do you know, leave home all day, 145
For fear of chancing on the Paris lords.
The best is when they pass and look aside;
But they speak sometimes; I must bear it all.
Well may they speak! That Francis, that first time,
And that long festal year at Fontainebleau! 150
I surely then could sometimes leave the ground,
Put on the glory, Rafael's daily wear,
In that humane great monarch's golden look,—
One finger in his beard or twisted curl
Over his mouth's good mark that made the smile, 155
One arm about my shoulder, round my neck,
The jingle of his gold chain in my ear,
I painting proudly with his breath on me,
All his court round him, seeing with his eyes,
Such frank French eyes, and such a fire of souls 160
Profuse, my hand kept plying by those hearts,—
And, best of all, this, this, this face beyond,
This in the background, waiting on my work,
To crown the issue with a last reward!
A good time, was it not, my kingly days? 165
And had you not grown restless . . . but I know—
'Tis done and past; 'twas right, my instinct said;
Too live the life grew, golden and not grey,
And I'm the weak-eyed bat no sun should tempt
Out of the grange whose four walls make his world. 170
How could it end in any other way?
You called me, and I came home to your heart.
The triumph was—to reach and stay there; since
I reached it ere the triumph, what is lost?

Let my hands frame your face in your hair's gold, 175
You beautiful Lucrezia that are mine!
"Rafael did this, Andrea painted that;
The Roman's is the better when you pray,
But still the other's Virgin was his wife—"
Men will excuse me. I am glad to judge 180
Both pictures in your presence; clearer grows
My better fortune, I resolve to think.
For, do you know, Lucrezia, as God lives,
Said one day Agnolo, his very self,
To Rafael . . . I have known it all these years . . . 185
(When the young man was flaming out his thoughts
Upon a palace-wall for Rome to see,
Too lifted up in heart because of it)
"Friend, there's a certain sorry little scrub
Goes up and down our Florence, none cares how, 190
Who, were he set to plan and execute
As you are, pricked on by your popes and kings,
Would bring the sweat into that brow of yours!"
To Rafael's!—And indeed the arm is wrong.
I hardly dare . . . yet, only you to see, 195
Give the chalk here—quick, thus the line should go!
Ay, but the soul! he's Rafael! rub it out!
Still, all I care for, if he spoke the truth,
(What he? why, who but Michel Agnolo?
Do you forget already words like those?) 200
If really there was such a chance, so lost,—
Is, whether you're—not grateful—but more pleased.
Well, let me think so. And you smile indeed!
This hour has been an hour! Another smile?
If you would sit thus by me every night 205
I should work better, do you comprehend?
I mean that I should earn more, give you more.
See, it is settled dusk now; there's a star;
Morello's gone, the watch-lights show the wall,
The cue-owls speak the name we call them by. 210
Come from the window, Love,—come in, at last,
Inside the melancholy little house
We built to be so gay with. God is just.
King Francis may forgive me; oft at nights
When I look up from painting, eyes tired out, 215
The walls become illumined, brick from brick
Distinct, instead of mortar, fierce bright gold,

That gold of his I did cement them with!
Let us but love each other. Must you go?
That Cousin here again? he waits outside? 220
Must see you—you, and not with me? Those loans?
More gaming debts to pay? you smiled for that?
Well, let smiles buy me! have you more to spend?
While hand and eye and something of a heart
Are left me, work's my ware, and what's it worth? 225
I'll pay my fancy. Only let me sit
The grey remainder of the evening out,
Idle, you call it, and muse perfectly
How I could paint, were I but back in France,
One picture, just one more—the Virgin's face, 230
Not yours this time! I want you at my side
To hear them—that is, Michel Agnolo—
Judge all I do and tell you of its worth.
Will you? To-morrow, satisfy your friend.
I take the subjects for his corridor, 235
Finish the portrait out of hand—there, there,
And throw him in another thing or two
If he demurs; the whole should prove enough
To pay for this same Cousin's freak. Beside,
What's better and what's all I care about, 240
Get you the thirteen scudi for the ruff!
Love, does that please you? Ah, but what does he,
The Cousin! what does he to please you more?

I am grown peaceful as old age to-night.
I regret little, I would change still less. 245
Since there my past life lies, why alter it?
The very wrong to Francis!—it is true
I took his coin, was tempted and complied,
And built this house and sinned, and all is said.
My father and my mother died of want. 250
Well, had I riches of my own? you see
How one gets rich! Let each one bear his lot.
They were born poor, lived poor, and poor they died:
And I have laboured somewhat in my time
And not been paid profusely. Some good son 255
Paint my two hundred pictures—let him try!
No doubt, there's something strikes a balance. Yes,
You loved me quite enough, it seems to-night.

241. Scudi: a coin

This must suffice me here. What would one have?
In heaven, perhaps, new chances, one more chance— 260
Four great walls in the New Jerusalem,
Meted on each side by the angel's reed,
For Leonard, Rafael, Agnolo and me
To cover—the three first without a wife,
While I have mine! So—still they overcome 265
Because there's still Lucrezia,—as I choose.

Again the Cousin's whistle! Go, my Love.

ROBERT BROWNING

1. What is the central conflict in this poem? In what lines is it foreshadowed? Where is it resolved?
2. How does Andrea reveal his character (a) by his attitude toward his wife? (b) by his attitude toward his art? (c) by his attitude toward himself?
3. Show how the speaker enlivens the narrative (a) by direct description of action; (b) by suggestive description of action.
4. What are the principal ironies in this poem? Where do they occur? How do they illuminate the action? the characterization?
5. How is Lucrezia's character revealed?
6. Compare this poem with "Tithonus," p. 114. Which is the more dramatic? Why?
7. How does the order of this poem differ from that of a narrative like "How They Brought the Good News from Ghent to Aix," p. 228?

PARADISE LOST

Book I

Of Man's first disobedience, and the fruit
Of that forbidden tree, whose mortal taste
Brought death into the world, and all our woe,
With loss of Eden, till one greater Man
Restore us, and regain the blissful seat, 5
Sing, Heavenly Muse, that, on the secret top
Of Oreb, or of Sinai, didst inspire
That shepherd who first taught the chosen seed
In the beginning how the heavens and earth
Rose out of Chaos: or, if Sion hill 10
Delight thee more, and Siloa's brook that flowed
Fast by the oracle of God, I thence

Invoke thy aid to my adventurous song,
That with no middle flight intends to soar
Above th' Aonian mount, while it pursues 15
Things unattempted yet in prose or rhyme.
And chiefly thou, Oh Spirit, that dost prefer
Before all temples th' upright heart and pure,
Instruct me, for thou know'st; thou from the first
Wast present, and, with mighty wings outspread, 20
Dove-like sat'st brooding on the vast Abyss,
And mad'st it pregnant: what in me is dark
Illumine, what is low raise and support;
That, to the height of this great argument,
I may assert Eternal Providence, 25
And justify the ways of God to men.
  Say first—for Heaven hides nothing from thy view,
Nor the deep tract of Hell—say first what cause
Moved our grand parents, in that happy state,
Favoured of Heaven so highly, to fall off 30
From their Creator, and transgress his will
For one restraint, lords of the World besides.
Who first seduced them to that foul revolt?
  Th' infernal Serpent; he it was whose guile,
Stirred up with envy and revenge, deceived 35
The mother of mankind, what time his pride
Had cast him out from Heaven, with all his host
Of rebel Angels, by whose aid, aspiring
To set himself in glory above his peers,
He trusted to have equalled the Most High, 40
If he opposed, and with ambitious aim
Against the throne and monarchy of God,
Raised impious war in Heaven and battle proud,
With vain attempt. Him the Almighty Power
Hurled headlong flaming from th' ethereal sky, 45
With hideous ruin and combustion, down
To bottomless perdition, there to dwell
In adamantine chains and penal fire,
Who durst defy th' Omnipotent to arms.
  Nine times the space that measures day and night 50
To mortal men, he, with his horrid crew,
Lay vanquished, rolling in the fiery gulf,
Confounded, though immortal. But his doom
Reserved him to more wrath; for now the thought
Both of lost happiness and lasting pain 55

Torments him: round he throws his baleful eyes,
That witnessed huge affliction and dismay,
Mixed with obdúrate pride and steadfast hate.
At once, as far as Angels ken, he views
The dismal situation waste and wild. 60
A dungeon horrible, on all sides round,
As one great furnace flamed; yet from those flames
No light; but rather darkness visible
Served only to discover sights of woe,
Regions of sorrow, doleful shades, where peace 65
And rest can never dwell, hope never comes
That comes to all, but torture without end
Still urges, and a fiery deluge, fed
With ever-burning sulphur unconsumed.
Such place Eternal Justice had prepared 70
For those rebellious; here their prison ordained
In utter darkness, and their portion set,
As far removed from God and light of Heaven
As from the centre thrice to th' utmost pole.
Oh how unlike the place from whence they fell! 75
There the companions of his fall, o'erwhelmed
With floods and whirlwinds of tempestuous fire,
He soon discerns; and, weltering by his side,
One next himself in power, and next in crime,
Long after known in Palestine and named 80
Beëlzebub. To whom th' Arch-Enemy,
And thence in Heaven called Satan, with bold words
Breaking the horrid silence, thus began,—
"If thou beest he—but Oh how fallen! how changed
From him who, in the happy realms of light 85
Clothed with transcendent brightness, didst outshine
Myriads, though bright!—if he whom mutual league,
United thoughts and counsels, equal hope
And hazard in the glorious enterprise,
Joined with me once, now misery hath joined 90
In equal ruin; into what pit thou seest
From what height fallen: so much the stronger proved
He with his thunder: and till then who knew
The force of those dire arms? Yet not for those,
Nor what the potent Victor in his rage 95
Can else inflict, do I repent, or change,
Though changed in outward lustre, that fixed mind,
And high disdain from sense of injured merit,

That with the Mightiest raised me to contend,
And to the fierce contentions brought along 100
Innumerable force of Spirits armed,
That durst dislike his reign, and, me preferring,
His utmost power with adverse power opposed
In dubious battle on the plains of Heaven,
And shook his throne. What though the field be lost 105
All is not lost—the unconquerable will,
And study of revenge, immortal hate,
And courage never to submit or yield:
And what is else not to be overcome?
That glory never shall his wrath or might 110
Extort from me. To bow and sue for grace
With suppliant knee, and deify his power
Who, from the terror of this arm, so late
Doubted his empire—that were low indeed;
That were an ignominy and shame beneath 115
This downfall, since, by fate, the strength of Gods,
And this empyreal substance, cannot fail;
Since, through experience of this great event,
In arms not worse, in foresight much advanced,
We may with more successful hope resolve 120
To wage by force or guile eternal war,
Irreconcilable to our grand Foe,
Who now triúmphs, and in th' excess of joy
Sole reigning holds the tyranny of Heaven."
So spake th' apostate Angel, though in pain, 125
Vaunting aloud, but racked with deep despair;
And him thus answered soon his bold compeer,—
"Oh Prince, Oh Chief of many thronéd Powers
That led th' embattled Seraphim to war
Under thy conduct, and, in dreadful deeds 130
Fearless, endangered Heaven's perpetual King,
And put to proof his high supremacy,
Whether upheld by strength, or chance, or fate,
Too well I see and rue the dire event
That, with sad overthrow and foul defeat, 135
Hath lost us Heaven, and all this mighty host
In horrible destruction laid thus low,
As far as Gods and heavenly Essences
Can perish: for the mind and spirit remains
Invincible, and vigour soon returns, 140
Though all our glory extinct, and happy state

Here swallowed up in endless misery.
But what if he our Conqueror (whom I now
Of force believe almighty, since no less
Than such could have o'erpowered such force as ours) 145
Have left us this our spirit and strength entire,
Strongly to suffer and support our pains,
That we may so suffice his vengeful ire,
Or do him mightier service as his thralls
By right of war, whate'er his business be, 150
Here in the heart of Hell to work in fire,
Or do his errands in the gloomy Deep?
What can it then avail though yet we feel
Strength undiminished, or eternal being
To undergo eternal punishment?" 155
Whereto with speedy words th' Arch-Fiend replied,—
"Fallen Cherub, to be weak is miserable,
Doing or suffering: but of this be sure—
To do aught good never will be our task,
But ever to do ill our sole delight, 160
As being the contrary to his high will
Whom we resist. If then his providence
Out of our evil seek to bring forth good,
Our labour must be to pervert that end,
And out of good still to find means of evil; 165
Which ofttimes may succeed so as perhaps
Shall grieve him, if I fail not, and disturb
His inmost counsels from their destined aim.
But see! the angry Victor hath recalled
His ministers of vengeance and pursuit 170
Back to the gates of Heaven: the sulphurous hail,
Shot after us in storm, o'erblown hath laid
The fiery surge that from the precipice
Of Heaven received us falling; and the thunder,
Winged with red lightning and impetuous rage, 175
Perhaps hath spent his shafts, and ceases now
To bellow through the vast and boundless Deep.
Let us not slip th' occasion, whether scorn
Or satiate fury yield it from our Foe.
Seest thou yon dreary plain, forlorn and wild, 180
The seat of desolation, void of light,
Save what the glimmering of these livid flames
Casts pale and dreadful? Thither let us tend

From off the tossing of these fiery waves;
There rest, if any rest can harbour there; 185
And, re-assembling our afflicted powers,
Consult how we may henceforth most offend
Our enemy, our own loss how repair,
How overcome this dire calamity,
What reinforcement we may gain from hope, 190
If not, what resolution from despair."
  Thus Satan, talking to his nearest mate,
With head uplift above the wave, and eyes
That sparkling blazed; his other parts besides
Prone on the flood, extended long and large, 195
Lay floating many a rood, in bulk as huge
As whom the fables name of monstrous size,
Titanian or Earth-born, that warred on Jove,
Briareos or Typhon, whom the den
By ancient Tarsus held, or that sea-beast 200
Leviathan, which God of all his works
Created hugest that swim th' ocean-stream.
Him, haply slumbering on the Norway foam,
The pilot of some small night-foundered skiff,
Deeming some island, oft, as sea-men tell, 205
With fixéd anchor in his scaly rind,
Moors by his side under the lee, while night
Invests the sea, and wishéd morn delays.
So stretched out huge in length the Arch-fiend lay,
Chained on the burning lake; nor ever thence 210
Had risen, or heaved his head, but that the will
And high permission of all-ruling Heaven
Left him at large to his own dark designs,
That with reiterated crimes he might
Heap on himself damnation, while he sought 215
Evil to others, and enraged might see
How all his malice served but to bring forth
Infinite goodness, grace, and mercy, shewn
On Man by him seduced, but on himself
Treble confusion, wrath, and vengeance poured. 220
  Forthwith upright he rears from off the pool
His mighty stature; on each hand the flames
Driven backward slope their pointing spires, and, rolled
In billows, leave i' th' midst a horrid vale.
Then with expanded wings he steers his flight 225

Aloft, incumbent on the dusky air,
That felt unusual weight; till on dry land
He lights—if it were land that ever burned
With solid, as the lake with liquid fire,
And such appeared in hue as when the force 230
Of subterranean wind transports a hill
Torn from Pelorus, or the shattered side
Of thundering Etna, whose combustible
And fuelled entrails, thence conceiving fire,
Sublimed with mineral fury, aid the winds, 235
And leave a singéd bottom all involved
With stench and smoke. Such resting found the sole
Of unblest feet. Him followed his next mate;
Both glorying to have scaped the Stygian flood
As gods, and by their own recovered strength, 240
Not by the sufferance of supernal Power.
"Is this the region, this the soil, the clime,"
Said then the lost Archangel, "this the seat
That we must change for Heaven?—this mournful gloom
For that celestial light? Be it so, since he 245
Who now is sovereign can dispose and bid
What shall be right: farthest from him is best,
Whom reason hath equalled, force hath made supreme
Above his equals. Farewell, happy fields,
Where joy for ever dwells! Hail, horrors! hail, 250
Infernal World! and thou, profoundest Hell,
Receive thy new possessor—one who brings
A mind not to be changed by place or time.
The mind is its own place, and in itself
Can make a Heaven of Hell, a Hell of Heaven. 255
What matter where, if I be still the same,
And what I should be, all but less than he
Whom thunder hath made greater? Here at least
We shall be free; th' Almighty hath not built
Here for his envy, will not drive us hence: 260
Here we may reign secure; and, in my choice,
To reign is worth ambition, though in Hell:
Better to reign in Hell than serve in Heaven.
But wherefore let we then our faithful friends,
Th' associates and co-partners of our loss, 265
Lie thus astonished on th' oblivious pool,
And call them not to share with us their part
In this unhappy mansion, or once more

With rallied arms to try what may be yet
Regained in Heaven, or what more lost in Hell?" 270
So Satan spake; and him Beëlzebub
Thus answered,—"Leader of those armies bright
Which, but th' Omnipotent, none could have foiled!
If once they hear that voice, their liveliest pledge
Of hope in fears and dangers—heard so oft 275
In worst extremes, and on the perilous edge
Of battle, when it raged, in all assaults
Their surest signal—they will soon resume
New courage and revive, though now they lie
Grovelling and prostrate on yon lake of fire, 280
As we erewhile, astounded and amazed;
No wonder, fallen such a pernicious height!"
He scarce had ceased when the superior Fiend
Was moving toward the shore; his ponderous shield,
Ethereal temper, massy, large, and round, 285
Behind him cast. The broad circumference
Hung on his shoulders like the moon, whose orb
Through optic glass the Tuscan artist views
At evening, from the top of Fesolé,
Or in Valdarno, to descry new lands, 290
Rivers, or mountains, in her spotty globe.
His spear—to equal which the tallest pine
Hewn on Norwegian hills, to be the mast
Of some great ammiral, were but a wand—
He walked with, to support uneasy steps 295
Over the burning marl, not like those steps
On Heaven's azure; and the torrid clime
Smote on him sore besides, vaulted with fire.
Nathless he so endured, till on the beach
Of that inflaméd sea he stood, and called 300
His legions—Angel Forms, who lay entranced
Thick as autumnal leaves that strow the brooks
In Vallombrosa, where th' Etrurian shades
High over-arched embower; or scattered sedge
Afloat, when with fierce winds Orion armed 305
Hath vexed the Red-Sea coast, whose waves o'erthrew
Busiris and his Memphian chivalry,
While with perfidious hatred they pursued
The sojourners of Goshen, who beheld
From the safe shore their floating carcases 310
And broken chariot-wheels; so thick bestrown,

Abject and lost lay these, covering the flood,
Under amazement of their hideous change.
He called so loud that all the hollow deep
Of Hell resounded,—"Princes, Potentates, 315
Warriors, the Flower of Heaven—once yours; now lost,
If such astonishment as this can seize
Eternal Spirits! Or have ye chosen this place
After the toil of battle to repose
Your wearied virtue, for the ease you find 320
To slumber here, as in the vales of Heaven?
Or in this abject posture have ye sworn
To adore the Conqueror, who now beholds
Cherub and Seraph rolling in the flood
With scattered arms and ensigns, till anon 325
His swift pursuers from Heaven-gates discern
Th' advantage, and, descending, tread us down
Thus drooping, or with linkéd thunderbolts
Transfix us to the bottom of this gulf?
Awake, arise, or be for ever fallen!" 330

. . . . .

JOHN MILTON

1. What characteristics of the epic, described on pp. 231 ff, are displayed in this passage?
2. Is the defiant speech of Satan (lines 84-124 and 157-192) designed to evoke admiration for the audacity of the speaker? Why or why not?
3. Show how Milton employs figurative language to intensify the description in lines 192-330.

THE FURNITURE OF A WOMAN'S MIND

1

A set of phrases learnt by rote;
A passion for a scarlet coat;
When at a play to laugh, or cry,
Yet cannot tell the reason why;
Never to hold her tongue a minute, 5
While all she prates has nothing in it.
Whole hours can with a coxcomb sit,
And take his nonsense all for wit.

2. Scarlet coat: soldier's uniform

Her learning mounts to read a song,
But half the words pronouncing wrong; 10
Has every repartee in store
She spoke ten thousand times before.
Can ready compliments supply
On all occasions, cut and dry.
Such hatred to a parson's gown, 15
The sight will put her in a swoon.
For conversation well endued,
She calls it witty to be rude;
And, placing raillery in railing,
Will tell aloud your greatest failing; 20
Nor makes a scruple to expose
Your bandy leg, or crooked nose.
Can at her morning tea run o'er
The scandal of the day before.
Improving hourly in her skill 25
To cheat and wrangle at quadrille.

2

In choosing lace a critic nice,
Knows to a groat the lowest price;
Can in her female clubs dispute
What lining best the silk will suit; 30
What colors each complexion match:
And where with art to place a patch.

3

In chance a mouse creeps in her sight,
Can finely counterfeit a fright;
So sweetly screams if it comes near her, 35
She ravishes all hearts to hear her.
Can dextrously her husband tease
By taking fits whene'er she please;
By frequent practice learns the trick
At proper seasons to be sick; 40
Thinks nothing gives one airs so pretty,
At once creating love and pity.
If Molly happens to be careless,
And but neglects to warm her hair-lace,
She gets a cold as sure as death, 45
And vows she scarce can fetch her breath;

[28]. Groat: coin of small value

Admires how modest woman can
Be so robustious like a man.

4

In party, furious to her power,
A bitter Whig, or Tory sour; 50
Her arguments directly tend
Against the side she would defend:
Will prove herself a Tory plain,
From principles the Whigs maintain;
And, to defend the Whiggish cause, 55
Her topics from the Tories draws.

5

Oh yes! If any man can find
More virtues in a woman's mind,
Let them be sent to Mrs. Harding;
She'll pay the charges to a farthing; 60
Take notice, she has my commission
To add them in the next edition;
They may outsell a better thing;
So, holla, boys! God save the King!

JONATHAN SWIFT

59. Mrs. Harding: a printer

1. Is this satire Horatian or Juvenalian? Why or why not?
2. Do the numbered divisions indicate the discussion of separate topics? Explain.
3. Does the geniality and exaggeration of this satire rob it of caustic bite? Explain.

THE VILLAGE

Theirs is yon house that holds the parish-poor,
Whose walls of mud scarce bear the broken door;
There, where the putrid vapours, flagging, play, 230
And the dull wheel hums doleful through the day;—
There children dwell who know no parents' care;
Parents who know no children's love, dwell there!
Heartbroken matrons on their joyless bed,
Forsaken wives, and mothers never wed; 235
Dejected widows with unheeded tears,

And crippled age with more than childhood fears;
The lame, the blind, and, far the happiest they!
The moping idiot and the madman gay.
Here too the sick their final doom receive, 240
Here brought, amid the scenes of grief, to grieve,
Where the loud groans from some sad chamber flow,
Mixed with the clamours of the crowd below;
Here, sorrowing, they each kindred sorrow scan,
And the cold charities of man to man: 245
Whose laws indeed for ruined age provide,
And strong compulsion plucks the scrap from pride;
But still that scrap is bought with many a sigh,
And pride embitters what it can't deny.
Say ye, oppressed by some fantastic woes, 250
Some jarring nerve that baffles your repose;
Who press the downy couch, while slaves advance
With timid eye, to read the distant glance;
Who with sad prayers the weary doctor tease,
To name the nameless ever-new disease; 255
Who with mock patience dire complaints endure,
Which real pain and that alone can cure;
How would ye bear in real pain to lie,
Despised, neglected, left alone to die?
How would ye bear to draw your latest breath, 260
Where all that's wretched paves the way for death?
Such is that room which one rude beam divides,
And naked rafters form the sloping sides;
Where the vile bands that blind the thatch are seen,
And lath and mud are all that lie between; 265
Save one dull pane, that, coarsely patched, gives way
To the rude tempest, yet excludes the day:
Here, on a matted flock, with dust o'erspread,
The drooping wretch reclines his languid head;
For him no hand the cordial cup applies, 270
Or wipes the tear that stagnates in his eyes;
No friends with soft discourse his pain beguile,
Or promise hope till sickness wears a smile.
But soon a loud and hasty summons calls,
Shakes the thin roof, and echoes round the walls; 275
Anon, a figure enters, quaintly neat,
All pride and business, bustle and conceit;
With looks unaltered by these scenes of woe,
With speed that, entering, speaks his haste to go,

He bids the gazing throng around him fly, 280
And carries fate and physic in his eye:
A potent quack, long versed in human ills,
Who first insults the victim whom he kills;
Whose murderous hand a drowsy bench protect,
And whose most tender mercy is neglect. 285
Paid by the parish for attendance here,
He wears contempt upon his sapient sneer;
In haste he seeks the bed where Misery lies,
Impatience marked in his averted eyes;
And, some habitual queries hurried o'er, 290
Without reply, he rushes on the door:
His drooping patient, long inured to pain,
And long unheeded, knows remonstrance vain;
He ceases now the feeble help to crave
Of man, and silent sinks into the grave. 295

. . . . .

GEORGE CRABBE

1. Is this passage more appropriately termed a verse essay with satirical touches or a genuine satire? Explain. If it is a satire, what kind is it?
2. Contrast the tone of this passage with that of "The Furniture of a Woman's Mind."

ENGLISH BARDS AND SCOTCH REVIEWERS

Still must I hear?—shall hoarse FITZGERALD bawl
His creaking couplets in a tavern hall,
And I not sing, lest, haply, Scotch Reviews
Should dub me scribbler, and denounce my *Muse*?
Prepare for rhyme—I'll publish, right or wrong: 5
Fools are my theme, let Satire be my song.

Oh! Nature's noblest gift—my grey goose-quill!
Slave of my thoughts, obedient to my will,
Torn from thy parent bird to form a pen,
That mighty instrument of little men! 10
The pen! foredoomed to aid the mental throes
Of brains that labour, big with Verse or Prose;
Though Nymphs forsake, and Critics may deride,
The Lover's solace, and the Author's pride.

What Wits! what Poets dost thou daily raise. 15
How frequent is thy use, how small thy praise!
Condemned at length to be forgotten quite,
With all the pages which 'twas thine to write.
But thou, at least, mine own especial pen!
Once laid aside, but now assumed again, 20
Our task complete, like Hamet's shall be free;
Though spurned by others, yet beloved by me:
Then let us soar to-day; no common theme,
No Eastern vision, no distempered dream
Inspires—our path, though full of thorns, is plain; 25
Smooth be the verse, and easy be the strain.

When Vice triumphant holds her sov'reign sway,
Obeyed by all who nought beside obey;
When Folly, frequent harbinger of crime,
Bedecks her cap with bells of every Clime; 30
When knaves and fools combined o'er all prevail,
And weigh their Justice in a Golden Scale;
E'en then the boldest start from public sneers,
Afraid of Shame, unknown to other fears,
More darkly sin, by Satire kept in awe, 35
And shrink from Ridicule, though not from Law.

Such is the force of Wit! but not belong
To me the arrows of satiric song;
The royal vices of our age demand
A keener weapon, and a mightier hand. 40
Still there are follies, e'en for me to chase,
And yield at least amusement in the race:
Laugh when I laugh, I seek no other fame,
The cry is up, and scribblers are my game:
Speed, Pegasus!—ye strains of great and small, 45
Ode! Epic! Elegy!—have at you all!
I, too, can scrawl, and once upon a time
I poured along the town a flood of rhyme,
A schoolboy freak, unworthy praise or blame;
I printed—older children do the same. 50
'Tis pleasant, sure, to see one's name in print;
A Book's a Book, altho' there's nothing in't.
Not that a Title's sounding charm can save
Or scrawl or scribbler from an equal grave:
This LAMB must own, since his patrician name 55

Failed to preserve the spurious Farce from shame.
No matter, GEORGE continues still to write,
Tho' now the name is veiled from public sight.
Moved by the great example, I pursue
The self-same road, but make my own review: 60
Not seek great JEFFREY'S, yet like him will be
Self-constituted Judge of Poesy.

. . . . .

Oh, SOUTHEY! SOUTHEY! cease thy varied song! 225
A bard may chaunt too often and too long:
As thou art strong in verse, in mercy spare!
A fourth, alas! were more than we could bear.
But if, in spite of all the world can say,
Thou still wilt verseward plod thy weary way; 230
If still in Berkeley-Ballads most uncivil,
Thou wilt devote old women to the devil,
The babe unborn thy dread intent may rue:
"God help thee," SOUTHEY, and thy readers too.

Next comes the dull disciple of thy school, 235
That mild apostate from poetic rule,
The simple WORDSWORTH, framer of a lay
As soft as evening in his favourite May,
Who warns his friend "to shake off toil and trouble,
And quit his books, for fear of growing double"; 240
Who, both by precept and example, shows
That prose is verse, and verse is merely prose;
Convincing all, by demonstration plain,
Poetic souls delight in prose insane;
And Christmas stories tortured into rhyme 245
Contain the essence of the true sublime.
Thus, when he tells the tale of Betty Foy,
The idiot mother of "an idiot Boy";
A moon-struck, silly lad, who lost his way,
And, like his bard, confounded night with day; 250
So close on each pathetic part he dwells,
And each adventure so sublimely tells,
That all who view the "idiot in his glory"
Conceive the Bard the hero of the story.

Shall gentle COLERIDGE pass unnoticed here, 255
To turgid ode and tumid stanza dear?

Though themes of innocence amuse him best,
Yet still Obscurity's a welcome guest.
If Inspiration should her aid refuse
To him who takes a Pixy for a muse, 260
Yet none in lofty numbers can surpass
The bard who soars to elegize an ass:
So well the subject suits his noble mind,
He brays, the Laureate of the long-eared kind.

Oh! wonder-working LEWIS! Monk, or Bard, 265
Who fain would make Parnassus a churchyard!
Lo! wreaths of yew, not laurel, bind thy brow,
Thy Muse a Sprite, Apollo's sexton thou.
Whether on ancient tombs thou tak'st thy stand,
By gibb'ring spectres hailed, thy kindred band; 270
Or tracest chaste descriptions on thy page,
To please the females of our modest age;
All hail, M.P.! from whose infernal brain
Thin-sheeted phantoms glide, a grisly train;
At whose command "grim women" throng in crowds, 275
And kings of fire, of water, and of clouds,
With "small grey men,"—"wild yagers," and what not,
To crown with honour thee and WALTER SCOTT:
Again, all hail! if tales like thine may please,
St. Luke alone can vanquish the disease: 280
Even Satan's self with thee might dread to dwell,
And in thy skull discern a deeper Hell.

. . . . .

GEORGE GORDON, LORD BYRON

1. What definition of satire is implied in lines 1-12?
2. Does Byron actually prove his charges against Southey, Wordsworth, Coleridge, and Lewis? Does satire require proof? Why or why not?
3. Compare the tone of Byron's satire with that of "To a Modern Poet" (p. 164) and "The Dunce" (p. 182).

CHAPTER XIII

The Language of Poetry—Style, Rhythm, Melody

IN THE PRECEDING chapters we have seen again and again just how language is the living tissue of a poem. The poet uses words in various combinations to present images, to convey ideas, and to express or suggest emotions. We have seen, too, how the language of poetry is exceptionally clear, vigorous and interesting. Your experience of the language of poetry may have convinced you of the aptness of Coleridge's saying that "Poetry equals the best words in the best order."

To determine more exactly what words are best, what order is best, that is, what style is most appropriate to poetry, let us first consider style in general.

STYLE IN GENERAL

In general style is, in Newman's phrase, "a thinking out into language," the discovery of the right word, the right construction, the right tone for an idea, a feeling, or impression. A good style, then, is the verbal expression of a good mind—that is, a mind that thinks accurately, feels intensely, and images vividly. Hence, grammarians and rhetoricians, no less than critics of poetry, have traditionally described the traits of a good style in terms of clarity, vigor, and interest. These traits correspond to the emotional, intellectual and imaginative elements of a poem, and like those elements, are closely related to each other.

Moreover, it is customary to speak of style in terms of diction, that is, words themselves, and of words in the larger context of the sentence and of sentences within the larger unit of the poem. We say that a word is clear when it exactly conveys an idea or impression. Here *exactly* means that a word not only *denotes* the object or action the writer has in mind, but also suggests, or *connotes,* the writer's attitude towards that object or action. Thus, in "The Echoing Green" (p. 126), Blake prefers the word *green* to *park,* because *green* not only denotes a piece of grassy land, as does a park, but it also connotes a public place where games are played. Hence, *green* is a more exact word for Blake's purposes than is *park.* Note how the italicized words in the sentence below clearly denote an historical event.

The *people* of Paris *approved* the *execution* in the Place de la Concorde.

But note how the italicized words in the next sentence not only denote the same historical event but also convey its emotional and imaginative overtones.

The Parisian *mob howled its approval* as the *guillotine slashed off the head* of Queen Marie Antoinette.

In the second sentence we know what happened and to some extent just how it happened. *Mob,* as opposed to the neutral word *people,* implies a cruel and disorderly rabble; *howled its approval,* as opposed to *approved,* suggests the noisy bestiality of the mob; *guillotine slashed off the head* of Queen Marie Antoinette compels us to visualize the act more vividly than the comparatively neutral word *execution.*

We have already seen in many different examples how figurative language—the metaphor and simile, personification and irony, paradox, and symbol—greatly extend the connotative meanings of language. We know, too, that the qualities of clarity, vigor and interest apply to the sentence order as well as to the choice of words. In poetry we have seen how the normal English word order of subject, verb, and complement may be altered by *inversion* of the usual word order, as in, "Yet ever runs she with reverted face" (Coleridge); by *antithesis* or the balance of equal but opposite ideas, as in "Oft she rejects, but never once offends." (Pope); by rhetorical exclamations, questions, exhortations, apostrophes, as in the lines from Act IV of *Hamlet:*

> How all occasions do inform against me,
> And spur my dull revenge! What is a man,
> If his chief good and market of his time

Be but to sleep and feed? . . .
How stand I then,
That have a father kill'd, a mother stain'd,
Excitements of my reason and my blood,
And let all sleep. . . ?
O, from this time forth,
My thoughts be bloody, or be nothing worth!

But these familiar, general characteristics of style, applicable to prose as well as poetry, take on a different color when we consider an individual poem.

Style Determined by the Context of a Poem

The poet does not normally employ words alone, or for their own sake, but rather in the context of a given poem and for the sake of that poem. Hence, a word acquires its poetic charge in the context of the poem, by association with other words whose sound and sense interact with it. Note below how the simple words in Walter de la Mare's "An Epitaph" work on each other.

Here lies a most beautiful lady,
Light of step and heart was she:
I think she was the most beautiful lady
That ever was in the West Country.
But beauty vanishes; beauty passes;
However rare, rare it be;
And when I crumble who shall remember
This lady of the West Country?

Not one word in the poem is unusual, learned, or "poetic." All are staples, some even the clichés of everyday speech. Yet, in the context of the poem the diction acquires a special lustre, solemnity and pathos. Notice how a very commonplace expression, "most beautiful lady," for instance, is endowed with new meaning in association with the title and the familiar "Here lies"—ritualistic words normally engraved on tombstones. Note, too, how the "beautiful lady" is repeated or echoed in line 3, in imitation of the way numbed mourners keep repeating the same epithets—(He was such a good man, she suffered so patiently). But then, after recalling that beauty vanishes and passes, de la Mare omits the word *beautiful* from the last line as if to imply that in time one can no longer call the dead lady *beautiful,* much less *most beautiful.*

Thus, in the context of the poem, this ordinary expression is endowed with pathetic irony, since it links beauty with death. Moreover, by virtue of the brief description in line 2, it evokes a sharp visual contrast between the quick and the dead. In like manner, "rare," used twice in line 6, expresses an attitude of quiet reverence, regret. In the last two lines the personification of the tombstone—"when I crumble"—intensifies the central idea, that even the most exquisite beauty vanishes, and the central emotion, that of poignant regret.

Even the tenses and moods of the verbs, and the pauses suggested by the punctuation help to establish the context of the poem. "Here *lies* a most beautiful lady"—the present tense is noncommittal. In the next three lines the repeated use of the past tense, "was," emphasizes the pathos of beauty's passing. In the fifth line the present tense accentuates the contrast between the permanence of death and the fleeting character of beauty. The present subjunctive, "be," in line 6 echoes grammatically the actual predicament of beauty—its dependence and contingency. In the last two lines the shift to the future tense points to the time when the lady's beauty will be forgotten. Closely connected with the time and mood of the verbs are the meaningful pauses in the rhythm. Note particularly how the semicolons and the comma in lines 5 and 6 allow time for compassionate sighs, whereas the last two lines suggest uninterrupted grief.

Much more could be said about the way the varied sentence arrangements, the rhythm and stress of the verse, the alliteration and assonance, the quality and quantity of the vowels, all work to endow familiar words with new meanings. Here let us conclude by emphasizing that the magic of poetry resides not in diction for its own sake, but in its relation to the poem as a whole. Those words are best that best serve the needs of a particular poem.

The diction that befits an epic (p. 233) may be too highly wrought for a simple lyric (p. 192). Or again, the plain language of a folk ballad (p. 221) may be ridiculously informal in a highly stylized verse essay like that of Alexander Pope (p. 234). By the same token, "the best order" of words, that is, the grammatical, rhetorical, and verse patterns of the sentences in a poem, are determined by the total context of the poem. The pattern of Milton's lines (p. 245) is intricate, periodic, ornate, in keeping with the sublimity of his central idea, whereas the pattern of "The Demon Lover" (p. 235) is simple, direct, and repetitive, in keeping with *its* purpose. The best order in a poem is an arrangement, or grammatical and rhetorical structure, that best presents the movement of image, thought and feeling from an effective beginning to an effective end.

Style Viewed in the Context of Language and Literature

Like all thoughtful men, a poet is at once the servant and the master of his language. He is the servant in the sense that he is obedient to the genius of language, to its vocabulary, syntax, literary forms, and types. Indeed, he is shaped by that language before he begins to think. Language provides him with the names of familiar things, the signals for necessary actions, the description of mental activity itself. In short, language embodies the bulk of his intellectual inheritance. In many instances he cannot alter language since words, constructions, and literary forms have an objective existence of their own and derive their authority from the community rather than the individual.

Sometimes that community insists upon hard and fast rules, as in a few periods of reaction, when some writers and readers regarded certain norms of diction and conventions of style as fixed forever. But even in less demanding periods, language in various ways is a master, a discipline, a standard that informs and regulates the poet's activities. All poets, however original, are in part the disciples of the language or languages, both popular and literary, in which they think, speak, and write. They succeed or fail in proportion to their ability to receive and preserve the expressive powers of language. By the same token, all readers of poetry are the pupils of language. To understand fully the poetry of a given poet they must understand the language of his time. Hence, the intelligent reader of poetry must remember that language changes throughout its development in vocabulary, syntax, spelling, and pronunciation.

But if the poet is, in some respects, a pupil and a servant of language he is, in other respects, its master. It is commonplace now to observe that one mark of a great poet is that he improves or purifies the language he has received. The fathers of poetry, a Dante or a Chaucer, for instance, raised rude provincial dialects to the level of polished national languages. Others, Shakespeare and Milton among them, ennobled a familiar vocabulary or assimilated the diction, syntax, and structure of other languages and thus extended the awareness of thought and feeling in their own language. Still others, Wordsworth and Coleridge, for instance, purified language by excluding from their poetry inflated, or shopworn, or inert diction and modes of expression that, at their particular moment of history, threatened to fossilize poetry.

The poet improves and purifies the language less by grammatical or critical arguments than by the persuasive power of his example. The successful poet lends himself to the genius of the particular language in which he writes by imitating and refining its inherent qualities of clarity, vigor, and interest. But he also lends his genius *to* the language. He gives new turns to old expressions and renewed life to perennial experience. Hence, the successful poet, no matter how traditional, possesses a style that at once reflects the genius of the language and his own genius, too. In Keats's sonnets, for instance, we may identify the tradition of English poetry and the individual talent that modifies, enlarges and continues that tradition. Thus, in the poem we have already examined, "On First Looking into Chapman's Homer," we encounter a poetic vocabulary that clearly refers to medieval and Elizabethan sources, a sentence structure that attests to the simplifying tendencies of the seventeenth and eighteenth centuries, a literary form, the sonnet, that reflects the historical development of that form, and the attitudes of a then contemporary nineteenth-century man. But all these traditional elements are informed, indeed transformed, by Keats's own genius so that past and present are united in the personal idiom of John Keats. The tradition of English poetry alone does not account for Keats's sonnet, but Keats's poem is indebted to that tradition, expresses itself in terms of that tradition—indeed, owes its very originality to the way it has continued and modified the tradition.

Of all the resources that literary tradition makes available to the poet, one of the most important is that summed up in the expression *the music of words*. Verbal music—the rhythm and melody of language—is one of the characteristics that distinguishes poetry from prose. By the right use of rhythm and melody the poet makes sound an echo of sense. His rhythms, that is, the regular recurrence of accent or stress, and his melodies, that is, the agreeable succession of vowels and consonants, enable him to present his ideas and feelings in an appropriate pace, tone, and pitch. Thus, the rhythm of a poem may be said to gallop, in imitation of a horseback ride, or to wind funereally, at the pace of mourners; to lisp like a child, or to pronounce solemnly in the manner of a prophet; to rise and fall like the sea, or to babble like a brook; to throb slowly with a serene pulse, or rapidly and irregularly with the pulse of terror; to glide and swoop with the energy of a falcon, or to fold and drop like the decayed leaf. Moreover, the sound pattern or melody of a poem ranges from loud and clear tones to muted and obscure ones, from high pitch to low pitch, from the direct reproduction of the rumble of thunder to the indirect evocation of the mood of lightness and serenity.

A successful rhythm must be discovered rather than imposed. A poet does not curb a poem with an arbitrary rhythm any more than the scientist predetermines the earth's spin, the succession of the seasons, the rate of a man's pulse. Rather, the poet finds the precise pattern of stress that will represent the impression and idea of a particular poem. Lear's speeches in *King Lear* differ from Hamlet's in *Hamlet,* though both are in blank verse. Even more to the point, Hamlet's speeches in the several parts of the play differ in rhythm, depending on the movement of the action and state of the hero's emotions. His speech rhythms vary from the wild and whirling words of his hysterical description of the ghost in Act I, to the tranquil sorrow of "Absent thee from felicity a while" in Act V.

RHYTHM

Although rhythm and melody are closely related in the structure of a poem, each presents special problems that should be discussed separately. Let us begin with rhythm.

The rhythm characteristic of English poetry is based primarily on word accent. Like prose, poetry stresses accented syllables in accordance with the normal rules of pronunciation. Unlike most prose, however, it occasionally stresses the secondary accents of a word too, as in the italicized words below, or gives special stress to monosyllables that are frequently unstressed in prose.

That to the height of this great *argument*
I may assert eternal *Providence.*

We note too that the rhythm or beat of the lines above is more regular than that of prose. To explain that regularity we must understand what is meant by meter and verse.

Meter and Verse

The two components of rhythm are *meter,* which is the measure of syllables in a *foot,* and *verse,* which is the measure of feet in a line. A *foot* is a unit that consists of one stressed (/) and one or more unstressed (◡) syllables. The four principal kinds of *feet** are:

the *iamb* (◡/), an unstressed syllable followed by a stressed syllable, as in

a wounded duck

the *anapest* (◡◡/), two unstressed syllables followed by a stressed syllable, as in

That he shouts with his sister at play.

the *trochee* (/◡), a stressed syllable followed by an unstressed syllable, as in

Willows whiten, aspens quiver.

the *dactyl* (/◡◡), a stressed syllable followed by two unstressed syllables, as in

This is the forest primeval: The murmuring pines and the hemlocks.

Verse is a line that consists of one or more feet. A line of one foot is a *monometer,* as in

Thus I
Pass by
And die . .

* We call these the principal feet in English poetry. While subject to many variations as we shall see, these feet alone can dominate the rhythm of a poem. Other kinds of feet, the spondee for instance, which consists of two stressed syllables (//), and the pyrrhic, which consists of two unstressed syllables (◡◡), may be used only as variations of the principal feet.

A line of two feet is a *dimeter,* as in

Who'er she be.

A line of three feet is a *trimeter,* as in

She neither hears nor sees.

In like manner a line of four feet is a *tetrameter,* five feet a *pentameter,* six feet a *hexameter,* and so on,* as in the examples below.

And mark in ev'ry face I meet.

The loneliness includes me unawares.

Or I shall drouse beside thee, so my soul doth ache.

Hence, to describe a line of verse fully, we mention the kind of foot that predominates and the number of feet in the line. (This full description, or the marking of the rhythmical components of a line, is called *scansion.*)

Metrical Variation

A majority of the poems in the previous sections of this book are written in a single predominant meter, but the metrical pattern is usually varied. Variation occurs not only in the more fluid patterns of blank verse and free verse, but also in the stricter forms of the sonnet and the rhyming couplet. Thus, in "On First Looking into Chapman's Homer" (p. 4), the predominant iambic movement is varied by occasional trochees, as in

Silent, upon a peak in Darien . . .

and spondees, as in

Round many western islands have I been.

Similarly, Alexander Pope varies the iambic meter by using other rhythms. Note the considerable variation in the lines below:

Not with more glories, in the etherial plain
The sun first rises o'er the purpled main,
Than, issuing forth, the rival of his beams
Launched on the bosom of the silver Thames.

Indeed, the variations are so many that we can name only a few of the principal ones. These are:

*Lines exceeding six feet are rare, since prolonged rhythms overtax the reader and tend to distract attention from the sense of the passage.

SUBSTITUTION, wherein the poet uses an iamb with an anapest, or a trochee with a dactyl, or vice-versa;

INVERSION, wherein the poet uses an iamb with a trochee, or a dactyl with an anapest, or vice-versa;

CATALEXIS, or the omission of the unstressed syllable or syllables at the beginning of iambic or anapestic verses, or of the unstressed syllables at the end of trochaic or dactyllic verses;

HYPERMETER, or the addition of unstressed syllables at the beginning of a trochaic line or at the end of an iambic line.

Nor should we ignore the variation that is sometimes achieved by a so-called musical pause, indicated by a caret (‸). This is a brief hesitation caused by the dilation of a strong sound. Such a pause occasionally takes the place of a short or unstressed syllable in a line, as in

˘ / ˘ / ˘ / /
John Anderson my jo,‸John.

Another kind of pause, the *caesura,* also contributes to the variation of the rhythmical pattern of the poem. The caesura is a pause or break. Sometimes it is demanded by the sense of the passage. Thus, we pause to indicate the logical word groups. Sometimes it is demanded for emphasis. Thus, we pause to give some special stress to a word whose importance might otherwise be missed. As in prose, punctuation helps us to identify a pause in poetry. The period indicates a full stop; the semi-colon and comma, a partial stop. But the caesural pause often occurs without punctuation.

There are two kinds of caesuras; that which occurs at the end of a line, in which case the line is called end-stopped, and that which occurs within the line. The second kind of caesura usually occurs in the middle of the line, and only for special reasons of sense or emphasis after the first and before the last syllables. In the passage below note how the various caesural pauses affect the rhythm of the verse and help to point up the logical and rhetorical meaning.

So Lycidas sunk low,// but mounted high
Through the dear might of Him that walked the waves;//
Where,// other groves and other streams along,//
With nectar pure his oozy locks he laves,//
And hears the unexpressive nuptial song//
In the blest kingdoms meek// of joy and love.//
There entertain him all the saints above//

In solemn troops,// and sweet societies,//
That sing,// and singing in their glory move,//
And wipe the tears forever from his eyes.//

The Characteristics of Meter

The several meters and the principal metrical variations are sometimes said to suggest certain moods or impressions. In Coleridge's famous mnemonic lines we gather that each basic meter has an affinity for a certain kind of poetic utterance.

Trochee trips from long to short.
From long to long in solemn sort
Slow spondee stalks; strong foot! yet ill able
Ever to come up with dactyl trisyllable.
Iambics march from short to long;
With a leap and a bound the swift anapests throng.

Thus, the trochee "trips" and gives an impression of lightness, whereas the iamb marches in a grave manner, and the spondee "stalks" even more slowly and solemnly. Dactyl and anapest, because of their greater number of unaccented syllables, have the leap and the thrust appropriate in verse that describes vivid action and excited feeling.

There is more than a measure of truth in this description of the inherent characteristics of the various verse movements. Yet the effect of any meter (save the unalterably slow spondee) may be modified by the melody, or the sound of the words, the meaning of the words, and the adroit variation of the meter by inversion, substitution and pause. As a result, the so-called grave iambic movement may be as tripping as the trochaic, as in Tennyson's "The Brook":

I come from haunts of coot and hern,
I make a sudden sally,
And sparkle out among the fern,
To bicker down a valley.

In this passage the large number of monosyllables, the concrete verbs in the active tense, the alliterations of *c*, *h*, and *s* sounds, the catalexis and the light feminine rhymes in lines 2 and 4 and, above all, the sense and spirit of the poem, all tend to transform the normally serious iambic movement into swift and lightsome verse. Contrariwise, the trochaic rhythm in the hymn *Dies Irae,*

/ ᴗ / ᴗ / ᴗ /
Day of wrath, that dreadful day,

is anything but cheerful in the context of the meaning and melody.

The foregoing discussion of rhythm is based on standard meters and metrical variation, by far the most common way of measuring rhythm. Readers of modern and Old English poetry, however, need hardly be told that different approaches to rhythm are found in modern experimental free verse and sprung rhythm, and in the ancient devices of alliterative verse and the so-called native meter.

Free Verse and Other Kinds of Rhythm

Free verse, first popularized in English by Walt Whitman and adopted by important twentieth-century poets like T. S. Eliot and Ezra Pound, follows no fixed pattern of meter, melody or stanza. It is distinguished from rhythmical prose only by retaining the line, which may be of any length. But if free verse lacks a fixed external pattern of meter and rhyme, it is not without its own inner discipline. Rather, the rhythms of successful free verse respond to the ebb and flow of the poet's thought and sensibility, sometimes strongly cadenced, as in Walt Whitman's prophetic verse, sometimes hardly accented at all, as in T. S. Eliot's conversational pieces. Yet in the freest verse, as Eliot himself remarks, the ghost of some simple meter lurks "behind the arras."

Sprung rhythm is a system of meter popularized and practiced by Gerard Manley Hopkins. In Hopkins's words, "It consists in scanning by accents alone or stresses alone, so that a foot may be one strong syllable or it may be many light and one strong." Theoretically, this description of sprung rhythm would also include prose. In practice, however, Hopkins often used trochees, dactyls, and paeons, that is, one stressed syllable followed by three unstressed ones, as well as single stressed syllables. Combined with his command of alliteration and assonance, pause and rhyme, sprung rhythm produced anything but prosaic effects. Sprung rhythm, like free verse, resembles natural speech and hence recommends itself to modern poets who write in a colloquial style.

In the *native meter* of Old English poetry the verse structure depends both on verse stress and on alliteration, that is, the repetition of identical consonant sounds separated by a caesural pause. Thus, in Langland, we read:

In a sómer sésun//whan sóft was the sónne, . . .

Few modern writers use alliteration as the basic structure of rhythm; rather, they use it as an aid to melody, as we shall see later. But the four-beat line characteristic of alliterative verse has been adopted by many poets. This line, like sprung rhythm, relies on four strongly accented syllables, and a varying number of unaccented syllables, with a pause between the second and third accent.

Ríde a cock hórse// to Bánbury Cróss
To sée a fine lády// upón a white hórse
Ríngs on her fíngers// and bélls on her tóes
And shé shall have músic// wherever she góes.

MELODY

Poetic rhythm, the regular, agreeable, and meaningful succession of stresses, establishes the movement, pace, and emphasis that harmonize with the ideas, expressions, and images of a poem. Melody—the regular, agreeable, and meaningful succession of tones or sounds—establishes the auditory pattern that harmonizes with the ideas, impressions, images and rhythms of a poem. Melody and rhythm are symbiotic; they live together in the sense that neither can rightly function without the other. Thus, rhyme, which is fundamentally melodic, also requires stress.

Melody is established by various patterns of agreeable sound. But before we investigate those patterns we should recall that individual vowel and consonant sounds themselves have their special properties. Vowels, for instance, many be ranged in a tonal scale, according to the intensity and duration with which each vowel is uttered.

The vowel sounds at the beginning of the scale are adapted to rapid, light movement, as in "The patter of feet in the dim-lit streets." On the other hand, the vowel sounds at the end of the scale are adapted to a slow, heavy movement as in "Bold Rome her doom pronounces." Consonants, too, have certain inherent characteristics. Thus, the liquid or unstopped consonants (*l, m, n, r*) and the sibilants (*s* and soft *c* and *z*) tend to create a soft flowing effect, as in "Summer lulls men to repose in uncertain satin zephyrs." On the other hand, the stopped or hard consonants (*p, t, k,* hard *c, b, d, g*) tend to slow up the movement of a line, as in "Scream, blow, blast thy cankered cheeks, thou wind unkind."

Onomatopoeia

When we say that weak vowels and strong vowels, soft consonants and hard ones possess *inherent* characteristics, we mean that they tend to reproduce natural sounds. Some sounds, indeed, are directly *onomatopoeic,* that is, they tend to reproduce the object or action producing the sound, as in the following expressions: frying pan *sizzles,* water *bubbles,* fire *crackles,* leaves *rustle,* geese *honk,* stones *thud* into earth, and so on. But, since human speech cannot directly reproduce many natural sounds, it is forced to imitate them, that is, to find a verbal counterpart rather than a verbal equivalent. Thus, we imitate a long bugle call by the word *blare.* Here the *bl* sound suggests blowing and the *are* sound, like a held note, suggests the prolonged effect of the bugle call. Hence, *The bugle's loud blare* contains indirect or *suggestive onomatopoeia.**

Alliteration and Assonance

Alliteration and assonance are the simplest forms of musical pattern in verse. Indeed, *alliteration,* the repetition of the same consonant sound in a line or in successive lines of verse, was one of the principal features of Old English poetry, as we have seen on p. 273. Modern poets, however, normally employ alliteration as a subordinate melody in verse, whose principal pattern is meter and rhyme, as in G. K. Chesterton's *Lepanto.*

Don John pounding from the slaughter-painted poop
Purpling all the ocean like a bloody pirate's sloop
Scarlet running over on the silvers and the golds,

* Suggestive onomatopoeia is found in numerous combinations of sounds. At the end of words, the *le* and *er* sounds often connote a continuous action, as in *dangle, linger, trickle, dicker, sparkle, flitter.* A concluding *ng* sound, after a vowel, connotes a prolonged sound, as in *gong, bang, clang, Ping-pong.*

Breaking of the hatches up and bursting of the holds,
Thronging of the thousands up that labor under sea,
White for bliss and blind for sun and stunned for liberty.

In the passage above note how varied is the alliteration. In each line several consonants are alliterated. Frequently the alliteration extends over several lines, as do the *p* sounds in lines 1 and 2. Note, too, that the resounding *nd* sounds and the abrupt *p, d, t* sounds are used several times.

Chesterton's alliteration, unusually forceful, underlines the violent action of a famous naval battle. Much alliteration, however, is like background music that merely suggests the mood of the poet, as in W. B. Yeats's "The Lake Isle of Innisfree" (p. 71), where the quiet *l, n, r* and *s* sounds help us to imagine the poet's solitary retreat.

I hea*r* *l*ake wate*r* *l*appi*n*g with *l*ow *s*ou*n*d*s* by the *s*ho*r*e.

Assonance is the repetition of the same vowel or diphthong sounds in a line or in successive lines of verse. In "Go Lovely Rose" (p. 31), the first line contains two long *o*'s and one short *o*, the second line three short *e*'s, the third line two *ow*'s, the fourth line three short *e*'s, the fifth line four open *e*'s. Note, too, each repeated vowel sound is contrasted with other sounds. Thus the strong *o* and *ow* sounds toll slow and solemn warnings while the weaker vowels strike a compassionate, indeed a plaintive, muted note.

Hence, assonance is not only a repetition of similar sounds but a balance or contrast of strong and weak sounds, the better to evoke a contrast of mood or meaning. Skillful poets, Tennyson for instance, often combine assonance with alliteration and onomatopoeia as in "The Bugle Song" (p. 133). Note how, in the lines below, the strong vowels are succeeded by weaker ones in a simulation of the loud first call and then the fading echo.

Blow, bugle, blow, set the wild echoes flying,
Blow, bugle; answer, echoes, dying, dying, dying.

RHYME

Rhyme, that is, the identity in the rhyming syllable of the accented vowel sounds and the consonant sounds that follow it, is at once a contribution to sound and to sense. Rhyming words harmonize, as in *Rome-dome, blew-few, cares-dares.* Moreover, rhymed words bind lines together.

The two chief types of rhyme are internal rhyme and end rhyme. In internal rhyme, the rhyming words are within the line, as in

> And all the *night,* 'tis my pillow *white,* . . .

In end rhyme, the rhyming words occur at the end of separate lines. Occasionally poets employ beginning rhyme, as in

> *From* round the camp
> *Come* warriors bold

Below note how the rhyming words *woe* and *blow* simultaneously provide a musical accompaniment and help to complete the idea.

> And I had done a hellish thing,
> And it would work 'em *woe;*
> For all averred, I had killed the bird
> That made the breeze to *blow.*

Woe and *blow* not only satisfy the ear but complete the sense by emphasizing contrast between the evil that followed the Ancient Mariner's killing of the albatross and the good that the albatross was believed to have accomplished.

While the ear is normally a safe guide in judging the melody of rhyme, we should know a few traditional rules, if only to establish a vocabulary for discussing melody. One, already stated above, is that the accented vowel sound in the rhyming syllables and the succeeding consonants and vowels be identical. A second is that the sounds preceding the vowel sound in the rhyming syllables should be different. Thus, *told* and *gold* are valid rhymes, whereas *told* and *tolled* are not. (Repetition of the same sound is of course an effective device but not rhyme.) Moreover, in multiple rhymes, those that contain two or three syllables, the accent of the rhyming words must fall on the penult or antepenult. Thus, *table–label,* and *battering–clattering* are valid rhymes, while *battery–very* or *tolerable–label* are not.

It is useful, too, to distinguish between masculine rhymes—wherein the rhymed syllables are the last syllables of the word, as in *intent–relent,* and feminine rhymes, wherein the rhymed syllables are followed by one or two unaccented syllables, as in *butter–flutter,* or *charity–clarity.* Sometimes masculine rhyme is called single rhyme, and feminine rhyme double or triple rhyme.

In most long poems, and in some shorter ones, the reader sometimes encounters *imperfect rhyme,* that is, one in which the vowel or consonant sounds in the rhyming words are approximate rather than identical. In Pope's *The Rape of the Lock,* we encounter imperfect rhymes like *air-star, long-tongue, adores-pow'r's.* Sometimes what is now an imperfect rhyme was perfect according to an earlier pronunciation. Sometimes, too, the poet wishes to avoid the strong stress created by a perfect rhyme, or the singsong effect of a series of perfect rhymes.

The Stanza

In general, a stanza is a group of lines centering, like the prose paragraph, on a single topic, thought, or mood. A stanza is a point of rest, or transition, or completion. It is the outer form or design that corresponds to developing mood, or movement, or meaning of the poem. In discussing successful poems, we may follow the stanzaic pattern as a normally reliable guide to the structure of a poem.

In English poetry, stanzas are of several kinds. Some are highly *irregular,* consisting of an indefinite number of lines, varied metrical patterns, and occasional rhymes, or, in some cases, no rhymes at all. Irregular stanzas are numerous and defy general description. While *regular* stanzaic patterns are also numerous, they are readily identified by a rhyme scheme, or by a pattern of rhymes, and by their predominant meter. Some of the principal varieties of the regular stanza are described below.

The *rhyming couplet* is a two-line stanza with a perfect end rhyme. Often the couplet is an iambic tetrameter, as in

> We must have silence where we go
> Like the hush that follows snow.

The term couplet also applies to any successive lines of poetry which rhyme, whether or not they constitute a separate stanza, as in

> But at my back I always hear,
> Times wingéd chariot hurrying near.

A very familiar type of couplet is the heroic couplet, which consists of iambic pentameters, as in

> Know thou thyself, presume not God to scan,
> The proper study of mankind is man.

Frequently, as in Pope's lines above, the rhyming couplet is closed, or end-stopped, that is, the thought ends within the couplet. Often, however, the rhyming couplet is open, or run-over; that is, the sense is carried beyond the couplets, as in

> Whatever spirit, careless of his charge,
> His post neglects, or leaves the fair at large,
> Shall feel sharp vengeance soon o'ertake his sins,
> Be stopped in vials, or transfixed with pins. . . .

A *tercet* is a three-lined stanza in which the rhyme scheme is *a a a* or *a b a,* as in the examples below.

> Oh, Galuppi, Baldassaro, this is very sad to *find!*
> I can hardly misconceive you; it would prove me deaf and *blind;*
> But although I take your meaning, 'tis with such a heavy *mind!*

> O wild West Wind, thou breath of autumn's *being*
> Thou from whose unseen presence the leaves dead
> Are driven, like ghosts from an enchanter *fleeing.*

When a tercet is linked with other tercets in a rhyme scheme *a b a, b c b, c d c,* and so on, the stanza is called *terza rima,* as in Shelley's "Ode to the West Wind" (p. 213).

By far the most common stanzaic pattern is the *quatrain,* a four-line stanza. The quatrain occurs in all meters, and in a great variety of rhymes. The most common are identified below.

Ballad meter, an iambic movement usually in four stress—or four and three stress—lines, employs various rhyme schemes.

> And every sand becomes a gem *x*
> Reflected in the beams *divine;* *a*
> Blown back, they blind the mocking eye, *x*
> But still in Israel's paths they *shine.* *a*

Another usual rhyme scheme in the ballad meter is *a b a b,* as in

> By brooks too broad for leaping *a*
> There lightfoot boys are laid, *b*

The rose-lipt girls are sleeping, *a*
In field where roses fade. *b*

Occasionally, the quatrain is rhymed *a b b a,* as in the *In Memoriam* of Tennyson (p. 307) or *a a b b.*

Five- and six-line stanzas are rarer than quatrains, but not unusual. See Josephine Miles's "The Lark" (p. 3), and William Wordsworth's "I Wandered Lonely as a Cloud" (p. 134).

The seven-line stanza, sometimes remembered because Poe used it in "The Raven," is more often associated with the *rhyme royal,* which consists of seven iambic pentameters with a rhyme *a b a b b c c.* A favorite stanza of medieval poets, it is still used by later poets like William Morris and John Masefield. The passage below conveys some of the effects characteristic of the rhyme royal.

Dreamer of dreams, born out of my due time,
Why should I strive to set the crooked straight?
Let it suffice me that my murmuring rhyme
Beats with light wing against the ivory gate,
Telling a tale not too importunate
To those who in the sleepy region stay,
Lulled by the singer of an empty day.

WILLIAM MORRIS

Eight-line stanzas occur frequently. Some, like Wordsworth's "The Solitary Reaper" (p. 189), resemble closely linked quatrains. Others, like Byron's *Beppo,* employ the *ottava rima* that is, iambic pentameters with the rhyme scheme *a b a b a b c c.*

"England! with all thy faults I love thee still,"
I said at Calais, and have not forgot it;
I like to speak and lucubrate my fill;
I like the government (but that is not it);
I like the freedom of the press and quill;
I like the Habeas Corpus (when we've got it);
I like a parliamentary debate,
Particularly when 'tis not too late . . . .

Nine-line stanzas include the well-known Spenserian stanza that consists of eight lines in iambic pentameter followed by a ninth line in iambic hexameter, called an *Alexandrine.* The rhyme scheme is *a b a b b c b c c.* This complex rhyme scheme was first popularized by Edmund Spenser, whose lines from *The Faerie Queene* below show how well suited it is for evocative description.

> That darksome cave they enter, where they find
> That cursèd man, low sitting on the ground,
> Musing full sadly in his sullein mind:
> His griesil locks, long growèn and unbound,
> Disordred hung about his shoulders round,
> And hid his face, through which hie hollow eyne
> Lookt deadly dull, and starèd as astound;
> His raw-bone cheekes, through penury and pine,
> Were shronke into his jaws, as he did never dyne.

Regular stanzas of ten and eleven lines are sometimes used, as in "The Scholar-Gipsy" (p. 89), which consists of ten lines, and "To Autumn" (p. 78), which consists of eleven lines. Regular thirteen-line stanzas are rare. The principal fourteen-line stanza is the sonnet, which is discussed in detail on pp. 192-96. Stanzas consisting of more than fourteen lines are rare, save for the *villanelle,* a French form consisting of nineteen lines: five tercets and a final quatrain. The exceedingly difficult rhyme scheme is: *a b a a b a a b a a b a a b a a b a a.* Line 1 reoccurs as a refrain in lines 6, 12, 18; line 3, in lines 9, 15, 19.

Blank Verse

Blank verse is unrhymed iambic pentameter that is not broken into regular stanzas. It was first used in drama because of its adaptability to dialogue. Shakespeare's blank verse is particularly notable for its fluidity, cadence, and rhythmical pause (p. 154). John Milton used blank verse for his epic poem *Paradise Lost* (p. 245). Since then it has been widely used in narrative and lyric poetry, particularly by Wordsworth, Shelley, Tennyson, Browning, and Arnold.

While blank verse lacks a regular stanzaic pattern, it may be divided into verse paragraphs, that is, groups of lines centering on a single thought or a single emotional impression. In Tennyson's "The Coming of Arthur" (p. 225), the verse paragraphs are partly indicated by the punctuation, partly by the sense of the individual lines and partly by a series of cadences, or rhythmic movements, proceeding from one pause to another, mounting to a climax and then a final stop. Another example occurs in Tennyson's "Ulysses."

> It may be that the gulfs will wash us down;//
> It may be we shall touch the Happy Isles,//
> And see the great Achilles,/ whom we knew.//
> Tho much is taken,/ much abides;// and tho
> We are not now that strength which in old days
> Moved heaven and earth,/ that which we are,/ we are://
> One equal temper of heroic hearts,//
> Made weak by time and fate,/ but strong in will
> To strive,/ to seek,/ to find,/ and not to yield.

Needless to say, a poem with an irregular stanzaic pattern, or no stanzaic pattern at all, may also be organized in units resembling the verse paragraph.

Characteristics of Rhyme and Stanzaic Patterns

Just as meter and verse may achieve certain characteristic effects (p. 271), so may rhyme and stanzaic pattern. In general, rhyme gives pleasure by its melody. The use of identical sounds arouses and fulfills our expectation. Moreover, since the rhyming words are normally the more important ones, rhyme reinforces the sense of a sentence. Again, rhyme links one sentence with another and helps reinforce the larger structure of a poem. By the same token, change of rhyme notifies the reader of a transition. Finally, rhyme is a great aid to memory.

Whether the various stanzaic forms are specially suited to certain subjects, moods, or methods of development is debatable. We should never forget that the external form or pattern of sound in a poem depends on its inner meaning. To reverse the procedure is equivalent to saying that a poet could write a successful poem by filling in the blank spaces in a rhyme scheme. Yet, it is a matter of history that many great poets have habitually selected particular patterns for some definite purpose, so that we have come to expect one kind of poem in one pattern, another in another. Thus, while the rhyming couplet has been used successfully in narrative and lyric verse, it seems especially adapted for thoughtful verse in general and the sententious expression of satire in particular. The Spenserian stanza, too, was first used in narrative, but in later times has been associated with descriptive or meditative verse. The ballad meter and rhyme scheme seem perfectly adapted to narrative, but not to the needs of meditative or "metaphysical" poetry. Finally, the sonnet, as we observed in a previous chapter (p. 193), is so well proportioned to the formal, melodious development of a single idea that its use for another purpose, to express the incoherency of a Lear, for instance, seems preposterous.

We will not be mistaken in our analysis of metrical and melodic patterns if we keep in mind what was said at the beginning of this chapter: Style in general is "a thinking *out* into language," not a filling *in* of external forms.

POEMS FOR DISCUSSION

The style of a poem—its diction, rhythm and melody—should not be divorced from the other elements in a poem. To emphasize this principle the study questions below refer to poems that have been studied in connection with the elements of emotion, thought, and imagination. The points for discussion follow the order presented in the chapter.

1. Compare the diction of "An Epitaph," p. 263, with that of "Here Lies a Lady" p. 217. What characteristics of diction do they have in common? In what points do they differ? Why?
2. Compare the diction of "The River of Life," p. 142, and "The Seven Ages of Man," p. 154.
3. Identify the rhythms in the poems listed below by indicating the stressed syllables (/) and the caesural pauses (// for full stop, / for partial stop). "Proud Maisie," p. 54; "Dover Beach," p. 64; "Tarantella," p. 127; "Tears, Idle Tears," p. 168.
4. Identify the principal metrical pattern in the poems listed below and point out several variations from that pattern.
   "A Valediction: Forbidding Mourning," p. 112; "Home Thoughts from Abroad," p. 133; "A Song of Divine Love," p. 174; "The Latest Decalogue," p. 181; "Pied Beauty," p. 195.
5. For each of the poems listed above show how the rhythm is or is not in harmony with the predominant thought or feeling.

6. Point out examples of onomatopoeia in each of the poems listed below. "Eight O'Clock," p. 47; "To a Snowflake," p. 74; "Tithonus," p. 114; "Full Fathom Five," p. 192.
7. Find examples of alliteration and assonance in the poems for discussion in Chapter X, pp. 180-83.
8. Identify the stanzaic patterns of the poems for discussion in Chapter IV, pp. 81-7. Point out examples of masculine and feminine rhymes.
9. Pick out three poems that illustrate an unusual harmony of rhythm and rhyme with sense. Show how that harmony exists.
10. Find three poems written in blank verse or free verse. Compare and contrast the musical qualities of these poems with those you have selected in answer to question 9.

CHAPTER XIV

An Ending, and a New Beginning

WE BEGAN our study by asking: Why do we read poetry? We read it because it embodies a total experience that compels us to feel intensely, to think profoundly, and to imagine vividly, in short, to bring all the powers of the human soul into activity. This activity, in turn, earns the reward of poetic experience, that possession of truth and beauty that we may call wisdom. In a sense, then, the full answer to the question is contained in the words—power and wisdom.

THE POWER OF POETRY

The power of poetry—the words have both a general meaning and the special meanings that have been established in the context of the previous chapters. In general, the power of poetry is the poet's art working within the poem. The poet is a man who not only sees, but also can tell us what he sees, and can make us see. His art, displayed in the successful poem, creates an object of knowledge and a meaningful structure of language, for the contemplation and delight of the reader. Hence, the power of poetry means all those artistic skills that translate a vision personal to the poet into a vision that is perceptible to a discerning reader.

Throughout this book we have studied the principal elements of poetic power. We saw how *emotion* is the power to respond justly to the situation presented in a poem. Emotion does not exist in isolation, but in association with thought and imagination. We examined the element of *thought* in poetry and discovered how thought is expressed in an organized movement of language toward a definite end. We recognized this *definite end* to be equivalent to some general truth of human nature and the organized movement of the language to be equivalent to the structure and style of a poem. Thus, while some poems are concerned with the actual truths of ordinary discourse, the specifically poetic truth is the fidelity of the situation imagined within the poem to a general truth of human nature.

Just as emotional power is organically related to the power of thought, so, too, both of these powers are closely related to the power of imagination. Imaginative power, we saw, expresses itself in various ways: in the vividness of sensory details and in the greater vividness and emphasis of figurative expressions, that is, simile, metaphor, personification, allegory, symbol, paradox, and irony. The creative power of the imagination combines intelligence and sense perception; it not only represents details vividly, but it envisions the whole structure of a poem—the development of resemblances in an allegory, the multiple meanings in a symbol and the sustained irony of a satire.

We saw, too, how these elements were employed in the various kinds of poetry; in the lyric, the narrative, and the dramatic narrative. Each type of poetry presents a different kind of poetic experience and a different attitude to that experience. For this reason, each type of poetry employs the power of poetry in certain special ways. Thus, the lyric is notable for its concentration on personal emotion; the narrative, for its unity and coherence of action; and the dramatic narrative, for its thoughtful development of character.

Finally, we examined the power of poetic language in terms of rhythm and melody, two characteristics that, in the context of the poem, also manifest the poet's power to express his vision. In short, we discovered that the principal elements of poetic power are intense emotion, thought, and imagination, expressed in the appropriate style, rhythm, and melody.

THE WISDOM OF POETRY

The wisdom of poetry—these words must be carefully understood. We mean here not the sagacity of the philosopher, nor the prudence of the saint, nor the shrewdness of the man of affairs, nor the teachings of the moralist, although all these qualities are sometimes found in poetry. We mean, rather, the wisdom inherent in the poetic experience.

As we have seen, poetry tends to provide a special kind of

knowledge. Through poetry, we come to *realize* the meaning of human life more vividly, more intensely and more profoundly. Truths of human experience, for instance, the perils of human destiny that Hamlet contemplates in his soliloquy, "To be or not to be . . . ," are burned into our own memory. We are enlarged by that knowledge, and thus become more truly, more sincerely, human. This knowledge is a kind of wisdom because it invites us to disregard trivial, superficial, or ephemeral realities and to concentrate on essential and eternal truths. Poetry also is charged with "a deep sympathy for truth," a love of truth, a desire to see the truth known, admired, accepted and, in the highest sense of the word, lived. The wisdom of poetry, then, consists in the possession and love of truth.

THE TESTS OF A SUCCESSFUL POEM

We have been summarizing what we have explored in earlier chapters, namely the elements of poetic power and wisdom. In effect these elements, taken together, are the very essence of a poem. A successful poem has power—the power of emotion, thought and imagination, together with the power of expressing those elements in an appropriate style, rhythm, and melody. Moreover, a successful poem manifests a knowledge and love of truth that is wisdom. A poem is more or less successful in proportion to its manifestation of power and wisdom.

These tests of poetry are intrinsic, that is, they are primarily concerned with the evidence contained within the poem itself. We may apply other tests as well, tests that are primarily concerned with evidence derived from sources outside the poem. Indeed, there are times when we must go beyond the poem itself to obtain satisfactory answers even to such simple questions as, What does the poem attempt to do? How well does it do it? To know what a poem intends we frequently must consult other works by the same poet, or the poetry that influenced his work, or even the facts about his own life and time.

Let us consider "Lycidas" again. By applying the intrinsic tests mentioned above we determined that the predominant emotion of the poem is grief at the death of his friend. We discovered the basic thought structure of the poem, as we have outlined it on p. 196-7. We traced the general imaginative conception, the fiction of the shepherds, and the abundant use of figurative language. We identified it as an elegy and recognized its rhythmical and melodic devices (p. 270) and its richness of diction. All these elements are contained within the poem.

But, we must go outside the poem for a fuller appreciation of John Milton's achievement. We must know something about his relations with Edward King, the friend whose death he is lamenting, because King, symbolized in the figure Lycidas, provides a clue to the poem's intention. We must know something about the convention of the pastoral elegy, for it is in terms of that convention that Milton's structure and style must be evaluated.

Furthermore, the relevance of St. Peter's denunciation of false shepherds (lines 103-131) must be determined by reference to the historical sensibility of the readers of Milton's time. Finally, Milton's highly ornate language reflects a pattern of usage, partly derived from the Renaissance rhetorical tradition, partly from Milton's own experience, and experiments, with language. Hence, satisfactory answers to the question—What does Milton's "Lycidas" attempt to do? and, How well does it succeed?—necessarily imply some knowledge of the poet's life and times and the tradition and conventions that affected him and his readers.

In short, a true criticism of poetry is primarily concerned with the poem itself, but also with the poem in the context of the literary and cultural tradition in which the poet worked. In one sense, an individual poem is a single, separate utterance, distinguishable from other utterances, and hence capable of being judged by itself. But, just as no man is an island sufficient unto himself, so no poem is wholly self-contained. Thus, in another sense, a poem is a part of a continuing series of utterances. Milton's voice is not restricted to "Lycidas;" it is heard, too, in the polemical sonnets, the religious hymns, and many other poems. The poet impersonates now one attitude, now another, so that, properly to understand one poem, we must see it in its relation to the others. By the same token, properly to understand the achievement of one poet, we must be aware of the achievements of other poets. How else would we know fully the characteristic excellences of T. S. Eliot's poems if we did not compare them with those of the many poets of the past whom he either quotes, or alludes to, or echoes, or paraphrases?

Thus, to widen the context of poetry we move from the study of the poem in itself to the study of the poem in the context of the other utterances of the poet, and then to the study of other poems by other poets. In doing this we necessarily cultivate the habit of comparison; and acquire, it may be, the power to discern the good from the bad and the best from the better and the good. To do this is to be a critic.

BECOMING A CRITIC

If poetry is the evaluation of human experience, then criticism is the evaluation of that evaluation. To say this is to imply that a true critic is a judge, not only of the technical aspects of poetry, but also of the values that poetry embodies. He distinguishes between non-literature and literature, and between literature and great literature. "The 'greatness' of literature," T. S. Eliot reminds us, "cannot be determined solely by literary standards, though we must remember that whether it is literature or not can be determined only by literary standards."* Hence, a true critic must not only know how to apply literary standards; he must also know how to apply standards based on philosophy, religion, and other relevant arts and sciences.

No one expects a beginning student to undertake the complete task of the critic. Nevertheless, there are many important critical responsibilities that he should be ready to assume. Chief among these is the responsibility to approximate, step by step, the ideal of the scholarly critic. This means wide reading, a scholarly understanding of that reading, and a systematic attempt to relate poetry with other arts.

It means, too, an ever-increasing capacity "to enjoy with discrimination, to discern value, to recognize and reject the spurious, to respond maturely to the genuine, never to be fooled by the shabby and the second-hand. . . ."**

The advanced study of poetry, and of related disciplines of language, literary history and criticism, need never interfere with the primary end of poetry—intellectual pleasure. Far from limiting the pleasure one derives from reading a poem for its own

* T. S. Eliot, *Essays Ancient and Modern* (New York, 1936), p. 92.

** David Daiches, *Critical Approaches to Literature* (New York, 1956), p. 393.

sake, these studies ultimately provide even greater delight. To become a critic is not to forsake one's personal attitudes, or to exchange them for the standard opinions of manuals and glosses. A scholarly critic brings to the art of reading and judging a poem a greater capacity to know and feel intensely.

Essentially, a successful poem is, in Charles DuBos' words, "the meeting ground of two souls." The poet or artist breathes life, born of his own intense experience, into his words. That life is begotten by love—the love of a vision that he must share with others. Moreover, it begets a kind of love in the reader—the love that displays itself in the admiring contemplation of the vision in a poem. The reader responds to that vision, quickens with it, joys or sorrows in it, is enlarged by its wisdom, assimilates its energy, and is thus united, within the poem, with another soul. That union, the meeting of minds in a common vision, is one of the great human values of poetry.

Each man seeks to escape the false isolation imposed upon him, at times by the cruelty of others, at times by his own selfishness or ignorance, at times by mere circumstance. He yearns to send messages from his own lonely island to those who live on other islands across "the unplumbed, salt, estranging sea." Out of Islands he would make a continent, a world, a union, wherein each person is his own inviolable self, yet one with others in a common human nature and in common aspirations.

Poems for Study

CONTENTS

⁜ Poems for Study ⁜

A
STUDENT'S ANTHOLOGY

UNDER THE GREENWOOD TREE

Under the greenwood tree
Who loves to lie with me,
And turn his merry note
Unto the sweet bird's throat,
Come hither, come hither, come hither! 5
Here shall he see
No enemy
But winter and rough weather.

Who doth ambition shun 40
And loves to live i' the sun,
Seeking the food he eats,
And pleased with what he gets,
Come hither, come hither, come hither!
Here shall he see 45
No enemy
But winter and rough weather.

WILLIAM SHAKESPEARE
(Act II, Scene V, *As You Like It*)

BLOW, BLOW, THOU WINTER WIND

Blow, blow, thou winter wind,
Thou art not so unkind 175
As mans' ingratitude;
Thy tooth is not so keen,
Because thou art not seen,
Although thy breath be rude.
Heigh-ho! sing, heigh-ho! unto the green holly. 180
Most friendship is feigning, most loving mere folly.
Then, heigh-ho! the holly!
This life is most jolly.

Freeze, freeze, thou bitter sky,
That dost not bite so nigh 185
As benefits forgot;
Though thou the waters warp,
Thy sting is not so sharp
As friend remember'd not.
Heigh-ho! sing, heigh-ho! unto the green holly. 190
Most friendship is feigning, most loving mere folly.
Then, heigh-ho! the holly!
This life is most jolly.

WILLIAM SHAKESPEARE
(Act II, Scene II, *As You Like It*)

FEAR NO MORE THE HEAT O' THE SUN

Fear no more the heat o' the sun,
Nor the furious winter's rages;
Thou thy worldly task hast done, 260
Home art gone, and ta'en thy wages;
Golden lads and girls all must,
As chimney-sweepers, come to dust.

Fear no more the frown o' the great;
    Thou art past the tyrant's stroke; 265
Care no more to clothe and eat;
    To thee the reed is as the oak:
The sceptre, learning, physic, must
All follow this, and come to dust.

Fear no more the lightning-flash, 270
    Nor the all-dreaded thunder-stone;
Fear not slander, censure rash;
    Thou hast finish'd joy and moan;
All lovers young, all lovers must
Consign to thee, and come to dust. 275

WILLIAM SHAKESPEARE
(Act IV, Scene II, *Cymbeline*)

THE DREAM

Dear love, for nothing less than thee
Would I have broke this happy dream;
    It was a theme
For reason, much too strong for fantasy.
Therefore thou waked'st me wisely; yet 5
My dream thou brok'st not, but continued'st it.
Thou art so true that thoughts of thee suffice
To make dreams truths and fables histories;
Enter these arms, for since thou thought'st it best
Not to dream all my dream, let's act the rest. 10

As lightning, or a taper's light,
Thine eyes, and not thy noise, waked me:
    Yet I thought thee—
For thou lov'st truth—an angel, at first sight;
But when I saw thou saw'st my heart, 15
And knew'st my thoughts beyond an angel's art,
When thou knew'st what I dreamt, when thou knew'st when
Excess of joy would wake me, and cam'st then,
I must confess it could not choose but be
Profane to think thee anything but thee. 20

Coming and staying show'd thee thee,
But rising makes me doubt that now
    Thou art not thou.

That Love is weak where Fear's as strong as he;
'Tis not all spirit pure and brave 25
If mixture it of Fear, Shame, Honour have.
Perchance as torches, which must ready be,
Men light and put out, so thou deal'st with me.
Thou cam'st to kindle, go'st to come; then I
Will dream that hope again, but else would die. 30

JOHN DONNE

TO CELIA

Drink to me only with thine eyes,
And I will pledge with mine;
Or leave a kiss but in the cup
And I'll not look for wine.
The thirst that from the soul doth rise 5
Doth ask a drink divine;
But might I of Jove's nectar sup,
I would not change for thine.

I sent thee late a rosy wreath,
Not so much honouring thee 10
As giving it a hope that there
It could not wither'd be;
But thou thereon didst only breathe
And sent'st it back to me;
Since when it grows, and smells, I swear, 15
Not of itself but thee!

BEN JONSON

THE FLAMING HEART

O thou undaunted daughter of desires!
By all thy dower of lights and fires;
By all the eagle in thee, all the dove; 95
By all thy lives and deaths of love;
By thy large draughts of intellectual day,
And by thy thirsts of love more large than they;
By all thy brim-filled bowls of fierce desire,
By thy last morning's draught of liquid fire; 100
By the full kingdom of that final kiss
That seized thy parting soul, and sealed thee His;

By all the Heav'n thou hast in Him
(Fair sister of the seraphim!);
By all of Him we have in thee, 105
Leave nothing of myself in me.
Let me so read thy life that I
Unto all life of mine may die!

RICHARD CRASHAW
(from "The Flaming Heart")

TO LUCASTA, GOING TO THE WARS

Tell me not (Sweet) I am unkinde,
That from the Nunnerie
Of thy chaste breast, and quiet minde,
To Warre and Armes I flie.

True; a new Mistresse now I chase, 5
The first Foe in the Field;
And with a stronger Faith imbrace
A Sword, a Horse, a Shield.

Yet this Inconstancy is such,
As you too shall adore; 10
I could not love thee (Deare) so much,
Lov'd I not Honour more.

RICHARD LOVELACE

A SONG FOR ST. CECILIA'S DAY

November 22, 1687

From Harmony, from heav'nly Harmony
This universal Frame began;
When Nature underneath a heap
Of jarring Atomes lay,
And cou'd not heave her Head, 5
The tuneful Voice was heard from high,
Arise, ye more than dead.
Then cold and hot and moist and dry
In order to their Stations leap,
And MUSICK's pow'r obey. 10

From Harmony, from heavenly Harmony
  This universal Frame began:
  From Harmony to Harmony
Through all the Compass of the Notes it ran,
The Diapason closing full in Man. 15

What Passion cannot MUSICK raise and quell?
  When *Jubal* struck the corded Shell,
 His listening Brethren stood around,
  And, wond'ring, on their Faces fell
 To worship that Celestial Sound: 20
Less than a God they thought there could not dwell
  Within the hollow of the Shell,
  That spoke so sweetly, and so well.
What Passion cannot MUSICK raise and quell?

  The TRUMPETS loud Clangor 25
   Excites us to Arms
  With shrill Notes of Anger
   And mortal Alarms.
  The double double double beat
   Of the thund'ring DRUM 30
   Cryes, heark the Foes come;
Charge, Charge, 'tis too late to retreat.

  The soft complaining FLUTE
  In dying Notes discovers
  The Woes of hopeless Lovers, 35
Whose Dirge is whisper'd by the warbling LUTE.

  Sharp VIOLINS proclaim
Their jealous Pangs and Desperation,
Fury, frantick Indignation,
Depth of Pains and Height of Passion, 40
  For the fair, disdainful Dame.

  But oh! what Art can teach
  What human Voice can reach
    The sacred ORGANS Praise?
   Notes inspiring holy Love, 45
Notes that wing their heavenly Ways
   To mend the Choires above.

Orpheus cou'd lead the savage race,
And Trees unrooted left their Place,
Sequacious of the Lyre; 50
But bright CECILIA rais'd the Wonder high'r:
When to her Organ vocal Breath was given,
An Angel heard, and straight appear'd
Mistaking Earth for Heav'n.

GRAND CHORUS

As from the Pow'r of Sacred Lays 55
The Spheres began to move,
And sung the great Creator's Praise
To all the bless'd above;
So, when the last and dreadful Hour
This crumbling Pageant shall devour, 60
The TRUMPET *shall be heard on high,*
The dead shall live, the living die,
And MUSICK *shall untune the Sky.*

JOHN DRYDEN

EPISTLE TO DR. ARBUTHNOT

Yet let me flap this bug with gilded wings,
This painted child of Dirt, that stinks and stings; 310
Whose buzz the witty and the fair annoys,
Yet wit ne'er tastes, and beauty ne'er enjoys;
So well-bred spaniels civilly delight
In mumbling of the game they dare not bite.
Eternal smiles his emptiness betray, 315
As shallow streams run dimpling all the way,
Whether in florid impotence he speaks,
And, as the prompter breathes, the puppet squeaks;
Or at the ear of *Eve*, familiar Toad,
Half froth, half venom, spits himself abroad, 320
In puns, or politics, or tales, or lies,
Or spite, or smut, or rhymes, or blasphemies;
His wit all see-saw, between *that* and *this*,
Now high, now low, now master up, now miss,
And he himself one vile Antithesis. 325
Amphibious thing! that acting either part,
The trifling head, or the corrupted heart;

Fop at the toilet, flatt'rer at the board,
Now trips a Lady, and now struts a Lord.
Eve's tempter thus the Rabbins have exprest, 330
A Cherub's face, a reptile all the rest;
Beauty that shocks you, parts that none will trust,
Wit that can creep, and pride that licks the dust.

ALEXANDER POPE
(From "Epistle to Dr. Arbuthnot")

LINES WRITTEN IN EARLY SPRING

I heard a thousand blended notes,
While in a grove I sat reclined,
In that sweet mood when pleasant thoughts
Bring sad thoughts to the mind.

To her fair works did Nature link 5
The human soul that through me ran;
And much it grieved my heart to think
What man has made of man.

Through primrose tufts, in that green bower,
The periwinkle trail'd its wreaths; 10
And 'tis my faith that every flower
Enjoys the air it breathes.

The birds around me hopp'd and play'd,
Their thoughts I cannot measure—
But the least motion which they made 15
It seem'd a thrill of pleasure.

The budding twigs spread out their fan
To catch the breezy air;
And I must think, do all I can,
That there was pleasure there. 20

If this belief from heaven be sent,
If such be Nature's holy plan,
Have I not reason to lament
What man has made of man?

WILLIAM WORDSWORTH

THE PRELUDE

Or, Growth of a Poet's Mind

BOOK TWO

Blest the infant Babe,
(For with my best conjecture I would trace
Our Being's earthly progress,) blest the Babe,
Nursed in his Mother's arms, who sinks to sleep 235
Rocked on his Mother's breast; who with his soul
Drinks in the feelings of his Mother's eye!
For him, in one dear Presence, there exists
A virtue which irradiates and exalts
Objects through widest intercourse of sense; 240
No outcast he, bewildered and depressed:
Along his infant veins are interfused
The gravitation and the filial bond
Of nature that connect him with the world.
Is there a flower, to which he points with hand 245
Too weak to gather it, already love
Drawn from love's purest earthly fount for him
Hath beautified that flower; already shades
Of pity cast from inward tenderness
Do fall around him upon aught that bears 250
Unsightly marks of violence or harm.
Emphatically such a Being lives,
Frail creature as he is, helpless as frail,
An inmate of this active universe:
For, feeling has to him imparted power 255
That through the growing faculties of sense
Doth like an agent of the one great Mind
Create, creator and receiver both,
Working but in alliance with the works
Which it beholds.—Such, verily, is the first 260
Poetic spirit of our human life,
By uniform control of after years,
In most, abated or suppressed; in some,
Through every change of growth and of decay,
Pre-eminent till death. 265

WILLIAM WORDSWORTH

LONDON, 1802

O Friend! I know not which way I must look
For comfort, being, as I am, opprest
To think that now our life is only drest
For show; mean handiwork of craftsman, cook,
Or groom!—We must run glittering like a brook 5
In the open sunshine, or we are unblest;
The wealthiest man among us is the best:
No grandeur now in Nature or in book
Delights us. Rapine, avarice, expense,
This is idolatry; and these we adore: 10
Plain living and high thinking are no more:
The homely beauty of the good old cause
Is gone; our peace, our fearful innocence,
And pure religion breathing household laws.

WILLIAM WORDSWORTH

KUBLA KHAN

In Xanadu did Kubla Khan
A stately pleasure-dome decree:
Where Alph, the sacred river, ran
Through caverns measureless to man
  Down to a sunless sea. 5
So twice five miles of fertile ground
With walls and towers were girdled round:
And there were gardens bright with sinuous rills,
Where blossomed many an incense-bearing tree;
And here were forests ancient as the hills, 10
Enfolding sunny spots of greenery.

But oh! that deep romantic chasm which slanted
Down the green hill athwart a cedarn cover!
A savage place! as holy and enchanted
As e'er beneath a waning moon was haunted 15
By woman wailing for her demon-lover!
And from this chasm, with ceaseless turmoil seething,
As if this earth in fast thick pants were breathing,
A mighty fountain momently was forced:
Amid whose swift half-intermitted burst 20
Huge fragments vaulted like rebounding hail,
Or chaffy grain beneath the thresher's flail:

And 'mid these dancing rocks at once and ever
It flung up momently the sacred river.
Five miles meandering with a mazy motion 25
Through wood and dale the sacred river ran,
Then reached the caverns measureless to man,
And sank in tumult to a lifeless ocean:
And 'mid this tumult Kubla heard from far
Ancestral voices prophesying war! 30
  The shadow of the dome of pleasure
  Floated midway on the waves;
  Where was heard the mingled measure
  From the fountain and the caves.
It was a miracle of rare device, 35
A sunny pleasure-dome with caves of ice!

  A damsel with a dulcimer
  In a vision once I saw:
  It was an Abyssinian maid,
  And on her dulcimer she played, 40
  Singing of Mount Abora.
  Could I revive within me
  Her symphony and song,
  To such a deep delight 'twould win me,
That with music loud and long, 45
I would build that dome in air,
That sunny dome! those caves of ice!
And all who heard should see them there,
And all should cry, Beware! Beware!
His flashing eyes, his floating hair! 50
Weave a circle round him thrice,
And close your eyes with holy dread,
For he on honey-dew hath fed,
And drunk the milk of Paradise.

SAMUEL TAYLOR COLERIDGE

ODE ON A GRECIAN URN

I

Thou still unravish'd bride of quietness,
  Thou foster-child of silence and slow time,
Sylvan historian, who canst thus express
  A flowery tale more sweetly than our rhyme:

What leaf-fringed legend haunts about thy shape 5
Of deities or mortals, or of both,
In Tempe or the dales of Arcady?
What men or gods are these? What maidens loth?
What mad pursuit? What struggle to escape?
What pipes and timbrels? What wild ecstasy? 10

II

Heard melodies are sweet, but those unheard
Are sweeter; therefore, ye soft pipes, play on;
Not to the sensual ear, but, more endeared,
Pipe to the spirit ditties of no tone:
Fair youth, beneath the trees, thou canst not leave 15
Thy song, nor ever can those trees be bare;
Bold Lover, never, never canst thou kiss,
Though winning near the goal—yet, do not grieve;
She cannot fade, though thou hast not thy bliss,
For ever wilt thou love, and she be fair! 20

III

Ah, happy, happy boughs! that cannot shed
Your leaves, nor ever bid the Spring adieu;
And, happy melodist, unwearièd,
For ever piping songs for ever new;
More happy love! more happy, happy love! 25
For ever warm and still to be enjoyed,
For ever panting, and for ever young;
All breathing human passion far above,
That leaves a heart high-sorrowful and cloyed,
A burning forehead, and a parching tongue. 30

IV

Who are these coming to the sacrifice?
To what green altar, O mysterious priest,
Lead'st thou that heifer lowing at the skies,
And all her silken flanks with garlands dressed?
What little town by river or sea shore, 35
Or mountain-built with peaceful citadel,
Is emptied of its folk, this pious morn?
And, little town, thy streets for evermore
Will silent be; and not a soul, to tell
Why thou art desolate, can e'er return. 40

V

O Attic shape! Fair attitude! with brede
  Of marble men and maidens overwrought,
With forest branches and the trodden weed;
  Thou, silent form, dost tease us out of thought
As doth eternity: Cold Pastoral! 45
  When old age shall this generation waste,
    Thou shalt remain, in midst of other woe
Than ours, a friend to man, to whom thou say'st,
  "Beauty is truth, truth beauty,"—that is all
    Ye know on earth, and all ye need to know. 50

JOHN KEATS

IN MEMORIAM

LXXXV

This truth came borne with bier and pall,
    I felt it, when I sorrow'd most,
    'Tis better to have loved and lost,
Than never to have loved at all—

O true in word, and tried in deed, 5
    Demanding, so to bring relief
    To this which is our common grief,
What kind of life is that I lead;

And whether trust in things above
    Be dimm'd of sorrow, or sustain'd; 10
    And whether love for him have drain'd
My capabilities of love;

Your words have virtue such as draws
    A faithful answer from the breast,
    Thro' light reproaches, half exprest, 15
And loyal unto kindly laws.

My blood an even tenor kept,
    Till on mine ear this message falls,
    That in Vienna's fatal walls
God's finger touch'd him, and he slept. 20

The great Intelligences fair
That range above our mortal state,
In circle round the blessed gate,
Received and gave him welcome there;

And led him thro' the blissful climes, 25
And show'd him in the fountain fresh
All knowledge that the sons of flesh
Shall gather in the cycled times.

But I remain'd, whose hopes were dim,
Whose life, whose thoughts were little worth, 30
To wander on a darken'd earth,
Where all things round me breathed of him.

O friendship, equal-poised control,
O heart, with kindliest motion warm,
O sacred essence, other form, 35
O solemn ghost, O crownéd soul!

Yet none could better know than I,
How much of act at human hands
The sense of human will demands
By which we dare to live or die. 40

Whatever way my days decline,
I felt and feel, tho' left alone,
His being working in mine own,
The footsteps of his life in mind;

A life that all the Muses deck'd 45
With gifts of grace, that might express
All-comprehensive tenderness,
All-subtilizing intellect:

And so my passion hath not swerved
To works of weakness, but I find 50
An image comforting the mind,
And in my grief a strength reserved.

Likewise the imaginative woe,
That loved to handle spiritual strife,
Diffused the shock thro' all my life, 55
But in the present broke the blow.

My pulses therefore beat again
 For other friends that once I met;
 Nor can it suit me to forget
The mighty hopes that make us men. 60

I woo your love: I count it crime
 To mourn for any overmuch;
 I, the divided half of such
A friendship as had master'd Time;

Which masters Time indeed, and is 65
 Eternal, separate from fears.
 The all-assuming months and years
Can take no part away from this;

But Summer on the steaming floods,
 And Spring that swells the narrow brooks, 70
 And Autumn, with a noise of rooks,
That gather in the waning woods,

And every pulse of wind and wave
 Recalls, in change of light or gloom,
 My old affection of the tomb, 75
And my prime passion in the grave.

My old affection of the tomb,
 A part of stillness, yearns to speak:
 "Arise, and get thee forth and seek
A friendship for the years to come. 80

"I watch thee from the quiet shore;
 Thy spirit up to mine can reach;
 But in dear words of human speech
We two communicate no more."

And I, "Can clouds of nature stain 85
 The starry clearness of the free?
 How is it? Canst thou feel for me
Some painless sympathy with pain?"

And lightly does the whisper fall:
 " 'Tis hard for thee to fathom this; 90
 I triumph in conclusive bliss,
And that serene result of all."

So hold I commerce with the dead;
Or so methinks the dead would say;
Or so shall grief with symbols play 95
And pining life be fancy-fed.

Now looking to some settled end,
That these things pass, and I shall prove
A meeting somewhere, love with love,
I crave your pardon, O my friend; 100

If not so fresh, with love as true,
I, clasping brother-hands, aver
I could not, if I would, transfer
The whole I felt for him to you.

For which be they that hold apart 105
The promise of the golden hours?
First love, first friendship, equal powers,
That marry with the virgin heart.

Still mine, that cannot but deplore,
That beats within a lonely place, 110
That yet remembers his embrace,
But at his footstep leaps not more,

My heart, tho' widow'd, may not rest
Quite in the love of what is gone,
But seeks to beat in time with one 115
That warms another living breast.

Ah, take the imperfect gift I bring,
Knowing the primrose yet is dear,
The primrose of the later year,
As not unlike to that of Spring. 120

ALFRED, LORD TENNYSON
(selection from "In Memoriam")

ASOLANDO

EPILOGUE

At the midnight in the silence of the sleep–time,
When you set your fancies free,
Will they pass to where—by death, fools think, imprisoned—

Low he lies who once so loved you, whom you loved so,
—Pity me? 5

Oh to love so, be so loved, yet so mistaken!
What had I on earth to do
With the slothful, with the mawkish, the unmanly?
Like the aimless, helpless, hopeless, did I drivel
—Being—who? 10

One who never turned his back but marched breast forward,
Never doubted clouds would break,
Never dreamed, though right were worsted, wrong would triumph,
Held we fall to rise, are baffled to fight better,
Sleep to wake. 15

No, at noonday in the bustle of man's work-time
Greet the unseen with a cheer!
Bid him forward, breast and back as either should be,
"Strive and thrive!" cry "Speed,—fight on, fare ever
There as here!" 20

ROBERT BROWNING

ISOLATION: TO MARGUERITE

Yes! in the sea of life enisled,
With echoing straits between us thrown,
Dotting the shoreless watery wild,
We mortal millions live *alone*.
The islands feel the enclasping flow, 5
And then their endless bounds they know.

But when the moon their hollows lights,
And they are swept by balms of spring,
And in their glens, on starry nights,
The nightingales divinely sing; 10
And lovely notes, from shore to shore,
Across the sounds and channels pour—

Oh! then a longing like despair
Is to their farthest caverns sent;
For surely once, they feel, we were 15
Parts of a single continent!

Now round us spreads the watery plain—
Oh, might our marges meet again!

Who ordered, that their longing's fire
Should be, as soon as kindled, cooled? 20
Who renders vain their deep desire?—
A god, a god their severance ruled!
And bade betwixt their shores to be
The unplumbed, salt, estranging sea.

MATTHEW ARNOLD

PHILOMELA

Hark! ah, the nightingale—
The tawny-throated!
Hark, from that moonlit cedar what a burst!
What triumph! hark!—what pain!

O wanderer from a Grecian shore, 5
Still, after many years, in distant lands,
Still nourishing in thy bewilder'd brain
That wild, unquench'd, deep-sunken, old world pain—
Say, will it never heal?
And can this fragrant lawn 10
With its cool trees, and night,
And the sweet, tranquil Thames,
And moonshine, and the dew,
To thy rack'd heart and brain
Afford no balm? 15

Dost thou to-night behold,
Here, through the moonlight on this English grass,
The unfriendly palace in the Thracian wild?
Dost thou again peruse
With hot cheeks and sear'd eyes 20
The too clear web, and thy dumb sister's shame?
Dost thou once more assay
Thy flight, and feel come over thee,
Poor fugitive, the feathery change
Once more, and once more seem to make resound 25
With love and hate, triumph and agony,
Lone Daulis, and the high Cephissian vale?

Listen, Eugenia—
How thick the bursts come crowding through the leaves!
Again—thou hearest? 30
Eternal passion!
Eternal pain!

MATTHEW ARNOLD

AFTER GREAT PAIN A FORMAL FEELING COMES

After great pain a formal feeling comes—
The nerves sit ceremonious like tombs;
The stiff Heart questions—was it He that bore?
And yesterday—or centuries before?

The feet mechanical 5
Go round a wooden way
Of ground or air or Ought, regardless grown,
A quartz contentment like a stone.

This is the hour of lead
Remembered if outlived, 10
As freezing persons recollect the snow—
First chill, then stupor, then the letting go.

EMILY DICKINSON

WONDER IS NOT PRECISELY KNOWING

Wonder is not precisely knowing,
And not precisely knowing not,
A beautiful but bleak condition
He has not lived who has not felt.

Suspense is his maturer sister; 5
Whether adult delight is pain
Or of itself a new misgiving—
This is the gnat that mangles men.

EMILY DICKINSON

HOPE

Hope is the thing with feathers
That perches in the soul,
And sings the tune without the words,
And never stops at all,

And sweetest in the gale is heard; 5
And sore must be the storm
That could abash the little bird
That kept so many warm.

I've heard it in the chillest land,
And on the strongest sea; 10
Yet, never, in extremity
It asked a crumb of me.

EMILY DICKINSON

FELIX RANDAL

Felix Randal the farrier, O he is dead then? my duty all ended,
Who have watched his mould of man, big-boned and hardy-handsome
Pining, pining, till time when reason rambled in it and some
Fatal four disorders, fleshed there, all contended?
Sickness broke him. Impatient he cursed at first, but mended 5
Being anointed and all; though a heavenlier heart began some
Months earlier, since I had our sweet reprieve and ransom
Tendered to him. Ah well, God rest him all road ever he offended!
This seeing the sick endears them to us, us too it endears.
My tongue had taught thee comfort, touch had quenched thy tears, 10
Thy tears that touched my heart, child, Felix, poor Felix Randal;
How far from then forethought of, all thy more boisterous years,
When thou at the random grim forge, powerful amidst peers,
Didst fettle for the great grey drayhorse his bright and battering sandal!

GERARD MANLEY HOPKINS

THE LEADEN ECHO AND THE GOLDEN ECHO

(Maidens' Song from St. Winefred's Well)

THE LEADEN ECHO

How to kéep—is there ány any, is there none such, nowhere known some, bow or brooch or braid or brace, láce, latch or catch or key to keep
Back beauty, keep it, beauty, beauty, beauty, . . . from vanishing away?
O is there no frowning of these wrinkles, rankèd wrinkles deep,
Dówn? no waving off of these most mournful messengers, still messengers, sad and stealing messengers of grey?
No there's none, there's none, O no there's none, 5
Nor can you long be, what you now are, called fair,
Do what you may do, what, do what you may,
And wisdom is early to despair:
Be beginning; since, no, nothing can be done
To keep at bay 10
Age and age's evils, hoar hair,
Ruck and wrinkle, drooping, dying, death's worst, winding sheets, tombs and worms and tumbling to decay;
So be beginning, be beginning to despair.
O there's none; no no no there's none:
Be beginning to despair, to despair, 15
Despair, despair, despair, despair.

THE GOLDEN ECHO

Spare!
There ís one, yes I have one (Hush there!);
Only not within seeing of the sun,
Not within the singeing of the strong sun, 20
Tall sun's tingeing, or treacherous the tainting of the earth's air,
Somewhere elsewhere there is ah well where! one,
One. Yes I can tell such a key, I do know such a place,
Where whatever's prized and passes of us, everything that's fresh and fast flying of us, seems to us sweet of us and swiftly away with, done away with, undone,
Undone, done with, soon done with, and yet dearly and dangerously sweet 25
Of us, the wimpled-water-dimpled, not-by-morning-matchéd face
The flower of beauty, fleece of beauty, too too apt to, ah! to fleet,

Never fleets móre, fastened with the tenderest truth
To its own best being and its loveliness of youth: it is an everlastingness of, O it is an all youth!
Come then, your ways and airs and looks, locks, maiden gear, gallantry and gaiety and grace, 30
Winning ways, airs innocent, maiden manners, sweet looks, loose locks, long locks, lovelocks, gaygear, going gallant, girlgrace—
Resign them, sign them, seal them, send them, motion them with breath,
And with sighs soaring, soaring síghs deliver
Them; beauty-in-the-ghost, deliver it, early now, long before death
Give beauty back, beauty, beauty, beauty, back to God, beauty's self and beauty's giver. 35
See; not a hair is, not an eyelash, not the least lash lost; every hair
Is, hair of the head, numbered.
Nay, what we had lighthanded left in surely the mere mould
Will have waked and have waxed and have walked with the wind whatwhile we slept,
This side, that side hurling a heavy headed hundredfold 40
Whatwhile we, while we slumbered.
O then, weary then why should we tread? O why are we so haggard at the heart, so care-coiled, care-killed, so fagged, so fashed, so cogged, so cumbered,
When the thing we freely fórfeit is kept with fonder a care,
Fonder a care kept than we could have kept it, kept
Far with fonder a care (and we, we should have lost it) finer, fonder 45
A care kept.—Where kept? Do but tell us where kept, where.—
Yonder.—What high as that! We follow, now we follow.
—Yonder, yes yonder, yonder,
Yonder.

GERARD MANLEY HOPKINS

THOU ART INDEED JUST, LORD

Justus quidem tu es, Domine, si disputem tecum: verumtamen justa loquar ad te: Quare via impiorum prosperatur? etc.

Thou art indeed just, Lord, if I contend
With thee; but, sir, so what I plead is just.
Why do sinners' ways prosper? and why must
Disappointment all I endeavour end?
Wert thou my enemy, O thou my friend, 5
How wouldst thou worse, I wonder, than thou dost

Defeat, thwart me? Oh, the sots and thralls of lust
Do in spare hours more thrive than I that spend,
Sir, life upon thy cause. See, banks and brakes
Now, leavèd how thick! lacèd they are again 10
With fretty chervil, look, and fresh wind shakes
Them; birds build—but not I build; no, but strain,
Time's eunuch, and not breed one work that wakes.
Mine, O thou lord of life, send my roots rain.

GERARD MANLEY HOPKINS

WHEN YOU ARE OLD

When you are old and grey and full of sleep,
And nodding by the fire, take down this book,
And slowly read, and dream of the soft look
Your eyes had once, and of their shadows deep;

How many loved your moments of glad grace, 5
And loved your beauty with love false or true;
But one man loved the pilgrim soul in you,
And loved the sorrows of your changing face.

And bending down beside the glowing bars
Murmur, a little sadly, how love fled 10
And paced upon the mountains overhead
And hid his face amid a crowd of stars.

WILLIAM BUTLER YEATS

BYZANTIUM

The unpurged images of day recede;
The Emperor's drunken soldiery are abed;
Night resonance recedes, night-walkers' song
After great cathedral gong;
A starlit or a moonlit dome disdains 5
All that man is,
All mere complexities,
The fury and the mire of human veins.

Before me floats an image, man or shade,
Shade more than man, more image than a shade; 10
For Hades' bobbin bound in mummy-cloth

May unwind the winding path;
A mouth that has no moisture and no breath
Breathless mouths may summon;
I hail the superhuman; 15
I call it death-in-life and life-in-death.

Miracle, bird or golden handiwork,
More miracle than bird or handiwork,
Planted on the star-lit golden bough,
Can like the cocks of Hades crow, 20
Or, by the moon embittered, scorn aloud
In glory of changeless metal
Common bird or petal
And all complexities of mire or blood.

At midnight on the Emperor's pavement flit 25
Flames that no faggot feeds, nor steel has lit,
Nor storm disturbs, flames begotten of flame,
Where blood-begotten spirits come
And all complexities of fury leave,
Dying into a dance, 30
An agony of trance,
An agony of flame that cannot singe a sleeve.

Astraddle on the dolphin's mire and blood,
Spirit after spirit! The smithies break the flood,
The golden smithies of the Emperor! 35
Marbles of the dancing floor
Break bitter furies of complexity,
Those images that yet
Fresh images beget,
That dolphin-torn, that gong-tormented sea. 40

WILLIAM BUTLER YEATS

STOPPING BY WOODS ON A SNOWY EVENING

Whose woods these are I think I know.
His house is in the village though;
He will not see me stopping here
To watch his woods fill up with snow.

My little horse must think it queer 5
To stop without a farmhouse near
Between the woods and frozen lake
The darkest evening of the year.

He gives his harness bells a shake
To ask if there is some mistake. 10
The only other sound's the sweep
Of easy wind and downy flake.

The woods are lovely, dark and deep,
But I have promises to keep,
And miles to go before I sleep, 15
And miles to go before I sleep.

ROBERT FROST

ENVOI (1919)

Go, dumb-born book,
Tell her that sang me once that song of Lawes:
Hadst thou but song
As thou hast subjects known,
Then were there cause in thee that should condone 5
Even my faults that heavy upon me lie,
And build her glories their longevity.

Tell her that sheds
Such treasure in the air,
Recking naught else but that her graces give 10
Life to the moment,
I would bid them live
As roses might, in magic amber laid,
Red overwrought with orange and all made
One substance and one colour 15
Braving time.

Tell her that goes
With song upon her lips
But sings not out the song, nor knows
The maker of it, some other mouth, 20
May be as fair as hers,
Might, in new ages, gain her worshippers,

When our two dusts with Waller's shall be laid,
Siftings on siftings in oblivion,
Till change hath broken down 25
All things save Beauty alone.

EZRA POUND

THE RECURRENCE

All things return, Nietzsche said,
The ancient wheel revolves again,
Rise, take up your numbered fate;
The cradle and the bridal bed,
Life and the coffin wait. 5
All has been that ever can be,
And this sole eternity
Cannot cancel, cannot add
One to your delights or tears,
Or a million million years 10
Tear the nightmare from the mad.

Have no fear then. You will miss
Achievement by the self-same inch,
When the great occasion comes
And they watch you, you will flinch, 15
Lose the moment, be for bliss
A footlength short. All done before.
Love's agonies, victory's drums
Cannot huddle the Cross away
Planted on its future hill, 20
The secret on the appointed day
Will be made known, the ship once more
Hit upon the waiting rock
Or come safely to the shore,
Careless under the deadly tree 25
The victim drowse, the urgent warning
Come too late, the dagger strike,
Strike and strike through eternity,
And worlds hence the prison clock
Will toll on execution morning, 30
What is ill be always ill,
Wretches die behind a dike,
And the happy be happy still.

But the heart makes reply:
This is only what the eye 35
From its tower on the turning field
Sees and sees and cannot tell why,
Quarterings on the turning shield,
The great non-stop heraldic show.
And the heart and the mind know, 40
What has been can never return,
What is not will surely be
In the chanted unchanging reign,
Else the Actor on the Tree
Would loll at ease, miming pain, 45
And counterfeit mortality.

EDWIN MUIR

POETRY

I, too, dislike it: there are things that are important beyond
all this fiddle.
Reading it, however, with a perfect contempt for it, one
discovers in
it after all, a place for the genuine. 5
Hands that can grasp, eyes
that can dilate, hair that can rise
if it must, these things are important not because a

high-sounding interpretation can be put upon them but because they are 10
useful. When they become so derivative as to become
unintelligible,
the same thing may be said for all of us, that we
do not admire what
we cannot understand: the bat 15
holding on upside down or in quest of something to

eat, elephants pushing, a wild horse taking a roll, a tireless
wolf under
a tree, the immovable critic twitching his skin like a horse
that feels a flea, the base- 20
ball fan, the statistician—
nor is it valid
to discriminate against "business documents and

school-books"; all these phenomena are important. One
must make a distinction 25
however: when dragged into prominence by half poets,
the result is not poetry,
nor till the poets among us can be
"literalists of
the imagination"—above 30
insolence and triviality and can present

for inspection, "imaginary gardens with real toads in them,"
shall we have
it. In the meantime, if you demand on the one hand,
the raw material of poetry in 35
all its rawness and
that which is on the other hand
genuine, then you are interested in poetry.

MARIANNE MOORE

JOURNEY OF THE MAGI

"A cold coming we had of it,
Just the worst time of the year
For a journey, and such a long journey:
The ways deep and the weather sharp,
The very dead of winter." 5
And the camels galled, sore-footed, refractory,
Lying down in the melting snow.
There were times we regretted
The summer palaces on slopes, the terraces,
And the silken girls bringing sherbet. 10
Then the camel men cursing and grumbling
And running away, and wanting their liquor and women,
And the night-fires going out, and the lack of shelters,
And the cities hostile and the towns unfriendly
And the villages dirty and charging high prices: 15
A hard time we had of it.
At the end we preferred to travel all night,
Sleeping in snatches,
With the voices singing in our ears, saying
That this was all folly. 20

Then at dawn we came down to a temperate valley,
Wet, below the snow line, smelling of vegetation;
With a running stream and a water-mill beating the darkness,
And three trees on the low sky,
And an old white horse galloped away in the meadow. 25
Then we came to a tavern with vine-leaves over the lintel,
Six hands at an open door dicing for pieces of silver,
And feet kicking the empty wine-skins.
But there was no information, and so we continued
And arrived at evening, not a moment too soon 30
Finding the place; it was (you may say) satisfactory.

All this was a long time ago, I remember,
And I would do it again, but set down
This set down
This: were we led all that way for 35
Birth or Death? There was a birth, certainly,
We had evidence and no doubt. I had seen birth and death,
But had thought they were different; this Birth was
Hard and bitter agony for us, like Death, our death.
We returned to our places, these Kingdoms, 40
But no longer at ease here, in the old dispensation,
With an alien people clutching their gods.
I should be glad of another death.

T. S. ELIOT

THE HOLLOW MEN

Mistah Kurtz—he dead.

A penny for the Old Guy

I

We are the hollow men
We are the stuffed men
Leaning together
Headpiece filled with straw. Alas!
Our dried voices, when 5
We whisper together
Are quiet and meaningless
As wind in dry grass
Or rats' feet over broken glass
In our dry cellar 10

Shape without form, shade without colour,
Paralyzed force, gesture without motion;

Those who have crossed
With direct eyes, to death's other Kingdom
Remember us—if at all—not as lost 15
Violent souls, but only
As the hollow men
The stuffed men.

II

Eyes I dare not meet in dreams
In death's dream kingdom 20
These do not appear:
There, the eyes are
Sunlight on a broken column
There, is a tree swinging
And voices are 25
In the wind's singing
More distant and more solemn
Than a fading star.

Let me be no nearer
In death's dream kingdom 30
Let me also wear
Such deliberate disguises
Rat's coat, crowskin, crossed staves
In a field
Behaving as the wind behaves 35
No nearer—

Not that final meeting
In the twilight kingdom

III

This is the dead land
This is cactus land 40
Here the stone images
Are raised, here they receive
The supplication of a dead man's hand
Under the twinkle of a fading star.

Is it like this 45
In death's other kingdom
Waking alone
At the hour when we are
Trembling with tenderness
Lips that would kiss 50
Form prayers to broken stone.

IV

The eyes are not here
There are no eyes here
In this valley of dying stars
In this hollow valley 55
This broken jaw of our lost kingdoms

In this last of meeting places
We grope together
And avoid speech
Gathered on this beach of the tumid river 60

Sightless, unless
The eyes reappear
As the perpetual star
Multifoliate rose
Of death's twilight kingdom 65
The hope only
Of empty men.

V

Here we go round the prickly pear
Prickly pear prickly pear
Here we go round the prickly pear 70
At five o'clock in the morning.

Between the idea
And the reality
Between the motion
And the act 75
Falls the Shadow
For Thine is the Kingdom

Between the conception
And the creation

Between the emotion 80
And the response
Falls the Shadow

Life is very long

Between the desire
And the spasm 85
Between the potency
And the existence
Between the essence
And the descent
Falls the Shadow 90

For Thine is the Kingdom

For Thine is
Life is
For Thine is the

This is the way the world ends 95
This is the way the world ends
This is the way the world ends
Not with a bang but a whimper.

T. S. ELIOT

THE SHOW

My soul looked down from a vague height with Death,
As unremembering how I rose or why,
And saw a sad land, weak with sweats of dearth,
Gray, cratered like the moon with hollow woe,
And fitted with great pocks and scabs of plagues. 5

Across its beard, that horror of harsh wire,
There moved thin caterpillars, slowly uncoiled.
It seemed they pushed themselves to be as plugs
Of ditches, where they writhed and shrivelled, killed.

By them had slimy paths been trailed and scraped 10
Round myriad warts that might be little hills.

From gloom's last dregs these long-strung creatures crept,
And vanished out of dawn down hidden holes.

(And smell came up from those foul openings
As out of mouths, or deep wounds deepening.) 15

On dithering feet upgathered, more and more,
Brown strings, towards strings of gray, with bristling spines,
All migrants from green fields, intent on mire.

Those that were gray, of more abundant spawns,
Ramped on the rest and ate them and were eaten. 20

I saw their bitten backs curve, loop, and straighten,
I watched those agonies curl, lift, and flatten.

Whereat, in terror what that sight might mean,
I reeled and shivered earthward like a feather.

And Death fell with me, like a deepening moan. 25
And He, picking a manner of worm, which half had hid
Its bruises in the earth, but crawled no further,
Showed me its feet, the feet of many men,
And the fresh-severed head of it, my head.

WILFRED OWEN

THE GROUNDHOG

In June, amid the golden fields,
I saw a groundhog lying dead.
Dead lay he; my senses shook,
And mind outshot our naked frailty.
There lowly in the vigorous summer 5
His form began its senseless change,
And made my senses waver dim
Seeing nature ferocious in him.
Inspecting close his maggots' might
And seething cauldron of his being, 10
Half with loathing, half with a strange love,
I poked him with an angry stick.
The fever arose, became a flame
And Vigour circumscribed the skies,
Immense energy in the sun, 15
And through my frame a sunless trembling.
My stick had done nor good nor harm.
Then stood I silent in the day

Watching the object, as before;
And kept my reverence for knowledge 20
Trying for control, to be still,
To quell the passion of the blood;
Until I had bent down on my knees
Praying for joy in the sight of decay.
And so I left; and I returned 25
In Autumn strict of eye, to see
The sap gone out of the groundhog,
But the bony sodden hulk remained.
But the year had lost its meaning,
And in intellectual chains 30
I lost both love and loathing,
Mured up in the wall of wisdom.
Another summer took the fields again
Massive and burning, full of life,
But when I chanced upon the spot 35
There was only a little hair left,
And bones bleaching in the sunlight
Beautiful as architecture;
I watched them like a geometer,
And cut a walking stick from a birch. 40
It has been three years, now.
There is no sign of the groundhog.
I stood there in the whirling summer,
My hand capped a withered heart,
And thought of China and of Greece, 45
Of Alexander in his tent;
Of Montaigne in his tower,
Of Saint Theresa in her wild lament.

RICHARD EBERHART

MUSEE DES BEAUX ARTS

About suffering they were never wrong,
The Old Masters: how well they understood
Its human position; how it takes place
While someone else is eating or opening a window or just walking dully
along;
How, when the aged are reverently, passionately waiting 5
For the miraculous birth, there always must be
Children who did not specially want it to happen, skating

On a pond at the edge of the wood:
They never forgot
That even the dreadful martyrdom must run its course 10
Anyhow in a corner, some untidy spot
Where dogs go on with their doggy life and the torturer's horse
Scratches its innocent behind on a tree.

In Breughel's *Icarus,* for instance: how everything turns away
Quite leisurely from the disaster; the ploughman, may 15
Have heard the splash, the forsaken cry,
But for him it was not an important failure; the sun shone
As it had to on the white legs disappearing into the green
Water; and the expensive delicate ship that must have seen
Something amazing, a boy falling out of the sky, 20
Had somewhere to get to and sailed calmly on.

W. H. AUDEN

BUICK

As a sloop with a sweep of immaculate wing on her delicate spine
And a keel as steel as a root that holds in the sea as she leans,
Leaning and laughing, my warm-hearted beauty, you ride, you ride,
You tack on the curves with parabola speed and a kiss of good bye,
Like a thoroughbred sloop, my new high-spirited spirit, my kiss. 5

As my foot suggests that you leap in the air with your hips of a girl,
My finger that praises your wheel and announces your voices of song,
Flouncing your skirts, you blueness of joy, you flirt of politeness,
You leap, you intelligence, essence of wheelness with silvery nose,
And your platinum clocks of excitement stir like the hairs of a fern. 10

But how alien you are from the booming belts of your birth and the smoke
Where you turned on the stinging lathes of Detroit and Lansing at night
And shrieked at the torch in your secret parts and the amorous tests,
But now with your eyes that enter the future of roads you forget;
You are all instinct with your phosphorous glow and your streaking hair. 15
And now when we stop it is not as the bird from the shell that I leave
Or the leathery pilot who steps from his bird with a sneer of delight,
And not as the ignorant beast do you squat and watch me depart,

But with exquisite breathing you smile, with satisfaction of love,
And I touch you again as you tick in the silence and settle in sleep. 20

KARL SHAPIRO

COLLOQUY IN BLACK ROCK

Here the jack-hammer jabs into the ocean;
My heart, you race and stagger and demand
More blood-gangs for your nigger-brass percussions,
Till I, the stunned machine of your devotion,
Clanging upon this cymbal of a hand, 5
Am rattled screw and footloose. All discussions

End in the mud-flat detritus of death.
My heart, beat faster, faster. In Black Mud
Hungarian workmen give their blood
For the martyre Stephen, who was stoned to death. 10

Black Mud, a name to conjure with: O mud
For watermelons gutted to the crust,
Mud for the mole-tide harbor, mud for mouse,
Mud for the armored Diesel fishing tubs that thud
A year and a day to wind and tide; the dust 15
Is on this skipping heart that shakes my house,

House of our Savior who was hanged till death.
My heart, beat faster, faster. In Black Mud
Stephen the martyre was broken down to blood:
Our ransom is the rubble of his death. 20

Christ walks on the black water. In Black Mud
Darts the kingfisher. On Corpus Christi, heart,
Over the drum-beat of St. Stephen's choir
I hear him, *Stupor Mundi,* and the mud
Flies from his hunching wings and beak—my heart, 25
The blue kingfisher dives on you in fire.

ROBERT LOWELL

STILL, CITIZEN SPARROW

Still, citizen sparrow, this vulture which you call
Unnatural, let him but lumber again to air
Over the rotten office, let him bear

The carrion ballast up, and at the tall
Tip of the sky lie cruising. Then you'll see 5
That no more beautiful bird is in heaven's height,
No wider more placid wings, no watchfuller flight;
He shoulders nature there, the frightfully free,

The naked-headed one. Pardon him, you
Who dart in the orchard aisles, for it is he 10
Devours death, mocks mutability,
Has heart to make an end, keeps nature new.

Thinking of Noah, childheart, try to forget
How for so many bedlam hours his saw
Soured the song of birds with its wheezy gnaw, 15
And the slam of his hammer all the day beset

The people's ears. Forget that he could bear
To see the towns like coral under the keel,
And the fields so dismal deep. Try rather to feel
How high and weary it was, on the waters where 20

He rocked his only world, and everyone's.
Forgive the hero, you who would have died
Gladly with all you knew; he rode that tide
To Ararat; all men are Noah's sons.

RICHARD WILBUR

Some Notes on Obscurity in Modern Poetry

THE QUESTION of obscurity in modern poetry may best be examined first by putting two views side by side; the parallel may help to dramatize certain issues that perplex many readers of poetry and may also suggest how these issues may be better understood.

The first view—perhaps the "official" view, since it is widely held by many critics and some teachers of poetry, is that which appeared in Louise Bogan's *Achievement in American Poetry 1900-1950*. Miss Bogan's attitude cannot be summed up in a few words without ignoring her fine discrimination between originality and mere eccentricity, between the genuinely experimental and the undisciplined self-expression. But the main drift of her argument is that American poetry has advanced from the Victorian night of 1900 when poetry "was imitative, sentimental and genteel," when its relation to the surrounding culture was superficial and its attitude towards genuine talent, such as Whitman, Melville and Emily Dickinson, was prejudiced in the extreme.

She traces this advance to the fusion of two revolutionary forces: the native American forces of liberation, that we encountered in E. A. Robinson, Edgar Lee Masters, Vachel Lindsay and Carl Sandburg, and the force derived, largely by way of Ezra Pound and T. S. Eliot, from the three successive French literary revolutions—the Romantic, the Parnassian and the Symbolist. As a result, she feels the status of poetry has advanced considerably beyond the aboriginal Victorian night. The work of other poets like Wallace Stevens, Marianne Moore, William Carlos Williams, and younger poets like Randell Jarrell, Karl Shapiro and Richard Wilbur encourages her to believe that twentieth-century poetry in English has achieved a great victory. Miss Bogan writes:

> At a first retrospective glance, the true triumph in every modern art appears to be that of sincerity over sham, of naturalness over affectation, of a striking turn toward precision, analysis, and structure; of a wider range of conception and idea; of a deeper apprehension of meaning. Poets writing in English during the last fifty years have freed themselves from a nineteenth-century role which rather comically combined the lay preacher, the parlor philosopher, and the seedy minstrel. Poets in all Western countries, along with artists in general, gradually took upon themselves tasks which required the complete strength of integrated personalities for their accomplishment; and they pushed through experiment and exploration despite the ridicule or the neglect of the public at large. The complexities of the time presented problems whose solution required endurance as well as insight. We are now able to recognize the steps by means of which complicated spiritual and even social situations were laid bare, if not entirely resolved; and the accompanying complicated artistic procedures which often had to be improvised by intuitive means. We can now perceive in what way
>
> . . . the forbidden,
> The hidden, the wild outside
>
> was grasped and absorbed into art; and how poets aided not only in the discovery of hidden truths, but had an important part in moulding such discoveries into accessible form.*

A second view may be deduced from a reading of the chapter on "The Modern Period" in Douglas Bush's *English Poetry.* I say *deduced* because this excellent short essay on the main currents of English poetry from Chaucer to the present is not conceived as an attack on, or a defense of, any one period of poetry; rather, it is an attempt to show that poetry is essentially a distillation of human experience that rises above its local conditions. "All great poetry," writes Mr. Bush, "is or may be [the reader's] present possession."** Nevertheless, his treatment of the successive ages of poetry implicitly rebukes the contemporary provincialism that some will detect in the passage quoted from Miss Bogan. For Mr. Bush, as for many other scholars and critics who have studied the Victorians, the work of nineteenth-century

* Louise Bogan, *Achievement in American Poetry 1900-1950* (Chicago, 1951), pp. 106-107.

** Douglas Bush, *English Poetry* (New York, 1952), p. viii.

poets like Tennyson, Browning, and Arnold cannot be characterized as sham, affectation or complacency. These Victorians—not to mention other intense, divided spirits like Thomas Hardy and Gerard Manley Hopkins, James Thomson and Francis Thompson—are no less agonized in spirit, no less sincere in reporting their own doubts and complexities (think of *In Memoriam, The Ring and the Book, Sohrab and Rustum*) and no less experimental in the light of their immediate situation than are twentieth-century poets. Indeed, Mr. Bush hints that the modern period has its own faults—and that these are perhaps graver than the faults of their romantic and Victorian predecessors—because they merely reproduce, instead of interpret, the moral confusion of our age.

> Poets, whether themselves distrusting traditional values and verities, or aware of general distrust, have been driven back to the irrefragable truth of concrete particulars and the data and symbols of private experience. Overt reflection and affirmation, in the past the products of relative assurance, have been either drastically limited in scope or replaced or enveloped by the oblique and noncommittal and ironical. Then, modern poems are likely to develop around and through images, instead of having a "logical" structure of ideas. Thus, unlike most earlier poetry, a modern poem may seem to be, in a sense, only half-written; much more is left to be done by the reader, and interpretation may (in the useful phrase of Sir Thomas Browne) admit a wide solution. Modern poets have often been accused of being excessively and wilfully difficult, but the same charge was lodged in earlier periods against poets who have long been acquitted; and time can always be relied upon to distinguish between authentic, inevitable obscurity and mere fashion.*

At first glance these views tilt in different directions. Miss Bogan asks us to believe that "modern" poets (not contemporary poets, we must note, for the bulk of poetry is still being written in a nineteenth-century tradition) have achieved a notable advance. Mr. Bush reserves judgment, but his tone suggests that much modern poetry lacks moral strength, intellectual vision and a poetic vocabulary. In effect, Miss Bogan argues that modern

* Bush, pp. 197-198.

poetry has registered growth and achievement because it represents what is happening to modern society. Like Archibald MacLeish, she appears to believe that, essentially, a poem must give us an image of our age in terms of the poet's personal perception. If the age is out of joint, the poet is blameless for reporting this fact. Indeed, he is equally blameless for being out of joint himself.

On the other hand, Mr. Bush argues that modern poetry does not necessarily achieve a high poetic status because it sincerely expresses the predicament of a cultivated sensibility in a time of spiritual confusion. For him the norm or measure of the poet's achievement is not only his awareness of his predicament, but his ability to judge it in terms of a central criterion. Thus he writes:

> If the predicament of the modern artist is to be attributed mainly to the character of modern civilization, the poets have perhaps been not entirely blameless, and we must hope for fuller rapprochement between the poet and the common reader for the sake of both poetry and society. And while our civilization is predominantly scientific, now as in former times poetry can break through the tyranny of the positivist intellect and claim to be the breath and finer spirit of all knowledge. Finally, now as always, a central criterion of the major poet is his recognition of the unceasing conflict between good and evil.*

In short, the contrasted views of Miss Bogan and Mr. Bush serve to dramatize a principal dispute in the field of contemporary poetry—a dispute as to the basic assumptions that underlie critical judgment. What is unquestionably growth and achievement for Miss Bogan is possibly regression or failure for Mr. Bush. Even when both writers admire the competence of individual poets (T. S. Eliot or W. H. Auden, for instance), they tend to admire them for different reasons. Thus, Miss Bogan admires T. S. Eliot's "The Love Song of J. Alfred Prufrock" because its style and tone are free from the mannerisms of late nineteenth-century English poetry. On the other hand, Bush regards this poem chiefly as a critique of an ugly, unheroic present. Miss Bogan is concerned with the poem's contempo-

* *Ibid.*, p. 218.

raneity, its esthetic opposition to the past; Mr. Bush, with its aptness as a criticism of life.

What we think of contemporary poetry, we may now infer, depends to a large extent on the questions we ask about it, and the questions we ask stem from our assumptions as to what poetry is, how it arises, how it is expressed, how it should affect the reader. If we assume that the poet should represent his attitude toward his time, that he should manifest the twentieth-century moods of anxiety and despair, its concern for the sub-conscious, its scepticism, its tensions, its fragmented characters, then we may conclude that a poet like Ezra Pound is an outstanding poet. But if we assume that a poet's thought should be clear, that his perceptions should be united in a coherent logical patten, that his allusions should be historically accurate, and that his work should be understandable to the intelligent general reader, then we may conclude that Pound is an eccentric, indeed, an enigmatic figure in contemporary writing.

Well, what assumptions are we to make? Miss Bogan's or Mr. Bush's? The assumptions of a professed symbolist like Ruth Zabriskie Temple who appears to identify poetry with the esthetic principles of French symbolism,* or the assumptions of an astute philosopher like Jacques Maritain?** This is to ask what assumptions are most relevant to the actual situation of contemporary poetry. This leads us to ask: What is that situation today? What does the situation call for?

But the *situation* of contemporary poetry is not primarily a problem of understanding the poet and his relation to the age, or of understanding the poet's technique. We are aware of an abundant biographical and historical commentary, and of detailed textual analysis that has brought the so-called "obscure" poet within the range of the interested reader. At one time T. S. Eliot needed interpreters. Now he needs defense from his interpreters. At one time we guessed wildly at Yeats's use of magical elements in his poetry. Now our guess is an educated one. Modern poetry does not need interpreters, biographical, historical or textual, so much as it needs readers. Modern poetry is not being read.

* *The Critic's Alchemy: A Study of the Introduction of French Symbolism into England* (New York, 1953).

** *Creative Intuition in Art and Poetry* (New York, 1953).

Why are there so few readers? The cause is frequently ascribed to the obscurity of modern poetry. Indeed, the defenders of modern poetry boast of its obscurity as openly as the attackers denounce it. For example, in his essay "Understanding Modern Poetry," Allen Tate insists that modern poetry, "must have the direct and active participation of a reader . . . it is a kind of poetry that requires of the reader the fullest cooperation of all his intellectual resources, all his knowledge of the world, and all the persistence and alertness that he now thinks of giving to scientific studies."* More recently Randall Jarrell** has argued that the general public, not the few trained readers, applies a false test of clarity to the poetry of today, forgetting that older poets like Donne or Browning, were, and still are, for those who do not take a predigested explanatory tablet, anything but clear. According to Jarrell, the general public means by clarity the kind of sub-intellectual plain talk that abolishes difficulty. Clarity of this sort is absence of meaning, absence of thought, a repose in slack, commonplace statement and a refusal of challenge. Small wonder, then, that the poet accused of obscurity may urge in his own defense Mr. Jarrell's estimate of the situation we are investigating.

> The poet lives in a world whose newspapers and magazines and books and motion pictures and radio stations and television stations have destroyed, in a great many people, even the capacity for understanding real poetry, real art of any kind. The man who monthly reads, with vacant relish, the carefully predigested sentences which the *Reader's Digest* feeds to him as a mother pigeon feeds her squabs—this man *cannot* read the *Divine Comedy,* even if it should ever occur to him to try; it is too obscure. Yet one sort of clearness shows a complete contempt for the reader, just as one sort of obscurity shows a complete respect. Which patronizes and degrades the reader, the *Divine Comedy* with its four levels of meaning, or the *Reader's Digest* with its one level so low that it seems not a level but an abyss into which the reader consents to sink? The writer's real dishonesty is to give an easy

* Allen Tate, "Understanding Modern Poetry," in *Reason in Madness,* (New York, 1941), p. 92.

** *Poetry and the Age,* (New York, 1953).

> paraphrase of the hard truth. Yet the average article in our magazines gives any subject whatsoever the same coat of easy, automatic, "human" interest; every year *Harper's Magazine* sounds more like *Life* and the *Saturday Evening Post.* Goethe said, "The author whom a lexicon can keep up with is worth nothing"; Somerset Maugham says that the finest compliment he ever received was a letter in which one of his readers said "I read your novel without having to look up a single word in the dictionary." These writers, plainly, lived in different worlds.
>
> Since the animal organism thinks, truly reasons, only when it is required to, thoughtfulness is gradually disappearing among readers; and popular writing has left nothing to the imagination for so long now that imagination too has begun to atrophy. Almost all the works of the past are beginning to seem to the ordinary reader flat and dull, because they do not supply the reader's response along with that to which he responds. Boys who have read only a few books in their lives, but a great many comic books, will tell one, so vividly that it is easy to sympathize: "I don't like books because they don't really show you things; they're too slow; you have to do all the work yourself." When, in a few years, one talks to boys who have read only a few comic books, but have looked at a great many television programs—what will they say?*

The situation, then, as Tate and Jarrell see it is that much modern poetry (charlatans are, of course, excluded) is obscure in the sense that it demands hard, disciplined reading. Readers today, so their explanation goes, will not cultivate their intellectual powers sufficiently to understand a T. S. Eliot or an Ezra Pound, an Allen Tate or a Randall Jarrell. Is there, however, another side of the case? Have some readers a just complaint? When we consider the other side of the case we encounter the charge that modern poetry is unintelligible, not because it is too intellectual, but because it is not intellectual enough, or even because it is not intellectual at all.

Oddly enough, the charge that modern poetry is not intellectual has been best stated by Sir Herbert Read, one of the most ardent defenders of the modern movement in poetry. In the concluding

* *Ibid.*, Jarrell, p. 18.

chapter of *Phases of English Poetry* Read sums up the historical development of English poetry in a series of diagrammatic statements:

> In the first [phase] the poet coincides with his circle; in the second he is a point within the circle; in the third he is a point on the circumference; and finally he is a point outside the circle. These are respectively the positions of the anonymous creator of ballad poetry, the humanist poet (with whom, for this purpose, we might associate the poets of love and sentiment), the religious poet, and the romantic poet. The humanist poet is the nucleus of his world, the focus of intelligence and intellectual progress. The religious poet lives at the periphery of his world—at the point where his world is in contact with the infinite universe. The romantic poet is his own universe; the world for him is either rejected as unreal in favour of some phantom world, or is identified with the poet's own feelings. The four phases complete a cycle, beginning with the world as poet and ending with the poet as world. My presumption is that the typical modern poet is aware of the completion of this cycle, and as a consequence either despairs of his function, or is desperately anxious to find a way out of the state of eccentricity.*

Read then goes on to point out that the poet, usually the sensitive recorder of spiritual directions, has in the past been representative of his time and nation. His signals once registered. But today he is ignored. "There has surely never been a period in our literary history when poetry was so little read and the poet so little recognized. . . . The last poet not to be regarded by the people at large as a social anomaly was Tennyson . . .**

What is the reason for this neglect of the poet and his work? Sir Herbert sees two possible explanations. Either society has surpassed the poet, and can now dispense with him, or the poet has developed his art beyond the needs or wants of the reading public. While he feels that both of these explanations are true, it is the second reason that is the more important. The modern poet is not only subjective, that is, concerned with what he alone thinks and feels, but he is also disillusioned, even embittered. He is isolated from society, and hence, intensely personal in his con-

* Herbert Read, *Phases of English Poetry* (New York, 1951), p. 166-167.
** *Ibid.*, p. 169.

cerns. His one belief is in his own sincerity and this sincerity, he feels, is at war with formal restraints of style, rhythm, rhyme, stanzaic pattern, logical structure—in short, with all the verbal and logical clarities. His effort to express his highly complicated self against the background of his highly complicated age, without rule or shape, necessarily makes the poet obscure.

"By definition," Read says, "a poet is a being of abnormal sensibility, and the reaction of such a being to the complex problems of existence, both personal and universal, are sure to be of a complexity quite beyond the normal limits of expression."* Hence, the very object of his vision—his complex interior world—is dark. How can he possibly express the dark world of intuition in neat logical outlines? He resorts, therefore, to indirect, oblique expression, to metaphor and myth, to highly personal symbols that often have only a shadowy meaning and often only for himself.

Read is aware that this intense privacy of the modern poet ignores the poet's public functions of story-teller, court-wit, popular jester, teacher, satirist, prophet and secular priest—public functions that helped to win for Chaucer, Spencer, Milton, Dryden, Wordsworth, Browning and many others their enduring place in our literary history. Moreover, the poet has abandoned these functions knowingly, if reluctantly. Something of this spirit of rejection appears in W. H. Auden's dedicatory epistle in *Nones* to Reinhold and Ursula Niebuhr.

> We, too, had known golden hours
> When body and soul were in tune,
> Had danced with our true loves
> By the light of a full moon
> And sat with the wise and good
> As tongues grew witty and gay
> Over some noble dish
> Out of Escoffier;
> Had felt the intrusive glory
> Which tears reserve apart
> And would in the old grand manner
> Have sung from a resonant heart.
> But, pawed-at and gossipped-over

* *Ibid.*, p. 184.

By the promiscuous crowd,
Concocted by editors
Into spells to befuddle the crowd,
All words like peace and love,
All sane affirmative speech,
Had been soiled, profaned, debased
To a horrid mechanical screech:
No civil style survived
That pandaemonium
But the wry, the sotto-voce,
Ironic and monochrome:
And where should we find shelter
For joy or mere content
When little was left standing
But the suburb of dissent.

It is this spirit of "pride of knowledge and exclusiveness of sensibility" that Read believes has isolated the poet from his public. "How then," Read asks, "can the modern poet, in the face of a hostile world, and with his doctrine of sincerity, find a means of reconciling his world and his art?"* Read would assign him the primitive role of ballad-maker, wherein he will divine the group-feeling and will "then create a poetry which not only satisfies the emotional needs of the populace, but which also possesses those universal elements of thought and feeling that ensure permanency."** This is what the poet must do; but that he can do it, given his present mode of thought, even Read doubts.

If we interpret Read, Jarrell and others correctly, their conclusion is that obscurity is authentic and inevitable when the poem is legitimately concerned with realities that admit of no facile statement. It is authentic, we may add, when the poet is attempting, in the manner of G. M. Hopkins and T. S. Eliot, "to purify the language of the tribe" by avoiding worn-out epithets, and rhythms in favor of fresh vocabulary and original modes of poetic speech.

But sometimes the obscurity in the poem is the fault of the poet. Not every poem, even of distinguished poets, is unified and coherent. Often, too, a poet commits himself to a theory of poetry

* *Ibid.*, p. 187.
** *Ibid.*, p. 189.

that leads him mistakenly to embrace obscurity for its own sake. Thus, the theory identified as "pure poetry" aimed at "an obscure enchantment independent of sense." Followers of this school not only shun rational statement, but avoid all the clarifications associated with the traditional art of poetry. Needless to say, this theory, if pursued consistently, leads to a cult of unintelligibility that has little or no connection with the authentic and inevitable obscurity of genuine poetry.

GLOSSARY

This glossary contains brief descriptions of some terms used frequently throughout this book. Many of these terms, however, are complex; some of them are treated throughout several chapters. Hence the reader may wish to consult the index for the principal discussions of the more important terms. Other terms may also be found in the index.

Abstract: general terms or statements that stand for or express ideas or concepts. The abstract is opposed to the concrete, that is, a term or statement that represents things, events, people, objects, or characteristics that can be apprehended by the senses.

Accent: the relatively different emphasis with which syllables are pronounced, as in *díffer* or *defér.*

Allegory: a sustained metaphor that establishes a precise, point-by-point correspondence between one action or object and another. See *Metaphor.*

Alliteration: the repetition of the same consonant sound in a line or in successive lines of verse. Often it is limited to mean the repetition of initial stressed syllables, as in *dreams of dreamers.*

Ambiguity: two or more possible meanings.

Amplification: the development of a subject by adding details; the achievement of a greater emotional effect by word choice, repetition, contrast and compression, climactic arrangement, and so on.

Analogy: a likeness that exists between objects or actions that are not in the same class. Analogy is the basis of figurative language.

Anapest: a metrical foot in which two unaccented syllables are followed by an accented syllable, as in *in thĕ sháde ŏf thĕ trée.*

Anaphora: forceful repetition.

Assonance: The repetition of the same vowel or diphthong sounds in a line or successive lines of verse, as in *Rōw us out to Dezanzanō.*

Ballad: originally a short folk tale of popular origin that was meant to be sung, chanted or recited. The so-called literary ballad is an artistic adaptation of the earlier folk ballad.

Blank verse: lines of unrhymed verse in iambic pentameter.

Caesura: a pause within a line of verse.

Cliché: an expression that is worn out through over-use, for example, *as good as gold.*

Climax: the point of highest interest or emotional intensity in a poem.

Compression: the fusion in poetry of many ideas, feelings, and images, usually achieved through figurative language.

Concentration: a focus on a single or main emotion or theme; a special characteristic of the simple lyric.

Concrete: a term that refers to some object, action, or characteristic that may be apprehended by the senses. See *Abstract.*

Connotation: the implied or suggested meaning of a word or expression as opposed to its explicit or denotative meaning.

Consistency: the coherence of part to part and of parts to whole in a poem.

Context: (1) the whole in which a word or expression or particular passage occurs; thus we study a stanza in the context of the whole poem; (2) the study of the poem in the context of the poet's whole body of work, and the poet's body of work in the context of other literary works.

Convention: a form of writing, such as the pastoral elegy or the sonnet, with fixed themes or procedures.

Couplet: two consecutive lines of verse bound together by rhyme.

Criticism: the evaluation of a work of art according to relevant standards or principles.

Dactyl: a metrical foot in which an accented syllable is followed by two unaccented syllables, as in *This is the forest primeval the . . .*

Denotation: the explicit meaning of a word or expression; the object, event or characteristic that a word specifically designates.

Design: the pattern or structure of the poem; the arrangement of the parts to achieve a unified, coherent whole.

Diction: the choice of words; in poetry diction is judged chiefly by its appropriateness in a given context.

Dramatic:

(1) a type of poetry that is suitable for presentation through action and dialogue on a stage;

(2) a poem whose structure resembles that of a drama;

(3) a poem that employs dramatic devices, such as dialogue, conflict, suspense, climax, and so on.

Elegy: a personal, serious, meditative poem, usually on death, containing an expression of grief.

Emotion: the feeling or tone that is evoked by the situation presented in a poem; the attitude that the writer takes toward an experience and that he attempts to induce in a reader.

Epic: a long narrative poem that centers on the exploits of an exalted character and aims to evoke admiration for the hero. It follows certain established conventions with regard to structure and style.

Epigram: a brief, witty, memorable statement, often a summary or general truth, frequently delivered in a rhyming couplet.

Episode: incidents in a long narrative poem, particularly in the epic, that are not directly related to the main action but contribute to the interest in the hero.

Epitaph: a brief, often epigrammatic, poem written on the occasion of a person's death.

Fable: a figure of speech in which an animal is endowed with human traits.

Figurative expression: fundamentally a comparison between two objects or incidents not in the same class. The main figures are simile, metaphor, personification, allegory, hyperbole, paradox, irony.

Foot: a metrical unit consisting of one stressed and one or more unstressed syllables. The common feet in English poetry are the iamb, trochee, anapest, dactyl, and spondee.

Form:
(1) the design or structure of a poem (see *Design*);
(2) the metrical pattern;
(3) the stanzaic pattern;
(4) the conventional order of development, as in the epic, pastoral, or sonnet;
(5) a combination of all these elements.

Free verse: verse that lacks regular meter, rhyme, or stanzaic pattern. Normally it is marked by cadence, that is, a rhythmical flow of irregularly stressed syllables.

Heroic couplet: an iambic pentameter couplet with end rhyme.

Hyperbole: an overstatement or exaggeration for the sake of emphasis.

Iamb: a metrical foot in which an unaccented syllable is followed by an accented syllable, as in *thĕ sún ĭs hót.*

Image:
(1) a word or expression that represents a sense experience, of sight, sound, touch, taste, and so on;
(2) a literal expression, as opposed to a figurative expression such as the metaphor;
(3) a symbol, that is, an object that stands for an idea.

Imagination:
(1) the power of representing an object mentally;
(2) a power of perceiving reality in a concrete way;
(3) the power to embody thought and feeling in a creative way.

Irony: (1) of speech, consists in a statement that says one thing but means the opposite; (2) of situation, consists in a contrast between what is expected and what actually happens. (3) Dramatic irony consists in the recognition by the audience of an outcome that the actor does not suspect, as in *Othello,* where the audience knows that Desdemona's expectations of allaying Othello's jealousy are impossible.

Literal: the usual or denotative meaning as opposed to the figurative, metaphorical, or symbolic meaning of a word or expression.

Litotes: an understatement.

Lyric: a brief poem, originally a song, that concentrates on a single emotion, sincerity of feeling, and universal appeal. It has a markedly musical quality.

Melody: (1) the music of words; (2) the agreeable succession of vowels and consonants. See *Alliteration, Assonance, Rhyme, Stanza.*

Metaphor: (1) a figurative expression in which one thing is identified with another; (2) an implied comparison between two things that are not in the same class; (3) a fusion of two objects or ideas in one image.

Meter: (1) the measure of syllables in a foot; (2) the regular grouping of stresses in a line; (3) the grouping of syllables in accordance with the normal rules of pronunciation into iambs, trochees, anapests, dactyls, spondees, and so on. See *Verse; Rhythm.*

Naturalness: (1) the fidelity of a poem to the general truth of nature; (2) the appropriateness of language to the character of the speaker, the nature of the subject, and the audience addressed.

Ode: a lyric poem that is formal, dignified, and often intricate in its metrical and stanzaic pattern.

Onomatopoeia: words that tend to reproduce, or suggest, natural sounds or the objects or actions that produce those sounds, as in *sizzle, bubble, blare.*

Paradox: (1) a statement that appears to be contradictory in a literal sense but in a figurative sense is true; (2) a situation that contains two apparently contrary aspects of reality.

Parody: an imitation of an author's theme or style, often for the purpose of satire.

Personification: a figure of speech in which an inanimate object or an abstract quality is endowed with human traits.

Plot: the interweaving of the several incidents or elements in a story or drama.

Poetry: the art or power of presenting an experience embodying emotion, thought, and imagination for the contemplation and delight of the reader. Poetry normally employs meter and verse, but compositions in meter and verse are not necessarily poetry.

Proportion: the degree of emotional intensity demanded by the situation presented in a poem.

Propriety: the appropriateness of the emotion to the situation presented in the poem.

Prose: language that avoids regular metrical pattern or rhyme.

Reasonableness: the adequacy of the motives, grounds, or proofs for the emotions, judgments, or conclusions suggested by the poem.

Rhyme: the identity in the rhyming syllables of the accented vowel sounds and the vowels and consonants that follow. Rhymes usually occur at the end of the line, sometimes within the line, occasionally at the beginning of the line.

Rhythm:

(1) The natural rise and fall of the sounds in language.

(2) In poetry, rhythm is marked by regular recurrence of stressed sounds; the measures of poetic rhythm are meter and verse.

(3) In prose, there is no regular recurrence of stress.

Romance: a story in verse, usually concerned with legendary heroes involved in chivalrous quests and adventures.

Satire: a type of poetry that ridicules vice or folly.

Scansion: the marking of the stresses in a line of verse; or the full description of a line.

Sensibility: the capacity to feel and to render the emotion appropriate to the situation represented in the poem. An excessive emotional response results in sentimentality; an inadequate emotional response in frigidity.

Sentimentality: an exaggerated emotional response to the situation presented in a poem.

Simile: a figurative expression in which two unlike objects are compared. Unlike the metaphor the comparison is expressed explicitly by the connectives *like, as,* and so on.

Sincerity: (1) in the poem, a quality similar to spontaneity; (2) in the author, intellectual honesty.

Sonnet: a poem in 14 lines in iambic pentameter. The Petrarchan form consists of an octave that rhymes *abbaabba* and a sestet that allows various rhyme schemes. The Shakespearean sonnet consists of three quatrains and a rhyming couplet.

Spondee: a metrical foot consisting of two accented syllables, as in *down deep.*

Stanza: a group of lines, often centering on a single thought, usually involving a regular rhyme scheme and a predominant meter.

Structure:

(1) The arrangement or order of the details, incidents, or subordinate elements or statements.

(2) The principle of organization that underlies the poem.

Style: (1) in general, the whole process of "thinking out into language"; (2) in particular, the choice of words and their arrangement within the poem.

Symbol: (1) an image or an object that stands for an idea; (2) an image that may have multiple meanings.

Synecdoche:

(1) A figure of speech, literally, *understood together.*

(2) An interchange of a term designating the part for the whole or the species for the genus.

Theme:

(1) The central idea or impression developed in the poem.

(2) The principle of unity according to which the poet selects details and harmonizes those details.

Thought:

(1) The body of ideas and judgments that are embodied in the poem.

(2) The organization of ideas and impressions in a poem.

See *Truth.*

Trochee: a metrical foot in which an accented syllable is followed by an unaccented syllable, as in *spléndid.*

Truth: in poetry, the fidelity of the imagined situation to a general truth of human nature.

Universality: the emotional, intellectual, and imaginative qualities in a poem that appeal to a great variety of readers.

Variation:

(1) The introduction of contrasting or slightly different tones, attitudes, or emotions to set off the main theme.

(2) The substitution of different metrical and stanzaic patterns consonant with the sense of the poem.

Verse:

(1) The measure of feet in a line.

(2) The numbering of feet in the line, as in the names monometer, dimeter, trimeter, tetrameter, pentameter, and so on.

(3) Broadly, any regularly recurrent rhythm as opposed to prose.

BIBLIOGRAPHY

THE books listed below have helped many students come to a fuller understanding of poetry and literature. Many of them have been cited in the text; others contain points of view that were considered indirectly in discussing various problems of poetry; still others present theories of poetry in an altogether different way. Books marked by an asterisk (*) are particularly helpful for beginning students.

Abrams, M. H. *The Mirror and the Lamp.* New York, 1953.
Aristotle. *Theory of Poetry and Fine Art,* ed. by S. H. Butcher. New York, 1902.
Barfield, Owen. *Poetic Diction: A Study of Meaning.* London, 1928.
Bogan, Louise. *Achievement in American Poetry 1900-1950.* Chicago, 1951.
Bowra, C. M. *From Vergil to Milton.* New York, 1946.
——— *The Heritage of Symbolism.* New York, 1943.
Bradley, A. C. *Oxford Lectures on Poetry.* New York, 1909.
Brémond, Henri. *Prayer and Poetry.* London, 1929.
Brooks, Cleanth. *The Well-Wrought Urn.* New York, 1956.
*Bush, Douglas. *English Poetry.* New York, 1952.
Coleridge, S. T. *Biographia Literaria,* ed. John Shawcross. Oxford, 1907.
Connell, F. M. *A Textbook for the Study of Poetry.* Boston, 1913.
*Daiches, David. *Critical Approaches to Literature.* New York, 1956.
Davie, Donald. *Purity of Diction in English Verse.* New York, 1953.
Deutsch, Babette. *Poetry in Our Time.* New York, 1952.
Dictionary of World Literature, ed. by Joseph Shipley. New York, 1943.
*Drew, Elizabeth. *Discovering Poetry.* New York, 1933.
Eliot, T. S. *Essays Ancient and Modern.* New York, 1936.
——— *On Poetry and Poets.* New York, 1957.
——— *Selected Essays.* New York, 1932.
Gilby, Thomas. *Poetic Experience.* New York, 1934.
Greene, T. M. *The Arts and the Art of Criticism.* Princeton, 1940.
Hamm, Victor F. *The Patterns of Criticism.* Milwaukee, 1951.
Horace. *Satires, Epistles, and Ars Poetica,* ed. H. Rushton Fairclough. Cambridge, Mass., 1936.
*Housman, A. E. *The Name and Nature of Poetry.* New York, 1948.
Intent of the Critic, The, ed. Donald Stauffer. Princeton, 1941.
Jarrell, Randall. *Poetry and the Age.* New York, 1953.
*Ker, W. P. *The Art of Poetry.* London, 1920.

Leavis, F. R. *New Bearings in English Poetry*. London, 1932, 1938.
Lewis, C., and Tillyard, E. *The Personal Heresy*. New York, 1939.
Literature and Belief, ed. by M. H. Abrams. New York, 1958.
Longinus. *On the Sublime*, tr. by W. Rhys Roberts. Cambridge, 1935.
Lowes, J. L. *Convention and Revolt in Poetry*. Boston, 1919, 1922.
——— *The Road to Xanadu*. Boston, 1927.
Lynch, W. F. *Christ and Apollo*. New York, 1960.
Maritain, Jacques. *Art and Scholasticism*. New York, 1930.
——— *Creative Intuition in Art and Poetry*. New York, 1953.
*Maynard, Theodore. *Preface to Poetry*. New York, 1933.
Murry, J. M. *The Problem of Style*. Oxford, 1922.
O'Connor, William Van. *Sense and Sensibility in Modern Poetry*. Chicago, 1948.
*Perry, Bliss. *A Study of Poetry*. Cambridge, Mass., 1920.
*Pottle, Frederick. *The Idiom of Poetry*. Ithaca, New York, 1946.
*Pound, Ezra. *The A B C of Reading*. New Haven, 1934; New York, 1951.
Read, Herbert. *Phases of English Poetry*. New York, 1951.
* Richards, I. A. *Practical Criticism*. New York, 1929.
——— *Principles of Literary Criticism*. New York, 1925.
Savage, D. S. *The Personal Principle*. London, 1944.
*Scott-James, R. *The Making of Literature: Some Principles of Criticism*. London, 1938.
*Stauffer, Donald. *The Nature of Poetry*. New York, 1946.
Tate, Allen. *Reason in Madness*. New York, 1941.
Temple, R. Z. *The Critic's Alchemy: A Study of the Introduction of French Symbolism into England*. New York, 1953.
Turnell, Martin. *The Poetry of Crisis*. London, 1938.
Warren, Austin, and Wellek, Rene. *Theory of Literature*, New York, 1949.
Wimsatt, William K., and Brooks, Cleanth. *Literary Criticism: A Short History*. New York, 1957.
Winters, Yvor. *In Defense of Reason*. New York, 1947.
Wood, Clement. *The Craft of Poetry*, New York, 1929.
Wordsworth, William. *Wordsworth's Literary Criticism*, ed. Nowell C. Smith. London, 1925.
Yeats, W. B. *Essays*. New York, 1924.

⁂ INDEX ⁂

SUBJECT, AUTHOR, TITLE, FIRST LINE

This index contains the names of authors, titles, and first lines of all poems, and the subjects discussed throughout the book. Bold-faced entries indicate the places where the topics are discussed at greater length. The poems included in the book may be found under the author entry. Exercise material is indicated by ex.